HOPE AND STRUGGLE IN THE POLICED CITY

Hope and Struggle in the Policed City

Black Criminalization and Resistance in Philadelphia

Menika B. Dirkson

NEW YORK UNIVERSITY PRESS
New York

NEW YORK UNIVERSITY PRESS
New York
www.nyupress.org

References to internet websites (URLs) were accurate at the time of writing. Neither the author nor New York University Press is responsible for URLs that may have expired or changed since the manuscript was prepared.

Please contact the Library of Congress for Cataloging-in-Publication data.

ISBN: 978-1-4798-2398-7 (hardback)
ISBN: 978-1-4798-2401-4 (library ebook)
ISBN: 978-1-4798-2399-4 (consumer ebook)

New York University Press books are printed on acid-free paper, and their binding materials are chosen for strength and durability. We strive to use environmentally responsible suppliers and materials to the greatest extent possible in publishing our books.

Manufactured in the United States of America

10 9 8 7 6 5 4 3 2 1

Also available as an ebook

For my grandmother, Ada Fernella

CONTENTS

At around 8:00 p.m. on April 20, 1971, Rafael Santiago and his brother Roberto were closing their three-story red-brick grocery store, located at 532 West Susquehanna Avenue in North Philadelphia, for the evening as their sons waited for them outside.[1] This day was particularly special for the Santiago family, since at 10:47 a.m., the birth of Gloria and Rafael Sr.'s fifth child had occurred at Northeastern Hospital. Nine-year-old Rafael Jr. was especially jubilant as he told his seven-year-old cousin Ramon and neighborhood friends about the birth of his sister.[2] Meanwhile, two rival gangs, Zulu Nation and the 8th and Diamond Streeters, began a shoot-out on the street. After two gunshots were fired, Rafael Jr. was hit by a stray bullet in the back and fell to the ground.[3]

At first, Ramon thought his cousin was playing a joke, until he saw blood flowing from Rafael's body. Soon Rafael Sr. and Roberto arrived and put the child in his uncle's car. As they traveled to St. Christopher's Hospital, Rafael Sr. attempted to give his son mouth-to-mouth resuscitation as blood gushed from Rafael Jr.'s mouth. When the Santiagos arrived at the hospital, Rafael Jr. was dead.[4] Later that evening, police and firemen searched for Santiago's killers and raided the 8th and Diamond Youth Center at 7th and Susquehanna Streets, where over four hundred members of Zulu Nation made their clubhouse in the basement.[5] In the raid, police found ten moth-riddled couches, a pool table covered with drug paraphernalia, a starter pistol, and heating pipes filled with bullet holes where gang members practiced their shooting.[6] Approximately ninety minutes after the shooting, eight members of Zulu Nation were arrested: seventeen-year-old Gary "Crip" Slocum was charged with murder, while the remaining seven were booked on narcotics charges.[7] This incident is one of thousands of stories that shocked the public and provoked communal introspection around the causes and solutions to violent crime in the 1970s.

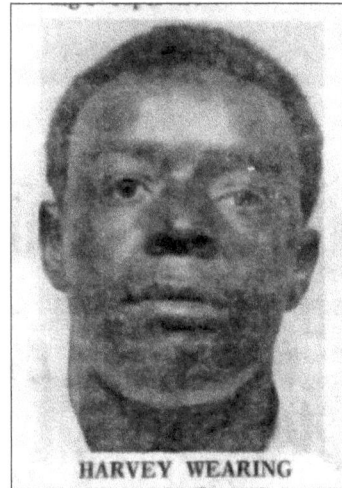

Newspaper images of four victims of gun violence in Philadelphia: Rafael Santiago, David Fineman, Antoinette Williams, and Harvey Wearing, 1970–73. *Philadelphia Inquirer / Philadelphia Daily News.*

As a historian, stories like the 1971 murder of Rafael Santiago haunt me. In fact, many ghosts from the 1970s haunt me: Everyday people like twenty-one-year-old Temple University graduate student David Fineman, who was targeted and killed by five members of the Gamma Phi United "club" as he was entering his car to go home from his Monday night class in April 1970.[8] Children like seven-year-old Antoinette Williams, who was killed by a stray bullet that struck her in the face as she sat on her North Philadelphia stoop occupied with her coloring book in June 1970.[9] And activists like twenty-seven-year-old social worker Harvey Wearing, who was murdered while talking to a group of juvenile gang members on a Southwest Philadelphia street corner in June 1973.[10] These tragedies are, in part, consequences of Philadelphia's history of segregation, poverty, slum housing, job discrimination, and racially biased policing that helped create the social conditions for these events to occur. For historians like me, it's our job to fill in the often obscured historical context surrounding seemingly isolated incidents by drawing out their roots in state-sanctioned social inequality and social justice. We write narratives demonstrating that the lives of those who were affected by historical events won't ever be forgotten. Journalists, community activists, city officials, and police have all used tragedy to spark change. Historians can do the same to advocate for causes we're passionate about and inspire a better world.

Issues of social inequality and racialized state violence that existed in major American cities like Philadelphia over a hundred years ago linger on in the present day. Many social activists recognize that social inequality, not racial inferiority, is responsible for the racial disparity that exists between white and nonwhite communities in regard to poverty, violence, and crime. From as early as 1899, sociological studies like W. E. B. Du Bois's *Philadelphia Negro* explained that socioeconomic inequality, housing discrimination, and racial violence often created the conditions in which black people fell into poverty, illiteracy, vice, and crime.[11] Du Bois also stressed that black people were not inherently immoral or criminal, as influential pseudoscientists of the era asserted.[12] Racist myths often encouraged wealthier residents to view the poor (who were often black) as threats to middle-class and all-white communities. This contributed to residents using the law and violence to strengthen residential segregation in their neighborhoods—notably during the Great Migration (1916–70), when 6.6 million black migrants, largely of rural origins, inhabited Northern cities above the Mason-Dixon Line where the percentage of African Americans was below 10 percent of the population.[13]

From the 1890s onward, black and white philanthropists, social workers, and college-aged volunteers established settlement houses like the

Octavia Hill Association, the Whittier Centre, and the Wharton Centre to provide the black poor with decent housing, employment, health care, and rehabilitation for juvenile delinquents.[14] From the 1920s through the 1960s, sociologists like Frederic Thrasher, William Foote Whyte, and Lewis Yablonsky determined that based on their research on crime—particularly as it relates to social, delinquent, and violent gangs in marginalized communities—youth often became gang members because they felt ostracized in their society and desired to be accepted in some sort of community. Influential sociologist Frederic Thrasher argued that poverty, social ostracism, and the desire for social belonging were influential factors in the formation of juvenile gangs. Thrasher's 1927 monograph *The Gang: A Study of 1,313 Gangs in Chicago* was particularly influential because it suggested that the establishment of inclusive institutions with positive and influential mentors was a solution to gang activity.[15]

In the 1930s, community activists from North Philadelphia's Wharton Centre created the antigang program Operation Street Corner to counteract the rise of youth gangs, which they attributed to the "social problems and neighborhood conditions" of generational unemployment, crime, and a lack of childcare for working adults. Furthermore, during the 1940s and 1950s, black social workers used participant observation to study, interact with, and rehabilitate gang members with athletics, weekly dances, trips, social clubs, and educational programs.[16] This tradition of black guardianship of juvenile gang members set a precedent for future Philadelphia activists to utilize rehabilitative social welfare programs rather than tough-on-crime policing in response to gang violence. Policymakers, however, have often rejected rehabilitative social welfare in favor of punitive policies intended to quickly curb crime and slow white flight.

In the 1960s, sociologists like Yablonsky argued that youth gang activity was a reaction to community ostracism and socioeconomic disadvantage. While some gangs were "friendship organizations" with supposed codes of brotherhood, other gangs functioned as outlets to channel the frustrations, aggressions, and hostilities they have about "school, family, the neighborhood, prejudice, or any other problems" into gang wars.[17] Furthermore, as many social scientists have pointed out, including historian Eric Schneider, there is a correlation between social ostracism (based on race, class, and wealth) and violence that beckons us to pay attention if we are to preserve human life by ensuring racial equity.[18]

In 1970, Philadelphia's poverty rate was 15.4 percent, while the national average was 12.2 percent. Along with poverty, gang violence was also a serious issue in the 1970s. Philadelphia's police department recorded the existence of over two hundred gangs and an average of 390 murders per year.[19] Even though 1.5 percent of all youth were involved in gang activity during that era, the Gang Control Unit (hereafter referred to as the Gang Unit) reported that up to 96 percent of gang members were black and over 50 percent of gang homicides occurred in deindustrialized North Philadelphia, where nearly two-thirds of the city's black population lived.[20]

By the 1970s, some journalists writing news articles about crime often featured provocative research data from social scientists to legitimize the belief that there was a correlation between increased migration and rising crime among different ethnic and racial groups. In 1975, gang research cultivated by anthropologist Walter B. Miller of Harvard Law School's Center for Criminal Justice was publicized in dozens of newspapers around the country, promoting the racist idea that new migrants brought violence and crime to urban cities. In Miller's 1975 monograph *Violence by Youth Gangs and Youth Groups as a Crime Problem in Major American Cities*, he explained how after studying the gang situation in twelve cities, including New York, Chicago, and Los Angeles, 1970s gang violence was greater than that of the 1950s because youth in gangs were less formally organized, more likely to use guns, and more active in schools.[21] Additionally, Miller's statistical and observational research identified "low-income ghettos" as havens for gang violence, suggesting that poverty begot crime but also arguing that youth of color were more prone to criminal activity than their white counterparts. In his study, Miller argued that ethnic populations with recent migrants and low-skilled laborers "produced" gangs. According to Miller, "white ethnics" dominated gangs in American society from the 1880s through the 1920s as a result of mass immigration from Eastern and Southern Europe, and during the 1970s, black youth were the "most heavily represented" in the gang populations because of the Great Migration of African Americans from the South.[22] In the 1970s, Miller's racially biased research triggered fear among city officials who wanted to curb gang violence to prevent white flight from neighborhoods adjacent to communities of color. Moreover, his report convinced journalists and city councils across America that the best way to retain the white and middle-class taxpayers was to invest in the police department.

In contrast, African American–led organizations like the Black Panther Party; the Nation of Islam; Safe Streets, Inc.; the House of Umoja; and the Black Liberation Army did not believe that criminality was an inherent trait of recent migrants or people of color, so they spent generations fighting poverty along with the intra- and interracial violent crime that touched their neighborhoods. The members of these organizations were conscious of the many ways that institutional racism, poverty, and police brutality damage the black community.[23] Therefore, they offered Philadelphia's black communities jobs, antigang activism, education, therapy sessions, recreation opportunities for juveniles, and antipoverty initiatives like food and clothing drives to curb crime. Despite all the programs these progressive groups fostered to facilitate change, we unfortunately still see some politicians, journalists, and everyday citizens continue to deploy stigmatizing crime narratives, endorse hypersurveillance, and support biased policing against communities of color.

Today, not much has changed. Philadelphia's poverty rate is approximately 23 percent, with some neighborhoods in places like North Philadelphia experiencing up to 45 percent of their residents living below the poverty line.[24] Additionally, poverty rates are disproportionate to the racial makeup of the city. Although black, white, and Latino residents compose 41.5 percent, 39 percent, and 15.2 percent of Philadelphia's population, respectively, among the over 354,000 people impoverished in Philadelphia, 47.8 percent are black, 26.5 percent are Latino, and 24 percent are white.[25] In the past five years, the average homicide rate has been approximately 417 murders per year, with at least 80 percent of the victims being black.[26] These statistics demonstrate there is clearly a racial disparity in the access white people and people of color have to social resources that determine an individual's ability to achieve financial stability and disinclination to engage in poverty-induced crime and violence.

For decades, major cities like Philadelphia have struggled with both poverty and gun violence. Social uplift organizations of the past like the Wharton Centre and the Black Panther Party spent decades demonstrating that racial equity is the key to ending socioeconomic ostracism and crime, but people in power are still investing more government money and resources in policing than social welfare programs. In fact, many American cities are allocating between 15 and 45 percent of their municipal budget spending for policing, resulting in hundreds of millions of dollars being divested from schools, libraries, community centers, and public housing each year.[27] Today, Philadelphia spends approximately 15 percent of its budget on policing—roughly over $700 million. Interestingly, over the years, community activists from groups like the Sultan Jihad Ahmad Community Foundation; Ready, Willing & Able; Cradle to Grave; and Mothers in Charge have demonstrated that social welfare programs offering food, housing, education, mentorship, recreation, and access to employment are still viable solutions to both poverty and violent crime. Nevertheless, my focus as a historian is to write in order to spark change. Inevitably, this for me means spending my career sharing the histories I know in an effort to position myself alongside community activists fighting to convince city officials, police officers, and the general public to be fully invested in and committed to social equality. Then just maybe there will be actual change—seen through decreased rates of poverty-induced crime, incarceration, unemployment, recidivism, and the loss of precious lives like Rafael Santiago.[28]

Introduction

[African Americans] You're living in poverty, your schools are
no good, you have no jobs, 58% of your youth is unemployed—
what the hell do you have to lose?
—Donald Trump, *Presidential Campaign Speech to American
Voters*, August 19, 2016

For more than fifty years, Philadelphia's route 33 bus, traveling from 23rd
and Venango to Penn's Landing, has been referred to by some SEPTA
(Southeastern Pennsylvania Transportation Authority) passengers as one
that you "ride at your own risk."[1] However, this bus route, with such a
stigmatized reputation, gives a vivid tour of how black bodies in urban
black spaces have been criminalized since the Great Migration (1916–70),
when nearly 75 percent of black migrants came to the city from the South
Atlantic states of Georgia, North Carolina, South Carolina, Virginia, and
Washington, DC.[2] The route begins in North Philadelphia, traversing the
low-income black neighborhoods of Nicetown-Tioga, Allegheny West,
Stanton, and Sharswood until it reaches the Benjamin Franklin Parkway,
located downtown in Center City.

From 1900 to 1970, these North Philadelphia neighborhoods went
from being segregated and middle-class all-white spaces to hypersegregated and impoverished all-black spaces as African Americans migrated
from the South to the North following the Civil War and Reconstruction and white flight occurred in response to their arrival up North. As
black migrants gradually changed North Philadelphia's demographics
over time, a slew of figures—social scientists, police, journalists, real
estate agents, city officials, and everyday citizens—spread popular narratives of "moral panic" laced with racial stereotypes to resist desegregation in their communities.[3] News media and popular culture promoted
racist narratives of uncontrollable "black crime" to trigger white fear,
criminalize African Americans, maintain segregation, and strengthen a

system of racial capitalism that relies on the exploitation of black people. Over time, these narratives influenced middle-class whites to resist their black neighbors with legalized segregation, violence, white flight, containment, hyperpolicing, and incarceration to maintain a racial hierarchy in which whites socioeconomically remain at the top while blacks stay at the bottom.[4]

For decades, the racialized stereotypes of poverty, filth, and crime bestowed on the route 33 bus mirror those placed on the North Philadelphia community it serves.[5] Along the route, neighborhood outsiders looking into North Philadelphia find poverty, filth, and vice showcased in the existence of housing projects, abandoned homes, trash-strewn streets and vacant lots, graffitied corner stores, liquor stores, and police patrols. When nonresidents see these elements in black neighborhoods (that look vastly different from Philadelphia's white communities) outside of their historical context, they are at *risk* of believing a stereotypical "single story" about the black working class and poor.[6] This "single story" of the black poor as impoverished, dirty, immoral, and criminal is often retold by people in power, who recycle racist stereotypes rooted in a social history of antiblackness. Nevertheless, the residents become voiceless while the police, journalists, and city officials who patrol, report, and represent these neighborhoods become the most influential narrators in the city. Oftentimes these narrators inform the public about these black urban spaces to criminalize them and further their political and financial goals.[7] In Philadelphia, these goals have been (and still are) about convincing white people that jobs, homes, and crimeless streets exist in the inner city to halt white middle-class flight to the suburbs and protect the city's tax base in times of economic downturn.

This book details how during the Great Migration of African Americans to the North, Philadelphia's police department, journalists, and city officials used news media to disseminate crime narratives laced with statistics and racial stereotypes of "black invasions," "urban neighborhood jungles," "roving black gangs," and the "culture of poverty" to convince the white middle class to resist desegregation and support tough-on-crime policing in the inner city from 1958 to the present day. This monograph argues that black people experienced double victimization: they were first stigmatized by the proliferation of the myth of inherent black inferiority and criminality, and they then faced a second round of victimization when local governments legitimized the myth cultivated from crime narratives and statistics by enacting socioeconomic policies that clearly disadvantaged and marginalized African Americans from the Civil Rights Movement era and beyond. In some instances, these two forms of victimization occurred simultaneously.

Beginning in the early 1900s, this narrative shows how Southern black migrants, labeled as members of a "black invasion," were first stigmatized by Northerners for their blackness in media, academic scholarship, and public discourse as they moved into the neighborhoods of majority-white Northern cities by the thousands. Reviewing the stigmatization and criminalization of blackness from the 1920s through the 1950s is crucial to understanding why African Americans faced tough-on-crime policing in the 1960s and 1970s. In the 1920s, black migrants were not only stigmatized for their slave heritage and Southern culture but also scapegoated for disrupting the labor and housing markets leading up to a period of economic turmoil that was out of their control: the Great Depression. From the 1930s through the 1970s, police and journalists gradually used crime narratives to justify the racially biased policing tactics of hypersurveillance, daily patrols, excessive force, and incarceration against black and poor residents in the postwar era when urban cities desegregated further.

During the Civil Rights Movement of the 1950s and 1960s, the civil unrest that occurred during some protests and uprisings against police brutality triggered the local government's usage of police power to maintain social order. Eventually, city officials noticed that job flight and white flight from Philadelphia caused a steady drop in tax revenues over time. They sought to curb these issues by not only implementing departmental cutbacks but also tightly managing crime with tough-on-crime policing that entailed officers receiving paid overtime to meet the city's perceived crime-fighting needs outside of their usual eight-hour schedule. Furthermore, the local government developed a system of racial capitalism in which City Council financially divested from social welfare programs, invested in the police department, and supported a tough-on-crime policing program that attempted to curb black crime, convince residents that city streets were safe, and generate wealth for Philadelphia's tax base by reattracting industries, businesses, consumers, and residents back to the city. The book ends in the 1970s, when African

Americans and the urban spaces they inhabited were criminalized and subsequently heavily policed following approximately two decades of well-documented media coverage of actual black crime along with civil rights protests (peaceful and violent) over issues like racial discrimination and police brutality.

Nevertheless, throughout this narrative are stories of resistance in which African Americans and their allies fought against racial and socioeconomic inequality in their communities. From the 1920s through the 1970s, community activists who were at times Quakers, social workers, college students, former gang members, politicians, and even police officers worked in community-led organizations to develop social welfare programs that improved the lives of black youth in the city. Other activists used their voices or pens to offer public testimony to the social ills of poverty-induced crime and police brutality in hopes of convincing the local government to create a socially just society for future generations. Nevertheless, their community activism, often informed by sociological research, around the issues of racism, poverty, juvenile delinquency, and crime challenged the myth that black people were inherently inferior and criminal while also provoking city officials to seek out strategies other than tough-on-crime policing to curb crime.

The History of the Criminalization of Blackness

The criminalization of black bodies and black urban spaces for socioeconomic gain is not a twenty-first-century invention. As writer Michael Harriot explained in his article "Maybe America Is Racist," it is easier to convince white people to believe racial stereotypes that portray black people as "inherently dumber, lazier, and more prone to violence" because it erases the "history of slavery, Jim Crow, redlining, voter suppression, and employment discrimination" that white people benefit from in a racial hierarchy constructed by white supremacy.[8] In America, racial stereotypes protect white supremacists from having a "crisis in whiteness" in which their racial privilege is denied and they must accept racial equality in the social, economic, and political realms of society.[9]

Furthermore, Harriot's argument coincides with social scientist Cedric J. Robinson's study of racial capitalism, an economic system of inequality that thrives on racism and labor exploitation to achieve profit and requires the erasure of history to "dispossess" and "expropriate" value from marginalized people cast as "different" from the majority that dominates a society.[10] In fact, even when black people rebel against multiple forms of oppression like segregation and police brutality, the memory of their resistance is often "systematically distorted and suppressed in the service of racialist, eurocentric, and ruling-class historiographies."[11] Crime narratives centered around historic racial stereotypes have particularly been used to not only cultivate division and adversarial interactions between black and white people but also justify political and economic programs that indefinitely disadvantage, marginalize, criminalize, and stigmatize African Americans while establishing a system of white privilege and entitlement to socioeconomic resources.

Racial stereotypes about black people as "dirty," "iniquitous," "deadly," and "wicked" were hatched as early as the 1500s. English traders and explorers like Richard Hakluyt and Richard Ligon, in their journals and travel accounts, portrayed West Africans as inferior people because they were of a different ethnicity, race, and culture.[12] However, racially biased discourses were used to not only other and misrepresent Africans as socially, morally, and religiously inept but also affirm the superiority of "white intelligence," legitimize European intolerance of African culture, and justify black slavery in the Americas and Europe.[13] These authoritative white narratives about black inferiority informed the public that black people had no natural right to "life, liberty, and property," and therefore the Anglo-American concept of civil rights became inapplicable to people of African descent. Moreover, the stigma of black inferiority these travelers and colonists cultivated in their narratives set the stage for the criminalization of black people in American society from the nineteenth century onward.

From the 1860s through the 1940s, scholars, journalists, police, and public officials used biased scientific research, social statistics, and crime narratives as so-called objective methods to measure and document black inferiority. This data was then used to justify white supremacist agendas to contain and control African Americans following their emancipation from slavery in 1865.[14] Physicians, naturalists, and demographers throughout the 1800s used scientific racism to prove that Anglo-Saxon and Germanic peoples had superior intellect and civility to govern society, while people of African descent were inferior beings prone to idleness, vice, and crime if not forcibly ruled over and put to work.[15] Physicians like Samuel George Morton (1799–1851) and Josiah Clark Nott (1804–73) analyzed human skulls and conducted patient observations on white and black people to disprove the fact that individuals of different races were physiologically the same and shared a common human ancestor. Although Morton and Nott's scientific methodology was wrought with discrepancies, their research supporting the white supremacist belief in polygenesis was published, read, and expanded upon by their contemporaries and many future scholars of the sciences and humanities.[16]

In the 1880s, naturalists like Nathaniel Southgate Shaler (1841–1906) described in his *Atlantic Monthly* article "The Negro Problem" how he used scientific research and his personal experiences with enslaved African Americans on his family's Kentucky plantation to argue that black people posed a threat to "civilized" society because their brains were less developed than whites' and their "African blood" made them unfit for "survival, labor, and citizenship" in America.[17] Shaler stated that although black people were "charming" and had "quick sensibilities," they were animalistic and childlike because they lacked the self-discipline necessary to control their sexual impulses, work industriously without guidance from a superior, or plan effectively for the future. Furthermore, he suggested there was a "white man's burden" in which white people had to contain and control black people with something greater than an "industrial education" and segregation or face the destruction of a "civilized" American society.[18] Nevertheless, Shaler, a Harvard College professor who taught over seven thousand students and authored numerous articles on "race relations," influenced future generations to follow in his tradition of social science and opinion-based narratives rooted in racist stereotypes and antiblackness.[19]

In the 1890s, demographers like Frederick Ludwig Hoffman (1865–1946) gathered statistics from the 1870, 1880, and 1890 US federal census reports along with mortuary reports from eight Southern states to analyze the "behavioral characteristics" of African Americans. Hoffman's overall goal was to evaluate how well black people survived independently from slave masters as freed people and determine whether they were able to "virtuously" overcome their "ancestral condition" by avoiding earthly vices.[20] In Hoffman's 1892 article for the Boston journal

The Arena, "Vital Statistics of the Negro," he argued that African Americans died at a rate twice that of whites because their poor health, "inferior constitution," and "gross immorality" made them susceptible to tuberculosis, maternal death during childbirth, and sexually transmitted diseases.[21] Throughout Hoffman's career as a statistician, he studied the work of Nathaniel Shaler of Harvard College; General Samuel Chapman Armstrong (1839–93), who founded the black industrial school Hampton Institute; and Alabama prison doctor Russell McWhortor Cunningham (1855–1921). Cunningham's 1894 journal article in *The Medical News*, in particular, inspired Hoffman to study black criminality.[22]

In Cunningham's "The Morbidity and Mortality of Negro Convicts," he argued that his observations of hundreds of black and white male convicts' bodies revealed that black men's physical deficiencies and asymmetrical bodies, seen in their "large stomachs and penises," made them "predisposed" to numerous diseases. Additionally, he claimed that as a prison doctor, he observed blacks to be more criminal than whites because, following emancipation, black people composed five times the prison population in comparison to whites, who made up 99 percent of convicts in Alabama prior to 1865.[23] Interestingly, when Cunningham came to these conclusions, he ignored the fact that approximately 90 percent of the African American population—four million—was enslaved prior to 1865, which explains why whites fully occupied Southern prisons. Cunningham also neglected to acknowledge that postemancipation, African Americans filled up prisons at higher rates than whites because Southern Black Codes established after slavery disproportionately incarcerated thousands of poor black men on trumped-up criminal charges like vagrancy, interracial sex, and gambling. These black men were then filtered into the convict leasing system, where they worked for months at a time in prison labor camps like Mississippi's Parchman Farm.[24] However, Cunningham still claimed that Alabama's laws were "impartially administered" in regard to race.[25]

A few physicians, like Philadelphia's Eastern State Penitentiary doctor Michael Valentine Ball (1868–1945), challenged Cunningham. In Ball's 1894 response to Cunningham's article in the *Medical News*, "Correspondence: The Mortality of the Negro," he explained that working-class black people *and* white immigrants often succumbed to illnesses earlier than whites of Anglo-Saxon and Germanic descent because they experienced lifelong poverty and "unsanitary" living conditions in overcrowded communities.[26] Furthermore, Ball stated that since black and white people were biologically the same, racial prejudice was the cause for African Americans being overrepresented in prisons, not black inferiority.[27] Unfortunately, Hoffman's racist views of black inferiority, promiscuity, and criminality prevailed into the twentieth century with his influential 1896 publication on African Americans postemancipation.

In Hoffman's 1896 monograph *Race Traits and Tendencies of the American Negro*, he reflected on the work of esteemed white supremacist scholars like Cunningham and argued that black people's "self-destructive tendencies" were responsible for their promiscuity, criminality, and overrepresentation in prisons, not white oppression or environmental factors.[28] Many of Hoffman's contemporaries accepted his findings because he described himself as an outsider from Germany who had no personal connections to slavery or racial discrimination against African Americans like many other whites in his field. Hoffman's statistical research later inspired his employer, Prudential Insurance Company of America, to charge African Americans higher premiums for life insurance than white people because they accepted his racially biased data describing black people as unhealthy and prone to illness.[29] Hoffman's research also encouraged scholars to collect biased crime statistics to justify disproportionate arrest and incarceration rates between blacks and whites. Moreover, Hoffman's work influenced future scholars in sociology and anthropology to use statistics to support the racist stereotype that people of Anglo-Saxon and German ancestry were superior to people of African, Asian, Hispanic, Eastern European, and Southern European descent.

In focusing on antiblackness during the twentieth century, the racialization of street crime by scholars and the media affected the method in which different racial groups were stereotyped and policed in major cities like Philadelphia. As 6.6 million African Americans migrated North during the Great Migration looking for wartime jobs and affordable housing, social Darwinists documented the "peculiarity and heightened rate" of black crime in New York, Chicago, and Philadelphia. The goal of these eugenicists was to convince white Northerners to resist integration with blacks.[30] Whites who feared social competition with blacks for jobs, housing, mates, and schools thrived on biased crime data because it justified their right to criminalize, police, and imprison blacks at higher rates than whites.[31]

When race-conscious social scientists highlighted the arrival of the "Negro Problem" to the North well into the 1940s, many white government and community officials began to view crime committed by blacks and whites differently. Following the Great Migration, Irish, Italian, Polish, and other non–Anglo Saxon whites who were once stigmatized as biologically vulnerable to criminal behavior were later viewed as victims of an unequal society who committed an individual failure and required charitable "redemption and rehabilitation" in a settlement house or Young Men's Christian Association (YMCA).[32] Conversely, society viewed African Americans as having a racially inborn defect that made them susceptible to crime and required imprisonment as a penalty. However, black social scientists like Anna J. Thompson and W. E. B. Du Bois countered those claims with statistical data arguing that crime among blacks and whites occurred at similar rates and for reasons such as inescapable poverty.[33] Furthermore, this continuation of the stereotypes of black inferiority, brutality, and criminality by eugenicists and social Darwinists during the Progressive era sparked the hyperpolicing and mass arrests of African Americans in cities, including Philadelphia.

During the pre- and post–World War II eras, news media, police, and the criminal justice system used adultification bias to justify the tough-on-crime policing and incarceration of black youth. In Chicago, Progressive-era reformers created the first juvenile court in 1899 with the mission to rehabilitate youth who committed crime. However, prejudice and racial discrimination played a role in the institution implementing different treatment for white and black children.[34] From 1899 to 1945, black youth were increasingly criminalized through inflated crime statistics and news stories, all while an influx of Southern black migrants were moving North during the Great Migration. Juvenile institutions justified rehabilitation for white youth from poor and immigrant families because juvenile court officials equated the children's "whiteness" with "childhood innocence."[35] On the other hand, black youth were often strictly disciplined, beaten, and tried as adults in court because juvenile officials in reformatories and the courts viewed their "blackness" as the cause of their "deviancy," which could not be reformed.[36] Furthermore, criminalized blackness took precedence over youth when social reformers confronted juvenile delinquency among African Americans.

The criminalization of black youth not only happened in Chicago but was also a national trend, common in several major urban cities during the Great Migration. From the 1930s through the 1970s, police, city officials, juvenile institutions, and journalists used inflated crime statistics and news stories to criminalize black youth and promote a tough-on-crime program against African Americans in New York City.[37] Since the 1930s, police stigmatized the black neighborhood of Harlem as a crime-ridden area threatening the city. Journalists portrayed Harlem as a place filled with jobless adults and "broken homes" where children lacked father figures. These accounts, along with biased crime statistics, led to tough-on-crime policing. Over the decades, police sought to control and contain crime in Harlem by preemptively sending additional police patrols to the area, which inevitably led to inflated crime rates and black residents facing increased police harassment. The police department also organized the Police Athletic League (PAL) to steer black youth away from crime.[38]

Following World War II, many African Americans who served in the military received benefits from the GI Bill, which enabled them to move out of all-black communities like Harlem to live in other neighborhoods in New York, desegregating them. However, police, journalists, and city officials criminalized black youth in the city through different methods, which kept black children in close contact with the criminal justice system. Police implemented preventative crime techniques like stop and frisk to get guns off the streets, while journalists and government officials like Mayor Fiorello LaGuardia (1934–45) portrayed black youths as "gang members" and "hoodlums" whose criminal behavior originated from excessive freedom and a culture based on "religion and sex."[39] Although African Americans and community activists from organizations like the YMCA, the Harlem Youth Citizens' Council (HYCC), and even sports teams like the Brooklyn Dodgers fought to end juvenile delinquency in the black community, black youth were often surrounded by a "cycle of crime" because they were born into an environment shaped by racial discrimination and discriminatory policing.[40]

While there is a substantial amount of analytical research on how African Americans have been criminalized throughout the twentieth century, few scholars have connected the political usage of stereotypical crime narratives in the 1960s to tough-on-crime policing initiatives that contribute to mass incarceration and racial capitalism in the present day. During the 1960s, conservative *and* liberal politicians under Lyndon B. Johnson's presidential administration sought a transition from the War on Poverty to the War on Crime in 1965 because of urban uprisings, gang violence, juvenile crime, and illegal gun sales throughout the country.[41] The federal government supported major cities with grants for antigang programs and job training for juveniles under the Law Enforcement Assistance Act (LEAA) of 1965. However, pressing concerns about crime and the gradual gains from rehabilitative programs for "inner-city" youth encouraged federal and local politicians to increase spending on police departments, military tanks, and other tough-on-crime policing initiatives. One narrative that reflected the racial stereotype of black criminality and inspired a call to action against black idleness and crime was Harvard University's president emeritus James B. Conant's 1961 description of unemployed and frustrated black youth as "potential social dynamite."[42]

Conant, who was a chemist and not a social scientist, suggested to policymakers at a May 1961 conference that the government assist black youth in getting jobs to prevent them from falling into delinquency and rioting in major urban cities.[43] However, the federal government later transitioned from a War on Poverty to a War on Crime when, by 1964, approximately 250 uprisings had occurred across the country following numerous incidents of police brutality against African Americans in cities like New York and Jersey City. The federal government's tough-on-crime initiatives involved offering major cities where African Americans were at least 33 percent of the population LEAA grants for not only antipoverty and anticrime programs for youth but also new surveillance technology and "military-grade weapons" for police departments.[44]

Additionally, some social scientists continued to produce data accepting the theory that poverty begot crime but also embracing the racial stereotypes of black inferiority and criminality. Furthermore, their biased research bolstered greater support for the War on Crime than the War on Poverty because it convinced policymakers that a rise in urban black crime was inevitable, as African Americans were inherently "culturally deficient."[45] In the 1960s, social scientists like sociologist and Assistant

Secretary of Labor Daniel Patrick Moynihan conducted studies on black families and youth that reflected a core belief in the "social pathology" of African Americans. In Moynihan's 1965 publication *The Negro Family: The Case for National Action* (popularly known as the *Moynihan Report*), he suggested that black immorality was responsible for higher rates of "female-headed households," unemployment, teen pregnancy, and high school dropouts among blacks than whites.[46] Although the *Moynihan Report* acknowledged that racial discrimination had a partial role in the marginalization of African Americans in "slums," Moynihan suggested that cultural inferiority was also to blame. According to his research, when blacks migrated from rural to urban cities, the first and second generations struggled to transition into their new environment. As a result of black people's difficulty in settling into their new community, they engaged in "drunkenness," "crime," and "juvenile delinquency."[47] Nevertheless, Moynihan's findings suggested that the federal government had a white man's burden to help African Americans live stable lives with proper education and jobs or watch black youth fall into criminality and inevitably incarcerate them.

Throughout the 1970s, social scientists like anthropologist Walter B. Miller collected biased statistics and observations of "black gangs" in neighborhoods and schools in Philadelphia, Chicago, and Los Angeles. His work highlighted higher rates of juvenile delinquency among blacks than whites and emphasized the racial stereotype of black criminality.[48] Miller, who worked with Moynihan at the Harvard-MIT Joint Center for Urban Studies during the 1960s, had research conclusions similar to Moynihan's on the issue of juvenile delinquency among youth of color. In Miller's 1975 publication *Violence by Youth Gangs and Youth Groups as a Crime Problem in Major American Cities*, he acknowledged that gang activity among youth of color was a product of poverty because juvenile delinquency was "concentrated in low-income ghettos." However, Miller suggested that youth of color, specifically black and Latino children, were inherently criminal because, in his opinion, most gang activities in nonwhite neighborhoods and schools were "non-criminal" but becoming more violent and dangerous.[49] Nevertheless, Miller's research not only described black gangs as imminent threats to urban cities over time but also criminalized both black bodies and hypersegregated black urban spaces as inseparable entities requiring police intervention.

Furthermore, politicians received the justification they needed from social scientists to spend hundreds of millions of dollars militarizing police departments and defund social welfare programs benefiting poor people of color because race-based statistics, observations, and crime narratives convinced them that the "culture of poverty" influenced black juvenile crime.[50] Nevertheless, this practice has resulted in the double victimization of urban low-income black communities. Black communities are criminalized because of not only the statistics and crime narratives police, journalists, and politicians share with the public but also the harmful public policies of government divestment from social programs, excessive force from militarized police, and stricter criminal sentences.

Most recently, urban historians have not only acknowledged statistical data documenting actual crime in black communities but also offered a contextual interpretation of black life that counters racial stereotypes and explains why there are vice and crime in hypersegregated low-income black neighborhoods. Black communities have become synonymous with crime because there is a complex history that explains how racial discrimination, violence, crime, and masculinity have played a role in the high rates of murder in places like Philadelphia's hypersegregated black neighborhoods from World War II to the early 1980s.[51] African Americans and their culture are not inherently violent. Although Southern black migrants came from a rural society with entrenched racial violence from white supremacist groups like the Ku Klux Klan (KKK), their culture of survival did not make them more likely than Northerners to commit crimes like murder.[52] Instead, high murder rates in marginalized black communities are a result of generations of social inequality that create an environment where life is uncertain and murder is performed as self-protection from physical violence and dishonor in the public and private spheres of society.

Segregation and ghettoization during the postwar era created the ecology for homicide to thrive in low-income African American neighborhoods. During World War II, African Americans migrating to Philadelphia looking for wartime industrial jobs were funneled into segregated neighborhoods. Government housing policies maintained residential segregation in the city, and white resistance to desegregation in the form of race riots and white flight made neighborhoods hypersegregated.[53] After World War II, African Americans were excluded from factory jobs when private enterprises, unbeholden to wartime production demands, offered positions to returning white soldiers seeking jobs despite civil rights protests for equal-opportunity employment. Deindustrialization, financial disinvestment, and the reduction of legitimate employment in black neighborhoods made room for "vice markets" of illegal drugs, alcohol, gambling, prostitution, and numbers games to "flourish" and inevitably bring residents in close contact with police.[54]

Black people were more likely than white people to carry weapons like knives and guns for self-protection because of underpolicing in their neighborhoods, racial violence when traveling through all-white neighborhoods, the existence of poverty-induced crime, and their mistrust of a racially biased criminal justice system.[55] Since black men had little control over their access to secure employment and financial stability, they "exercised" their masculinity through violence when they faced confrontations in the street and at home that threatened their social reputation. Moreover, murder was about not only self-protection but also asserting one's manhood through the display of dominance over adversaries who challenged their masculinity, such as friends, domestic partners, romantic rivals, police, and strangers.[56]

Moreover, the scholarship of academics like Khalil Gibran Muhammad, Tera Agyepong, Carl Suddler, Elizabeth K. Hinton, and Eric C. Schneider on the criminalization of black people in urban spaces has set the stage for new research on how police, journalists, and city officials have used crime narratives about black people to stigmatize neighborhoods and housing projects highly populated by poor African Americans and expropriate value from them through tough-on-crime policing. Academic disciplines within the social and natural sciences have already debunked generations of racist ideological rhetoric circulated in media, political discourse, and everyday conversation detailing the myth of black inferiority and stereotypical characterizations of all-black communities as "ghettos" filled with poverty, crime, juvenile gang activity, and gun violence. However, these racist ideas about African Americans are still embedded in our minds as schema (or collective knowledge) we may have learned in our neighborhoods, schools, religious institutions, community centers, or the media. Unfortunately, people in power, especially government officials, often use that schema to justify political goals like tough-on-crime policing and racial capitalism against people of color, the working class, and the poor. Nevertheless, this fight against antiblackness in education, government, and our society as a whole remains with us in the present day.

A New Intervention: Racial Stereotypes, Criminalized Bodies, and Racial Capitalism

For generations, police, journalists, and city officials used crime narratives featuring antiblack stereotypes to promote tough-on-crime policing against African Americans beyond the post–World War II era. Crime narratives influenced white backlash to desegregation and the formation of poor, marginalized, and overpoliced black communities in urban postwar cities. The result of the public's consumption of these narratives was hypersegregation, the stigmatization of black neighborhoods, the adultification of criminal black youth, and tough-on-crime policing. This race- and class-based tough-on-crime program against African Americans as a group and later as individuals was justified and city-financed because of their mythologized identity of racial inferiority.

Scholarship from historians, sociologists, anthropologists, and criminologists are the foundation of this monograph. Additionally, original research based on an interdisciplinary and investigative analysis of primary sources like newspaper articles, archived news reels, municipal court dockets, census records, oral histories, interviews, police investigation reports, housing project pamphlets, and maps uplift this narrative. These primary sources serve as concrete evidence that the most visible consequences of tough-on-crime policing were hypersurveillance, the use of excessive force, and neglect by officers in the most disadvantaged areas of the city: poor, segregated, and black-inhabited housing projects and neighborhoods.

By looking through the lens of Philadelphia specifically, I emphasize that the budgetary strategy of a city government spending more money on policing and corrections than social welfare programs is ineffective and a form of racial capitalism that relies on criminal scapegoating, continues the cycle of poverty-induced crime, inflates rates of incarceration and police brutality, and marginalizes poor people of color. However, over time, community activists fought against the stigmatization and criminalization of blackness and even established their own social welfare programs when city officials defunded public resources that largely benefited people of color. Nevertheless, these activists functioned as agents of resistance in an era when big cities like Philadelphia were more focused on achieving a balanced city budget than resolving issues of poverty, racial discrimination, racial tension, and the racial wealth gap between white and black people in the city.

Hope and Struggle in the Policed City is divided into two parts and has six chapters. Part 1 explains how African Americans experienced and resisted the victimizing stigma of mythologized black inferiority along with gradual criminalization from police, journalists, city officials, citizens, and the media in Philadelphia from approximately 1900 to 1970. Chapter 1 explores how from the 1910s to 1935, the myth of a "black invasion" of African Americans into all-white neighborhoods following the Great Migration triggered resistance from white segregationists in the form of race riots, police power, and discriminatory housing laws. However, all these efforts failed, as black people persistently found ways to bypass those impediments and desegregate white communities. Although black people faced de facto segregation in Center City, where they were banned from patronizing lunch counters, hotels, restaurants, and theaters, many African Americans were still able to overcome those racial restrictions and achieve middle-class status.

Chapter 2 discusses how from 1935 through 1957, racial tension between black and white people in residential neighborhoods intensified as desegregation expanded, postwar crime among juveniles increased, and police and journalists cultivated the stereotype of "the jungle"—a crime-ridden, gang-active, impoverished black slum—to keep white people out of black neighborhoods in North and West Philadelphia. Once newspapers like the *Philadelphia Evening Bulletin* and the *Philadelphia Inquirer* published crime narratives about violence and murder committed by black juvenile gang members in the city, the stereotype of "the jungle" was spread by everyday citizens to maintain racial and class solidarity against desegregation and promote tough-on-crime policing against African Americans.

Chapter 3 continues the saga by demonstrating how from 1958 to 1969, police and journalists shifted from disseminating criminal narratives about neighborhood jungles to publicizing a new threat to society: "roving black gangs." When a University of Pennsylvania graduate student was murdered in an integrated West Philadelphia neighborhood by a group of black teenagers, city officials feared white flight and white middle-class disinvestment from the inner-city institutions that fed Philadelphia's tax base. Nevertheless, while community groups sought to eliminate black gang violence through education, recreation, social welfare, and job training, police and public officials responded to the murder with tough-on-crime policing and incarceration.

Part 2 explains how double victimization occurred when African Americans experienced and fought against not only criminalization but also tough-on-crime policing, actual black crime, poverty, and the defunding of much-needed social welfare programs in black neighborhoods, at housing projects, and on city streets from approximately 1970 to 1979. Chapter 4 shows how the gang-related deaths of innocent young people inspired city officials, police, former gang members, and community activists to solve juvenile gang violence through community-led peaceful initiatives like Safe Streets, Inc., instead of brute police force. Although Safe Streets, Inc., was largely successful in rehabilitating black youth, it failed to convince City Council and the police department to make long-term financial investments in the organization because it didn't swiftly lower the rate of violent crime, totally eradicate gang activity, or erase the stigma of black gang violence attached to North and West Philadelphia.

Chapter 5 explains how African Americans already facing poverty, housing inequality, and residential isolation in places like South Philadelphia's Wilson Park housing project experienced race- and class-biased excessive force and criminalization from police during criminal investigations. Crime narratives and the existence of actual black crime at housing projects, including the murder of a police officer by a black youth, made it easy for police to justify the use of excessive force in these black-inhabited spaces. Nevertheless, the police department's use of the crime-fighting strategy Operation FIND (Fugitive Interception Net Deployment) stigmatized poor black communities, terrorized black residents, and criminalized not only black gangs but also black individuals who were found in hypersegregated environments like housing projects.

Lastly, Chapter 6 describes how tough-on-crime policing led to surveillance, hyperpolicing, and police brutality in black and poor neighborhoods. Although many Philadelphians resisted corrupt police officers by pursuing court cases, producing editorials and investigative reports, and giving testimonies at town hall meetings about the issue of police brutality, this tough-on-crime program would support a system of racial capitalism that expropriated value from black communities and bestowed financial wealth to the police department and City Council. The arrest and incarceration of residents for real and manufactured crime provided police officers with extra income through paid overtime for hours served during criminal interrogations and court appearances. City Council also benefited from tough-on-crime policing because the crime-prevention program worked to convince the white middle class to stay in the inner city, pay taxes, and protect the tax base as Philadelphia struggled with financial debt.

Today, crime narratives about African Americans are less racially stigmatizing, but these narratives are still used to support tough-on-crime policing in major urban cities like Philadelphia. Crime narratives facilitate a system of racial capitalism that promotes the expropriation of value from low-income black communities, condones police brutality to prevent black crime, and heaps countless socioeconomic and judicial benefits onto militarized police departments at the expense of everyday citizens. Furthermore, the overall goal of this book is to be more than fodder for academic discussions on race and policing in America. The stories told here are meant to be provocative and memorable, as they were written in the spirit of James Baldwin's description, "To be a Negro in this country and to be relatively conscious is to be in a state of rage almost all of the time and in one's work."[57] Moreover, my hope is that this book ultimately sparks a moral imperative in city officials, police, journalists, policymakers, and everyday citizens to rightfully and wholeheartedly upend structures of social inequality concerning poverty, mass incarceration, and the policing system.

PART I

Black Migration, Settlement, and Stigmatization (1900–1970)

Yes we are going north!
I don't care to what state,
Just so I cross the Dixon line,
From this southern land of hate,
Lynched and burned and shot and hung,
And not a word is said.
No law whatever to protect—
It's just a "nigger" dead.
Go on, dear brother; you'll ne'er regret;
Just trust in God; pray for the best,
And at the end you're sure to find
"Happiness will be thine."
—William Crosse, "The Land of Hope"

1

"The Great 'Black Invasion'"

In 1920, twenty-one-year-old Howard Crosby Brittenum left his parents' sharecropping farm in Holly Grove, Arkansas, to create a new life in Philadelphia.[1] With a seventh-grade education and some training in "hotel work," which consisted of waiting tables and taking care of banquets, Brittenum's only expectation upon arriving in Philadelphia was to "get a job."[2] His step-uncle had recently married a woman with family there, and since the couple couldn't read very well, they bought Brittenum a train ticket so he could become their "interpreter" as they adjusted to life in the North.

During World War I and beyond, black Arkansans from Monroe County often migrated to Kansas City, Saint Louis, and Chicago, but by the Second World War, African Americans from rural communities were traveling to California for a new beginning, where the threat of white racial violence seemed to be minimal, wages were higher, and black populations were growing. From 1865 to 1950, there were approximately 6,500 lynchings in America, with Mississippi, Georgia, Louisiana, and Arkansas being the top four states in the country where this extralegal violence occurred.[3] Living in the South was dangerous for African Americans, where, in the words of historian Leon Litwack, white supremacists found "slow, methodical, sadistic, often highly inventive forms of torture and mutilation" to reestablish the racial hierarchy in local communities after the Civil War ended slavery.[4] African Americans often faced violent backlash for challenging the repressive Jim Crow laws of segregation and attempting to exercise their civil rights to vote, hold public office, own property, and demand fair wages from white employers. But there was also the constant threat of a white mob torturing, murdering, and desecrating the body of a black person who engaged in social interactions across the color line (including friendship, flirtation, sex, and cohabitation) or was falsely accused of "high crimes" like rape, robbery, and murder against a white person.[5] For example,

Kathryn "Kitty" Woodard's family left Fort Valley, Georgia, for Philadelphia in 1919 after her Uncle Leon was nearly lynched by a white mob of "hoodlums" in town. A white waitress falsely accused Woodard's uncle of "bothering" her when he rejected her romantic advances. Woodard's father secretly drove the man (who hid on the floor of the car under a rug) to safety in the nearby city of Macon, where he later traveled to Baltimore. Although Woodard had a "comfortable" life—her father ran a taxi business, her mother owned a grocery store, and the family lived in a house her grandfather built—the sentiment of "I'm not gonna raise my children up like this," her father lamented, captured the disgust and fear that motivated the family's move up North.[6]

For "refugees of the Jim Crow South," migrating North meant escaping not only racial intimidation but also socioeconomic oppression.[7] In the North, black migrants could find industrial and service jobs that paid as much as quadruple the wages a farm laborer would make in a day. Although the cost of living in the urban North was much more expensive than life in the rural Deep South, wages and housing opportunities were considerably better in the North. A farmer could see his salary increase from $0.75 to $4.50 a day as a factory worker in Illinois, or a migrant without housing could earn "$2.75 a day plus a rent-free room" as a dye plant laborer in New Jersey.[8] For example, young widow Beulah Collins was a migrant from Snow Hill, Maryland, whose brothers and sisters convinced her to travel to Wilmington, Delaware, and then Philadelphia for better domestic work and health care options after her husband died of pneumonia while stationed at Camp Meade during World War I. However, Collins decided to stay in Philadelphia permanently for the educational opportunities that would benefit her young son: "I had poor education and I wanted my child to have better."[9]

Urban cities in the North and West were also gradually cultivating large African American communities. From 1780 to 1900, over 90 percent of African Americans lived in the South, and by 1900, approximately 80 percent of black people lived in rural communities.[10] However, from 1900 to 1930, during the Great Migration, cities like Detroit, Cleveland, Chicago, and Philadelphia saw their black populations double and even quadruple. Philadelphia, in particular, witnessed its black population increase from 4.8 percent to 11.3 percent during those three decades.[11] Despite the 6.6 million black people who traveled North during the Great

Migration, many African Americans remained in the South, but by 1970, 80 percent of African Americans lived in cities where governmental services were centralized and social, political, and economic opportunities were better than in the countryside.

Prior to receiving his step-uncle's invitation, Brittenum had already lived and worked in Memphis and Saint Louis, but his goal was to move to Chicago. For years, white and black newspapers like the *Arkansas Gazette* and the *Chicago Defender*, respectively, informed Arkansans about life in the North, and with this information, Brittenum could plan a new life outside of Southern society that would inevitably take place in Philadelphia. Once he arrived, Brittenum lived with his step-aunt and uncle at 34th and Wharton Streets in the South Philadelphia neighborhood of Grays Ferry, where African American, Italian, Irish, and Polish families lived. Then he got an eight-dollar-a-week job as a dishwasher at Green's Hotel at 8th and Chestnut Streets in downtown Philadelphia.[12]

Over the course of twelve years, Brittenum became accustomed to city life and accepted his acculturation to Northern traditions and social mores—he believed Southern migrants like himself needed "eight to ten years mostly at that time to learn how to live in a city." In Philadelphia, working-class and poor blacks and whites sometimes lived in proximity to one another, but the Fourth, Fifth, Seventh, and Eighth Wards were historic black communities located between Pine and Bainbridge Streets in South Philadelphia. In Brittenum's neighborhood, he witnessed Philadelphia's racial segregation and had to navigate traveling to and from home, work, and the dance hall to avoid violent confrontations with white people:

> West Philadelphia was considered a nice neighborhood. North Philadelphia was considered the roughest neighborhood, worst neighborhood. Especially among colored people there. . . . South Philadelphia . . . until you got below Washington Avenue was tough down there. . . . You might have—put up a fight if you got down in there . . . [the black area was bounded] from 19th Street [to the west] to Carpenter Street [to the south] back to Pine Street [to the north]. Didn't hardly get no further than Pine because I think white people was on Spruce Street more or less . . . all the way back to Fifth Street going east . . . pretty well colored population in there.[13]

At Green's Hotel, he received his first experience working with white people in menial labor jobs. Prior to the Great Migration, African Americans in Philadelphia were either educators, self-made caterers, ministers, "professionals, small business owners, and domestic servants" of highly esteemed white families, or unskilled laborers who worked as chauffeurs, porters, maids, butlers, cleaners, and postal workers.[14] However, wealth and sociopolitical power were heavily concentrated in white society. The racial hierarchy at Brittenum's workplace restricted black people to jobs as waiters, busboys, bellboys, and maids, while white people held jobs as janitors and storeroom laborers at the hotel. Eventually, Brittenum worked at a local YMCA doing banquet work in the facility's dining room, earned extra money on the weekends doing barbering, and acquired single housing for himself near 16th and Catharine Streets, where he rented a room in a private house. He discontinued several rural customs and began to "act" and "dress" in a Northern fashion, which for him, in particular, included sleeping in actual pajamas instead of his underwear. By 1932, Brittenum, upon the advice of a friend, pursued a barber's license and maintained that profession until his retirement in 1980. With this career, he was able to get married, start a family, and live in his own home.[15]

Once Brittenum settled in Philadelphia for a few years, he began to notice how rural black migrants like himself were different from native-born black Philadelphians. Over time, he learned that the agrarian lifestyle was stigmatized in the North's urban metropolises as backward and a symbol of poverty. Northern whites and blacks often viewed the majority of black migrants as culturally inferior and socially awkward because of their farming attire, Southern accents, and lack of belongings and money upon arrival. Many migrants like Brittenum either had a limited education or were illiterate because rural children were often pulled out of school during the winter and summer seasons to assist their sharecropper parents with planting and harvesting crops. When Brittenum (now reinvented as a Northern city dweller) saw black migrants regularly "pour" out from trains at Philadelphia's Broad Street Station, he immediately noticed how socioeconomically disadvantaged they were, since many arrived with no suitcases but a "big bundle" of their clothing wrapped in a sheet along with a prepared homemade lunch so they did not have to spend money on food during their journey.[16] Ralph Harold Jones, a black "Old Philadelphian" whose family lived in the city for several generations prior to the Great Migration of rural black Southern-ers, recalled seeing them arrive in Philadelphia "dusty and dirty" wearing "rustic clothing," with some migrants settling in the city with a wartime job promised to them but nowhere to live in South Philadelphia:

> They came up in coveralls and overalls . . . you could tell they were from the country and they would gravitate to the black neighborhoods which was South Street . . . about 8th and 9th Street to Broad Street [east to west] and Bainbridge and Pine [south to north], you'd find them all there. At that time, Philadelphia was a crossroads for the northeastern states. Peo-ple from Boston and New Haven. . . . even New York State, if they were coming to Philadelphia, would say, "I'll meet you at Broad and South."[17]

When black migrants found housing and settled into their new homes in Philadelphia, they were often criticized for their Southern culture and

Philadelphia's Broad Street Station, date unknown. Special Collections Research Center, Temple University Libraries, Philadelphia, PA / George D. McDowell *Philadelphia Evening Bulletin* Collection.

traditions that many Northerners viewed as threats to their neighbor-hoods' real estate value. Aside from rural migrants wearing their work clothing all day, every day (except for Sunday, when formal dress was required for church), many kept farm animals for food sustainability, lived in housing units as intergenerational families, sheltered fel-low migrants who needed a "stopover" while they looked for work in another Northern city, and sometimes painted their homes in unique colors that disrupted the visual uniformity of a series of rowhomes on a city block.[18] Even the oft-quoted scholar, civil rights activist, and black elite Sadie Tanner Mossell referred to the newcomers as a "group generally uneducated and untrained."[19] By the 1930s, black enclaves spread throughout Philadelphia, and certain blocks within these spaces would acquire monikers like "Little Georgia" (between York Street and Susquehanna Avenue in North Philadelphia), as they were identified as areas where migrants from similar states could find community in their newly adopted city.[20] Nevertheless, as thousands of black rural migrants arrived in Philadelphia, the more segregated the city became as racist white residents along with middle- and upper-class black citizens con-cerned about their racial reputation resisted these newcomers.

From 1905 to 1915, white supremacist literature and film mythologized black people as racially inferior and inherently criminal while also cel-ebrating white mob vigilante groups like the Ku Klux Klan that "pro-tected" white supremacy in American society. In 1905, white supremacist and lawyer Thomas Dixon Jr. released the book *The Clansman: A His-torical Romance of the Ku Klux Klan*, subscribing to the Dunning school interpretation of the Civil War, which argued that although the war was a "Lost Cause" for Southerners, the Confederate States of America (CSA) fought gallantly to defend slave owners' state right to enslaving African Americans as their property.[21] Dixon's narrative celebrated men like his fa-ther and uncle, who retaliated against the social reforms of Reconstruc-tion by participating in Klan parades and the lynchings of alleged "black [male] rapists" of white women.[22] After Dixon's novel sold over a million copies nationwide, director D. W. Griffith transformed it into the 1915 film *The Birth of a Nation*.[23] By 1920, approximately fifty million people saw the 193-minute propaganda film that offered viewers a Confederate apologist's recollection of Reconstruction, including sitting president Woodrow Wil-son, who authorized a White House screening of the photoplay.[24]

During the 1910s and 1920s, journalists and scholars described how the arrival of hundreds of thousands of rural black migrants to the North would be detrimental to the socioeconomic lives of people native to the region. Iterations of the "Negro Problem" had already been circulating around the country when newspapers like the *Philadelphia Public Ledger* argued that the city's housing market was overwhelmed and ill resourced because of the new migrants' demand for lodging. In one case, the newspaper reported that twenty men were "herded together like cattle" into a sixteen-by-twenty-foot room where they slept on the floor and paid the proprietor $1.50 a week.[25]

When scholars, white and black, analyzed the effects of the Great Migration on urban cities, they highlighted not only the causes of black migrants' move up North but also the potential consequences their presence would have in disrupting the established racial order, social politics, and economy of urban cities. However, some black social scientists were particularly concerned about Southern black migrants unintentionally provoking white Northerners to rescribe racial stereotypes onto the entire Northern black population because the socioeconomic status and cultural mores of the majority of rural black Southerners were stigmatized as inferior to the lifestyle of Northerners, white and black alike. Black sociologist E. Franklin Frazier referred to the migration as "changing the whole structure of the Negro community," while economist Sadie Tanner Mossell described it as "crushing and stagnating the progress of Negro life" because, from their perspective, Southern blacks appeared to be overwhelming urban populations and damaging the racial reputation of African Americans by refusing to conform and submit to the perceived expectations of white society.[26]

Locally, Mossell explained in her 1921 doctoral thesis in economics, "The Standard of Living among One Hundred Negro Migrant Families in Philadelphia," that "dissatisfaction with the tenant and crop sharing system," segregation, and "mistreatment and persecution by representatives of the law" were some of the economic, social, and political reasons why black migrants traveled North. However, from Mossell's viewpoint, black migrants supposedly threatened the "social and educational facilities" black Old Philadelphians enjoyed along with "courteous treatment" from white people because their presence in large numbers and social traits triggered white racist sentiments of black inferiority.[27] At that time, Mossell was convinced that black people had to prove their humanity and perfect their fluency in white Anglo-Saxon Protestant culture to win white social acceptance and equality in the North. Nevertheless, black scholars like Mossell believed rural black migrants were jeopardizing all the hard work long-standing black Northerners had put in to acculturate to perceived white standards before the Great Migration upset the historic demography of cities like Philadelphia.

When the manufacturing and construction sectors in Philadelphia declined and the Great Depression of 1929 launched millions of Americans nationwide into poverty, black migrants became "scapegoats" for the socioeconomic problems that developed during this era. From 1929 to 1933, business activity in Philadelphia dropped by approximately 33 percent, and about 20 percent of homeowners lost their abodes to foreclosure and eviction. By March 1933, roughly 40 percent of Philadelphians were unemployed and 20 percent were part-time laborers.[28] While manufacturing jobs were in decline, the demand for service jobs increased and more women gained employment, particularly in domestic labor. Consequently, factory workers and marginalized groups like people of color, immigrants, and the elderly (who faced racial discrimination, xenophobia, and ageism in the job market) suffered greatly during this economic shift. For African Americans living in Philadelphia during the Great Depression, approximately 50 percent were unemployed and 60 percent qualified for work relief and public assistance.[29] Nevertheless, as education scholar John P. Spencer explained, native-born Philadelphians blamed black migrants for "rising crime rates, a booming underground economy, public disorder, and deteriorating neighborhoods" because the migrants' arrival coincided with the beginning of an economic downturn. Black migrants were also scapegoated for altering the city's labor market (which originally consisted of locally employed laborers) and, from the perspective of native black Philadelphians, triggering "antiblack attitudes" that would curtail African Americans' efforts to achieve full equality and respect from white people in the city.[30] Nevertheless, journalists and social scientists greatly shaped the low expectations many everyday citizens had of black migrants. They were, as journalist Isabel Wilkerson explained, "cast as poor illiterates who imported out-of-wedlock births, joblessness, and welfare dependency" despite the fact that in comparison to their Northern black counterparts, they had similar years of schooling and were more likely to be married, be employed, and raise children in a two-parent household.[31]

For many of these black migrants, their drive for success reflected an "emigrant psyche" that produced countless businessmen, activists, entertainers, and politicians, including seven of the first black mayors in the North and West, who were the progeny of migrants of the Great Migration.[32] Although there were black migrants who faced unemployment, engaged in vice, and/or delved into criminality, their black Southern culture did not catapult them into those life experiences or corrupt the Northern black population to stereotypically engage in vice and crime. Instead, as historian Florette Henri argued, black migrants of the Great Migration weren't "passive reactors" to race-based social, political, and economic inequality in the South but go-getters like the "American blacks" who emigrated to Canada, the West Indies, Sierra Leone, and Liberia throughout American history to achieve freedom from slavery and racial oppression and acquire the American Dream by "making it happen" on their own.[33]

During the 1920s, urban elites, journalists, scholars, and everyday people labeled Southern black migrants of the Great Migration as a plague that brought vice and crime, along with a backward and corruptible culture, to urban Northern cities. Although these issues, along with racial segregation and discrimination, existed in the North prior to these migrants' arrival, black Southerners became scapegoats for the urban problems that existed in society. Eventually, the stereotypes and stigmas placed on rural black migrants stigmatized the entire black population in Northern cities like Philadelphia regardless of their social, political, economic, or nativity status. The racist and classist stereotypes of rural black migrants as impoverished, unclean, lazy, welfare dependent, violent, and criminal helped expand, intensify, and solidify racial segregation and prejudice against African Americans in public spaces and residential communities through the 1930s.

Philadelphia: A Segregated City of Neighborhoods

In the nineteenth century, Philadelphia was a city of diverse ethnicities, with many being foreign-born and working-class white ethnics fleeing famine, political unrest, and religious persecution in their home countries. Among all the ethnicities present in the city, "old-stock" Philadelphians of English and German descent had ancestors who lived in America for more than seven generations. German Americans, specifically, had been in the Philadelphia area since the 1600s, when Germantown was established as a community for German immigrants, especially those tied to religious organizations such as the Quakers and Lutherans.[34] By the 1860s and lasting until the 1890s, the Irish, who had first started coming to Philadelphia to escape the Potato Famine, were the largest immigrant group in the city as their population grew from 16.9 percent to 41 percent.[35] From 1870 to 1960, most city blocks in Philadelphia were segregated by race, class, and ethnicity. North, West, South, and Central Philadelphia were highly populated by white immigrants or native-born citizens whose families had been in America for three to seven generations.[36]

Although Philadelphia was home to predominantly Anglo-Saxons and Irish, several other European descendants resided in the city.[37] In North Philadelphia, there were Irish, Eastern European, and Jewish enclaves in Kensington and Port Richmond where the proliferation of synagogues, kosher meat markets, and Jewish-owned businesses made the area colloquially known as "Jewtown" and "Jerusalem."[38] During the twentieth century, Puerto Ricans from the rural areas of Salinas and San Lorenzo migrated to North Philadelphia to find jobs as factory workers, domestics, white-collar professionals, and agricultural laborers as Puerto Rico pursued mass urbanization, since sugar, tobacco, and coffee industries were declining on the island.[39] They settled in Spring Garden, Kensington, Port Richmond, and Fairhill and, by the 1960s, had established their own commercial corridors like Centro de Oro where other Latinos from primarily Cuba, Mexico, Dominican Republic, and Central America also arrived and opened grocery stores, movie theaters, and department stores.[40]

In the center of the city, "The Tenderloin," located within the borders of 6th and 12th Streets and Callowhill to Arch Streets, encompassed Chinatown, where Asian Americans as early as 1870 fled the racial violence of the Driving Out on the West Coast to create a new life in a segregated area near Skid Row, a "vice district" known for its "burlesque houses," "gin joints," and flophouses.[41] Chinatown later grew into a residential community and a commercial district surrounded by community centers, churches, and legal agencies.[42] Over time, Asian immigrants from Korea and Vietnam would become the second and third largest Asian populations in the city (after Chinese), but since the city had no historic enclaves for them to settle in similar to Chinatown, they often lived throughout the city, clustered in North, South, and West Philadelphia neighborhoods alongside whites or blacks based on their class status.[43]

In West Philadelphia, there were majority Irish residents who lived in the "Top" beyond 52nd Street, while African Americans lived within the borders of 32nd to 40th Streets and Market Street to Powelton Avenue in an area known as the "Black Bottom." In South Philadelphia, there were Italian, Irish, Jewish, Polish, and Lithuanian residents living in conditions as diverse as "one-story white houses with ducks, pigs, and chickens in 'The Neck,'" located south of Moore Street and between the Schuylkill and Delaware Rivers, to tar paper shacks surrounded by "unpaved roads, pig farms, trash dumps, and outdoor toilets" in the Southwest, known as "The Meadows."[44] Neighborhoods outside of these locations, like Germantown, Mount Airy, and Chestnut Hill, usually housed Philadelphians of English and German descent.[45] These neighborhoods were also stratified by class. In Germantown alone, the neighborhood was divided into three class-distinct areas: "Dogtown" referred to the upper edge between Upsal and Johnson Streets, where "proud dog owners" lived in single and multifamily homes; "Smearsburg" (named after smearcase, a German-style cottage cheese) was known as a working-class area south of Penn Street; and "Brickyard" referred to a blue-collar community at the lower edge (bordering Nicetown) at Germantown and Wister Avenues, where businessman Samuel Collum operated his brickmaking facility near the Reading Railroad train station, Wayne Junction.[46]

As early as the 1890s, African Americans from Southeastern states like North and South Carolina, Virginia, and Georgia steadily traveled to Philadelphia, often by train, for better employment, housing, and educational opportunities while also escaping the debt-inducing poverty of the sharecropping system, segregation, and racial violence from white supremacist groups like the Ku Klux Klan.[47] When working-class African Americans arrived in Philadelphia, they often lived in tenements, shacks, and rowhomes in segregated all-black neighborhoods or side by side with white immigrant families in South and North Philadelphia, where housing was affordable, crowded, and located in "undesirable" places, often near dockyards, rivers, and swampland.[48] When Marcus Foster migrated with his family from Athens, Georgia, to South Philadelphia as a child in the 1920s, his neighborhood was "full of Italian and Jewish migrant families" where, despite a few "turf battles" between the Irish and Italians, different ethnic groups largely lived in peace and children played "street games like rugby, stickball, and jump rope" in the desegregated community.[49] Similar to native-born black Philadelphians, black migrants acquired service jobs in white-owned businesses or were employed at industrial centers, railroads, shipyards, and steel companies like the Pennsylvania and Erie Railroads and Midvale Steel, where they were traditionally given the dirtiest jobs, paid less than their white counterparts, and sometimes blocked from joining unions.[50] When "old-stock" working-class whites gained upward social mobility by acquiring jobs as policemen, firemen, and watchmen, white immigrants (like the Irish and Italians) and African Americans competed for the jobs in the construction of brickwork, bridges, and railroads and domestic labor they left behind. Nevertheless, "old-stock" politicians gave ethnic privilege to Irish and Italian Americans by gradually promoting them through the ranks of government in areas like City Council and the police department.[51]

Although black migrants left the Jim Crow South to escape racial segregation, racial and class biases awaited them in the North. However, some white immigrants also encountered segregation, employment discrimination, and economic exploitation too because their foreign origins and culture were stigmatized as "other." Nevertheless, many migrants and immigrants (white and black) relied on social welfare institutions like settlement houses to provide them assistance with housing, employment, health care, education, and recreation to keep them out of poverty, homelessness, and criminality.[52] As early as the 1880s, black and white activists in Philadelphia were concerned about the existence and effects of poor housing on newcomers to the city, particularly African Americans. Since homes in the city's black neighborhoods were often dilapidated and exorbitantly priced, black churches, settlement houses, and local philanthropists often worked with community activists and professionals trained in the health and social sciences to improve the quality of life for black residents of the slums. These organizations and activists were not able to eradicate the slums, but they provided charitable outreach to African Americans who sought out their help.[53]

As early as 1880, banker and philanthropist Theodore Starr purchased a lot on Saint Mary Street in South Philadelphia, built several homes, and sold them to African Americans at a low cost.[54] Starr's initiative influenced Susan Parrish Wharton, a Quaker philanthropist and graduate of Vassar College, to establish the Octavia Hill Association in 1888 with her cousin Helen Parrish to renovate dilapidated homes to rent and sell to poor and working-class black families at an affordable rate.[55] In 1893, Wharton and several other social reformers established the Whittier Centre in South Philadelphia, a settlement house that offered social programs to help recent black migrants from the South adjust to their new lives in Philadelphia. Among the social welfare services offered at the Whittier Centre were affordable and decent housing programs, tuberculosis testing and treatment, and financial savings clubs facilitated by black staff who were professionally trained social workers and medical officials.[56] Additionally, as historian Matthew J. Countryman has explained, the city's black elite ran social organizations like the Citizen's Republican Club, the Philadelphia Association for the Protection of Colored Women, and the Armstrong Association during the Great Migration era to assist black Southerners in voting and finding employment, despite any ambivalence or contempt they had for rural black migrants.[57] Moreover, these social services offered by philanthropists and social workers, medical officials, and community activists enabled black migrants to adjust to their new lives in Philadelphia despite the difficulties they encountered in housing, employment, and health care.

At the start of the twentieth century, blackness and poverty became social stigmas often equated with immorality and crime. In sociologist W. E. B. Du Bois's 1899 monograph *The Philadelphia Negro*, he discussed the competing theories of nature versus nurture in regard to the "submerged tenth," a term coined by English theologian William Booth in his 1890 book *In Darkest England, and the Way Out* referring to the bottom tenth of the population that remained entrenched in poverty.[58] Du Bois argued that the intersecting stigmas of blackness and poverty led to stereotyping African American residents of South Philadelphia's Seventh Ward as inherently vulnerable to vice and crime. From August 1896 to December 1897, Du Bois, with the help of his assistant Isabel Eaton, conducted five thousand interviews, mapped landmarks and social institutions, and administered questionnaires to residents of the Seventh Ward, an area bordered by Spruce Street to the north and South Street to the south and extending from the Schuylkill River east to 7th Street.[59] Through his research, he determined that there was no "Negro Problem" wherein poor black people were a threat to the morality and safety of society. However, as Du Bois explained in the final chapter of *The Philadelphia Negro*, "ignorance, poverty, crime, and the dislike of the stranger" were factors supporting white racism against African Americans through socioeconomic inequality, housing discrimination, and racial violence that created conditions in which black people fell into poverty, illiteracy, vice, and crime.[60] Nevertheless, he concluded that while there were African Americans who engaged in crime, black people were not inherently immoral or criminal because of their race, as naturalists, eugenicists, and social Darwinists of the time used pseudo-science to argue as fact.[61] These racist myths encouraged many outside of the "submerged tenth" to view the poor (who were often black) as threats to middle-class and all-white communities, which resulted in residents of different races and classes using the law and violence to strengthen residential segregation in their neighborhoods.[62]

From 1900 to 1935, white segregationists noticed the migration of thousands of Southern blacks to Philadelphia and responded with not just violence but also laws enforcing residential segregation. In 1910, Philadelphia's population was nearly 1.5 million, and residents of European descent were the racial majority living in distinct ethnic enclaves in South, North, and West Philadelphia. The population of specifically white ethnic immigrants from Eastern and Southern Europe steadily increased into 1930.[63] In 1920, Philadelphia's Russian community was the largest immigrant group due to Jewish people escaping pogroms in the Soviet Union. By 1930, the Italian immigrant population in Philadelphia was significant following war along with political and social unrest associated with the Risorgimento (unification of Italy from 1848 to 1871), when it increased from 5 percent to 9.3 percent in twenty years. Prior to the Great Migration, Philadelphia's black population was small in comparison to that of the entire white immigrant community from 1900 to 1920, although it increased from 4.9 percent to 7.3 percent over the span of ten years.[64]

When the United States became involved in World War I (from 1917 to 1918), the war triggered the First Great Migration (1916–30), in which 1.6 million African Americans were inspired to leave the entrenched racism of the rural South and relocate to Northern industrial cities like Philadelphia, looking for wartime jobs and decent, affordable housing. From May 1916 to May 1918 alone, over fifteen thousand black migrants arrived in the city at a rate of approximately 150 people per week. In the summer of 1918, over eight thousand African Americans migrated to the city within three months.[65] As African American migration to Philadelphia continued, profit-seeking landlords capitalized on segregation by offering recent black migrants slum shacks and bandbox houses, often converted into tiny apartments, in exclusively black neighborhoods that were overpriced, overcrowded, and in desperate need of repair.[66] In South Philadelphia, where many migrants first settled, tenement homes were overcrowded, expensive, and lacked modern amenities. Journalists often wrote exposés on the numerous tenement homes along Lombard, Rodman, and Iseminger Streets where multiple families lived in buildings with stagnant water, dark rooms, crumbling walls, winding stairs, and no baths.[67] Despite the decrepit conditions of these tenements, many landlords made a 100 to 200 percent profit each year by overrating the rental price for rooms. For example, in 1935, a one-hundred-room tenement house with no baths at 219 Lombard Street had a real estate value of $4,000, but the landlord earned approximately $10,400 a year with 50 percent occupancy by renting rooms at $4 a week![68]

When African Americans attempted to move into all-white neighborhoods, municipal segregation zoning ordinances usually banned "black occupancy" in those communities, until the Supreme Court made the practice unconstitutional in 1917.[69] When city ordinances were inapplicable, racist white residents protested the arrival of black neighbors with cross burnings, arson, bombings, and stonings at the homes of black families.[70] By the 1920s, restrictive covenants found in the home deeds of nearly every new private housing development built between 1920 and 1948 barred African Americans from living in white neighborhoods.[71] These restrictive covenants consisted of overtly classist and racist clauses requiring homeowners to prohibit multiple-family housing, restrict household animals like pigs and chickens (which some rural migrants owned to maintain their livelihood), and ban home rentals and sales for nonwhite people such as "Africans, Negroes, Ethiopians" and, to a lesser extent, "Asians, Mexicans, and Jews."[72] To make matters worse, federal housing policies established during the Great Depression (1929–41) declared that racial homogeneity existed in new developments, while real estate agents protected the rights of developers and homeowners who desired racially segregated neighborhoods by "steering blacks into racially mixed or all-black neighborhoods."[73]

Southern Black Migrants Are "Invaders"

From as early as 1909, white resistance to black migrants moving into white neighborhoods happened not only in Philadelphia but in other Northern cities across the country. In 1910, Baltimore's Mayor J. Barry Mahool implemented the first residential racial zoning ordinance in America, making it the first city where redlining became legal.[74] The Home Owners' Loan Corporation (HOLC) denied African Americans home loans in white neighborhoods, but middle-class African Americans often found ways to circumvent legal and economic barriers to homeownership in all-white neighborhoods despite white supremacists resisting their black neighbors with threats, rioting, and flight from their own communities. News reporters from New York, Baltimore, and Chicago described how the influx of black families into all-white Northern communities was a "black invasion" that triggered lawsuits, white rioting, and white flight. For example, in 1910, educator of phrenology Adena C. E. Minott bought a house at 121 West 136th Street in an all-white neighborhood of Harlem to house black students from her school, the Clio School of Mental Sciences.[75] According to a journalist from the *Evening World* who covered the story in the 1911 article "Black Invasion of Harlem Stirs Up a Bitter Feud," six hundred white members of the Harlem Property Owners' Protective Association spent a year trying to "oust" Minott from the neighborhood. The organization pursued lawsuits against Minott, and members pledged to not rent or sell their homes to African Americans for fifteen years. However, Minott overcame those challenges with support from the New York branch of the National Association for the Advancement of Colored People (NAACP). The NAACP later created a vigilance committee to file a lawsuit against the property owners' association to guarantee

African Americans the right to purchase homes on 132nd and 139th Streets in Harlem.[76]

On November 2, 1914, twenty-eight-year-old James H. Teagle, the "colored" chauffeur for Philadelphia City Controller John Walton, left his trinity house at 215 South Delhi Street in South Philadelphia to move into a home at 6112 Spruce Street in West Philadelphia with his white wife, Laura, and mother-in-law, Aurelia Jones.[77] The next day, a white mob gathered outside their home, broke their windows, and demanded the family "vacate immediately." On November 4, another white mob of approximately one thousand people surrounded the Teagle home.[78] Unfortunately, Teagle was not home, and his family was left unprotected as he went to work. The white mob taunted the family, and soon, people began to throw sticks, bricks, and stones at the house. One youth used an axe to shatter the glass on the front door.[79] The stoning of the Teagle house damaged windowpanes and furniture and injured Teagle's mother-in-law, who was knocked unconscious by a stone or brick that came through a window. Around 8:00 p.m., Teagle arrived home, and upon seeing the riot, he called the police. When Eighteenth District police arrived, they dispersed the mob but made no arrests. Two days later, the Teagles agreed to move, and their white neighbors raised money to purchase their home and pay for the damages made by the white mob.[80] Following the incident, the local chapter of the NAACP investigated the riot and offered legal support, but Teagle refused and later moved into an apartment located in a black neighborhood in North Philadelphia.[81]

On March 4, 1922, black principal Harry T. Pratt and his family moved into a "solid white" block at 527 Stanford Place in Baltimore. Three days later, a group of white neighbors carrying bricks and pistols attacked the Pratt home, shattering its windows, unhinging the front door, and splattering ink on its marble steps.[82] Like Teagle, Pratt's white neighbors used violence to convince him and his family to leave the neighborhood so that the white residents who opposed desegregation would not have to move out or risk real estate agents devaluing their home's property value.

And in March 1923, two white Chicagoans, identified as "Yanker" and "An Evader" in the *Chicago Tribune*, wrote letters to the editor detailing how the "invasion" of black migrants from the South to white neighborhoods in Chicago inspired them to move elsewhere.[83] In Yanker's letter, "Moving," he described himself as a "white man" who moved four times in six years (with plans to move again) to "evade the black invasion" of the South Side.[84] In An Evader's letter, "Race Irritation," the author complained that African Americans were moving to all-white residential communities all over Chicago.[85] An Evader further stated that other non–Anglo Saxon groups had stayed in their own communities, like Chinatown and Little Italy, but African Americans refused to settle completely in the Black Belt (located on the South Side of Chicago). An Evader summed up the letter in a protest for segregation, stating, "If the Negroes would pick a certain section of the city and stay there, all this argument would be passe. Instead, they keep up their invasion of the white neighborhoods, north, south, east, and west."[86] Furthermore, both authors, who read newspaper articles laced with racist narratives of black migration, were convinced that African Americans were encroaching upon their communities and white people had to resist in any way possible. Moreover, the white residents across the country who evolved from antidesegregation lawsuits and riots to white flight facilitated the process of inner-city neighborhoods gradually becoming hypersegregated prior to World War II.

Additionally, some white journalists who covered news stories about racial desegregation were highly vocal about their resentment regarding the gradual migration of middle-class black families into all-white neighborhoods throughout the country. As one journalist from the *Birmingham News* explained in his 1918 article about a reported incident of white resistance to black neighbors in South Philadelphia, "A Different Black Invasion," black migrants had no right to "impose" on whites in cities like Philadelphia and "invade" districts "long occupied" by the white community.[87] The author further argued that white people had a right to "indignant protest," or to riot against their black neighbors because the "consequences" of accepting racial desegregation were a "bad feeling," a "depreciation of real estate values, and an increase of lawlessness." The underlying sentiment in this article was that black people were inherently criminal regardless of their character, social status, or profession. Since African Americans themselves were racially stigmatized as criminals, the spaces they occupied were also marked as criminal areas. Furthermore, the author concluded that white residents should use armed resistance to prevent their neighborhoods from becoming "a perfect haven for the most disreputable negroes" or look forward to their communities becoming desegregated, financially devalued criminal spaces where "dope-smoking, crap-shooting, gun-fighting, razor-cutting, and joy-riding" were commonplace.[88] Moreover, the news reports of lawsuits, riots, and white flight were examples of how false crime narratives laced with racial stereotypes persuaded some white people to fear and resist desegregation in neighborhoods and, to a greater extent, in schools and government, which middle-class black people would eventually populate if they lived in the same communities as white people.

From 1908 to 1935, many black Philadelphians achieved middle-class status—2,009 were teachers, policemen, businessmen, physicians, and clergymen. Additionally, black homeownership in Philadelphia increased by over 1,200 percent, making it an exceptional yet capitalist-driven city with the most black homeowners above the Mason-Dixon Line.[89] In the 1930s, some black families witnessed violent backlash from their neighbors in all-white communities, while others experienced white flight from their neighborhood block after they settled into their new homes. When the Great Migration brought black migrants from the South into Philadelphia's inner-city communities surrounding Center City, many white residents moved out to all-white neighborhoods on the margins of the city in a phenomenon historian James Wolfinger describes as the "black core–white periphery form of many of America's postwar cities."[90] White real estate agents, who knew how to profit from segregation and integration, noticed the demand for housing "went sky high" and catered to black families who had the money to rent and buy homes in any neighborhood the families desired.[91] As a result of black settlement in all-white neighborhoods, white families panicked and sold their homes to realtors at prices below market value and moved to other racially homogenous communities. It wasn't overcrowding that initiated this pre–World War II white flight but racial prejudice against African Americans (like the narratives about black primitivism and criminality presented in *The Birth of a Nation*) because the suburbanization of counties outside of Philadelphia with new and affordable housing had not occurred until the postwar era.[92]

For example, in 1900, the Thirty-Second Ward of North Philadelphia, in the area bounded by Norris Street to the north and Montgomery Avenue to the south and extending from 19th Street east to 18th Street, was an all-white neighborhood. Among the two hundred English, German, and Irish American families that lived there, the only African Americans who resided there were nineteen servants in private households. By 1930, at least 50 percent of the neighborhood contained African American families, many of whom were working-class renters from the Carolinas, Virginia, Maryland, Mississippi, and West Virginia.[93] Twenty-nine-year-old Riley Posey, a laundryman from South Carolina, was one of these newcomers. He rented a house for his wife, Lelia, and son, Melvin, at 1949 North 19th Street for twenty-six dollars per month. Among the new arrivals to the neighborhood were also black people with middle-class status who could afford to purchase their own homes instead of renting from a landlord. Music teacher John M. Boiling, his wife, Edna, and their six children moved from South Philadelphia to a home at 1927 North 19th Street, which the family purchased for $6,000. Another black family new to the area was Randolph Thompson, a Virginia-born construction worker and World War I veteran, and his wife, Ethel, who moved from Southwest Philadelphia to a home at 1813 Berks Street, which they purchased for $5,000.[94] Other new black homeowners in the Thirty-Second Ward were thirty-four-year-old real estate agent Elizabeth A. Madison of 1815 Berks Street, sixty-one-year-old roofer William Stewart and his fifty-two-year-old wife, Leenma, of 1945 North 19th Street, and forty-one-year-old dressmaker Maggie E. Cook of 1947 North 19th Street.[95]

As African Americans moved into the Thirty-Second Ward, many white families moved out. In 1900, fifty-two-year-old shirt salesman Francis C. Brooker lived with his fifty-two-year-old wife, Maria, and twenty-one-year-old son, William, at 1909 North 19th Street. Brooker lived in his Stanton house over the span of twenty years, where he experienced three major life events: the deaths of his wife and son, his remarriage to Sara Elizabeth Rhoads, and his entrance into retirement.[96] Although Brooker had many familial and emotional ties to Philadelphia, he and his wife sold their home and moved to Doylestown, where he died in 1929.[97] Brooker was not the only white resident to break long-standing ties with their neighborhood to escape their black neighbors. From 1900 to 1930, Philadelphia-born dyer William Pascoe Childs lived with his wife, Caroline, and daughter, Caroline, at 1913 North 19th Street, where they gradually witnessed desegregation in their neighborhood.[98]

By 1940, Childs, now a widower, sold his home and moved to Abington, where his daughter and brother-in-law lived.[99] While some white residents moved to suburban areas to avoid desegregation, others like jewelry engraver Thomas Washington Hitchcock frantically moved multiple times throughout the city to find "peace" by living in an all-white neighborhood.

In 1900, forty-four-year-old Tennessee-born Hitchcock lived with his wife and four children in a home at 2047 North Gratz Street, located in an all-white community.[100] By 1910, Hitchcock sold his house and moved with his family to another home in North Philadelphia located at 1929 North 19th Street.[101] At this Stanton home, the same one James Teagle would eventually live in by 1920, Hitchcock was unsatisfied with the demographic change in the area and decided to sell the house and move again to 3403 North 15th Street in Nicetown-Tioga.[102] Then at the time of Hitchcock's death in 1924, he and his family were living in a new home two doors down, at 3407 North 15th Street.[103] Furthermore, Hitchcock's death did not end the family's instinct to engage in white flight. In 1930, Hitchcock's wife, Anna, moved with her family for a fourth time to 3414 North Carlisle Street, where there were still *affordable* homes for working-class people in an all-white neighborhood![104] Moreover, racism and irrational fears of a "black invasion" drove thousands of white residents like Hitchcock, Childs, and Brooker to leave their neighborhoods during the early years of the Great Migration.

In March 1935, the black-owned, middle-class-conscious newspaper *Philadelphia Tribune* published its investigation into the housing situation in the article "Slums No Accident Claims Tribune Housing Investigator." In the article, journalist Harry B. Webber explained that real estate agents were aware of the racial prejudices many white residents had about black people, and they capitalized on those proclivities and profited from "black and white alike" by engaging in blockbusting.[105] According to Webber, realtors were known to "plant" a "colored family" in a "lily white block" in North and West Philadelphia neighborhoods and wait for white families to respond with panic selling: "Real estate men saw on the one hand a horde of Negro families demanding decent houses. On the other hand they saw long clean blocks of white dwellings in West and North Philadelphia and in Germantown. They quickly learned that when a colored family moves into an all-white block, the rest of the block quickly begins to show 'For Rent' and 'For Sale' signs."[106] Real estate agents knew that white residents viewed black people as inferior, unclean, uncivilized, and prone to engaging in crime, so they "played upon white residents' prejudices" and offered them cash for their homes. The white families took the cash and put down payments on new homes in white neighborhoods while the realtors sold the vacated homes to black families who unknowingly bought them at a rate of at least a thousand dollars more than what the real estate agents paid.[107] Although many realtors were consciously engaging in the lucrative practice of "block emptying" all-white neighborhoods to provide housing options for black families, real estate agents maintained the class status of the existing community by planting a "high-class colored family" in a "high-class" white neighborhood and a "colored laborer family" in a working-class white neighborhood. In working-class white neighborhoods, realtors sometimes further aggravated racial tensions by "planting" a black family with several children because white residents would have a greater chance of discovering their presence when the youths played outside on the street. Furthermore, Webber's article also explained that by 1935, this realtor scheme was a citywide practice done on approximately 5,500 residential blocks in Philadelphia.[108] Nevertheless, when discriminatory housing laws and racially biased policing could not keep black families out of white neighborhoods, white segregationists resorted to white flight to avoid living with African Americans and risking the devaluation of their homes in the midst of residential desegregation.

Conclusion

Black migration and settlement into all-white neighborhoods during the Great Migration triggered resistance from white segregationists in the form of race riots, police power, and discriminatory housing laws. Black people faced de facto segregation in Northern cities, where they were banned from patronizing lunch counters, hotels, restaurants, and theaters. In researcher Charles J. Storey's 1929 investigative report *A Study of Municipal Recreation in Philadelphia*, he discovered that African Americans were excluded from multiple forms of recreation, like "moving picture houses" and "most Y.M.C.A. gymnasiums," leading him to subsequently argue in his pamphlet that it was "the responsibility of the city to provide public recreation."[109] Furthermore, African Americans faced even more stigmatization when newspapers, academic scholarship, and even films like *The Birth of a Nation* spread racist and classist propaganda that convinced white citizens to view groups of black migrants and residents as threats to not only racial purity and segregation but also public safety in the North.

When Edgar Campbell, a native of Savannah, Georgia, lived in Philadelphia during the 1930s and 1940s, black people were not only restricted to living in certain communities because of segregation but also often received no service at restaurants in Center City, had to sit in the "attic" of movie houses like the 1,300-seat Goldman Theatre at 15th and Ranstead Streets, and even traveled frequently from place to place on the subway to specifically avoid walking through a hostile all-white neighborhood. In Northern cities like Philadelphia, white racist beliefs about black inferiority played out in plain view, as Campbell experienced when, in 1934, he and a friend patronized a Center City restaurant with a "public reputation" of providing equal service to whites and blacks:

> They [black migrants] came North, and they were painted a beautiful picture of the North, everything wide open. But then there were places they couldn't even go in and eat . . . right here in Philadelphia. Horn & Hardarts, 1508 Market Street. We used to go in there after dinner dance, and whatever we ordered, they didn't have. . . . I ordered a cup of coffee, and we drank it. We said, "Give us another." They'd break that cup up. We made them break up all the dishes in the place one night . . . the guy [waiter] would do everything he can to keep from waiting on you. But then when you decide to create a scene, he'd wait on you. So, a lot of times, they'd break the glasses up, the dishes up, whatever you used . . . we'd know they were going to do it.[110]

While black Philadelphians like Campbell peacefully protested racial discrimination on an individual level, lawyers and activists like Raymond Pace Alexander, John Francis Williams, Hobson R. Reynolds, and Cecil B. Moore (who were active in the NAACP and state government) successfully protested and sued white businesses and institutions that practiced racial discrimination. State Representative Reynolds' civil rights activism, in particular, encouraged the passage of legislation like the Pennsylvania Equal Rights Bill of 1935, which vowed "to provide civil rights for all people, regardless of race or color" by punishing any owner of a "public accommodation, resort, or amusement" with a fine and/or imprisonment if they violated the act.[111] However, as many black Philadelphians would soon realize, they were effectively living in what poet and educator Sonia Sanchez describes as a "disguised Southern city."[112]

Although some African Americans were successful in integrating public spaces in the North, white segregationists, police, and realtors capitalized on racist and classist stereotypes of black migrants to resist desegregation and encourage white flight. When white supremacists cast black migrants as "invaders" in their neighborhoods and communal spaces during the 1920s and 1930s, they also criminalized them as harbingers of urban decline. This criminalization later morphed into focusing on isolating, containing, and policing not just black adults but also black youth as poverty, inequality, and poverty-induced crime became more noticeable while the American economy recovered and stabilized during World War II.

2

"Thugs," "Bandits," and Gang Attacks

In March 1935, *Philadelphia Tribune* journalist Harry B. Webber wrote a six-part series for the black-owned newspaper about North Central, a neighborhood in lower North Philadelphia colloquially known to police as "Blood Hill," with black residents, slum housing, and alleged rampant crime.[1] According to Webber, Blood Hill was a community east of Broad Street where over twenty-four thousand African Americans (and a few whites) lived in overcrowded bandbox homes (often converted into apartments) spread out across 198 acres of land. Police identified Blood Hill as a slum because of the neighborhood's vacant and crumbling homes, high crime, and desolation. Webber described the neighborhood as the place where working-class migrants from South Philadelphia came to find better homes.[2] Since housing in places like South Philadelphia's Navy Yard consisted of three- to four-room apartments and "wood and coal-burning stoves" without gauges through the 1950s, moving to North Philadelphia seemed like a great opportunity for black families to have modernized homes.[3] Consequently, when black residents left South Philadelphia for North Philadelphia, they unknowingly faced housing discrimination, with realtors and slumlords forcing them to pay several thousand dollars more to mortgage and rent two- and three-story homes that were once owned by white residents.

As more black people occupied the slum area known as Blood Hill, the neighborhood became synonymous with crime. According to Webber, newspaper reporters identified this area as a "happy hunting ground" for big crime stories and tragic accounts of human suffering.[4] Many of the narratives surrounding Blood Hill involved abject poverty along with the constant presence and fear of violent crime. According to Webber, the most "newsworthy" stories of Blood Hill involved joblessness, homelessness, teen pregnancy, kidnapping, robbery, and murder. It was labeled as a place of high unemployment where "jobless men" lived in vacant lots under the railroad, a neighborhood of danger where "women walked in pairs at night," and a den of moral defilement where "honky tonk cabarets" and "odorous movie houses" operated at night.[5] In some instances, the residents of Blood Hill were reportedly so poor that some slept in alleys, while others ripped apart their homes to secure firewood on cold nights.

Throughout Philadelphia, the Great Depression hit many neighborhoods hard. As historian Roger D. Simon explained, some families who experienced eviction were able to "double up" and stay in homes with nearby family and friends, while individuals in abject poverty and facing homelessness built "shacks and shanties" on vacant land and even established encampments along the banks of the Schuylkill River. Settlement houses, churches, missions, political clubs, and lodge halls offered soup kitchens, bread lines, and daily necessities for the working class and poor who desperately needed them, but de facto racial segregation at many of these institutions made survival even more difficult for people of color to navigate no matter where they lived in the city.[6]

Despite the financial turmoil white *and* black Philadelphians were clearly experiencing during this era, Webber learned from his conversations with police that Blood Hill was documented by the Bureau of Crime Prevention as a crime hotspot where "uncivilized" people lived. For the police, residents of Blood Hill who engaged in crime were, by nature, criminals. The fact that many residents lived in crumbling homes built of wood and sandstone while youth had few yards or playgrounds for recreation was not a significant excuse for descent into crime. From 1908 to 1953, the city's carceral system dealt with juvenile delinquency at Philadelphia's House of Detention (located at Front and Arch Streets), where detained youth awaiting criminal trials in juvenile court were offered room and board, schooling, recreation, and discipline.[7]

By 1932, private citizens and police were so concerned about juvenile delinquency among boys, particularly between the ages of sixteen and twenty-one, that they developed two separate units under the police department's newly established Crime Prevention Association (CPA) to rehabilitate youth identified as at risk of engaging in criminal behavior.[8] The main goal of CPA was to prevent "criminal development among older boys" in "four bad spots" in one section of the city.[9] In June 1932, CPA's civilian unit (consisting of two private citizens whose part-time work was financed by private contributions) and police unit (composed of a county detective and two patrolmen) organized a program of "recreation, investigation, and supervision" where staff members attended magistrate court hearings, interviewed and investigated the home environments of delinquent boys, and acquired unoccupied buildings and vacant lots to erect boys' clubs of recreation. By December 1933, CPA acquired eighty-four Civil Works Administration (CWA) workers (through President Franklin D. Roosevelt's New Deal program to lift unemployed Americans out of poverty) who supervised the use of seventy-nine vacant lots as baseball fields and managed the operation of twenty-four boys' clubs that offered gymnasium work, boxing, billiards, dancing, and table games to approximately 1,400 youth. Unfortunately, racial discrimination and segregation stymied people of color's access to this rehabilitation program for juveniles when *only* one out of the twenty-four boys' clubs offered by CPA admitted "Negro boys."[10] Four years later, CPA established a separate division where female officers focused on rehabilitating boys under sixteen years old and girls between the ages of sixteen and twenty-one. By 1950, CPA expanded its operations citywide when it became the Juvenile Division.[11] Nevertheless, the Philadelphia Police Bureau's racial and gender prejudice limited the access black youth had to public recreation and rehabilitation that would keep them out of crime and the carceral system.

In the context of juvenile delinquency among African Americans in Blood Hill, Webber claimed that the housing crisis produced a series of crimes where "roving boy gangs" roamed the streets and "party girl" gangs rented rooms and old houses to host unsupervised late-night get-togethers for teenagers under sixteen years old.[12] According to Webber, the cruelty of slum life made gang membership enticing to youth in Blood Hill. Through his research, he uncovered that there were "hundreds of child criminals" who by the age of ten had been arrested and paroled approximately twenty times. Several youth gangs existed in North Philadelphia and were known for congregating on street corners and committing petty crimes like theft. According to Webber, gangs like the Muggers, 40 Thieves, and Black Hawks had up to one hundred members who were mostly twelve or thirteen years old.[13] Many gang members were arrested, but oftentimes, youth were paroled to their parents' homes because institutions like the House of Correction were regularly overcrowded and Philadelphia's county jail only accepted inmates who were at least sixteen years old.[14]

Over the course of Webber's six-part muckraker series, he maintained the belief that African Americans were not inherently criminal and that poverty begot crime. However, he argued in his articles that slum residents had a personal responsibility to avoid crime and corruptible influences. Webber, who represented the *Philadelphia Tribune* as a reporter to the black middle class, harkened back to the supposed "middle-class values" of morality and self-sufficiency to question the effectiveness of neighborhood churches and disavow movie theaters that permitted youth to view "Wild Wild West"–themed films because, in his estimation, those institutions were failing to instill positive values to shape residents into law-abiding citizens.[15] Additionally, Webber suggested that black leaders, presumably from the middle class, should engage in social activism to uplift Blood Hill residents. He described North Philadelphia as a huge area of "amazing life, possibilities, and people" where "leadership worthy of the name" could contribute to the "better life of the city" by redeeming the reputation of the working-class African American community.[16] Furthermore, while Webber's 1935 report critiqued the moral compass of adults and youth in Blood Hill, Webber primarily blamed slumlords who used blockbusting and redlining to trigger white flight and create a hypersegregated environment where poverty and crime could thrive.

As a housing investigator for the *Philadelphia Tribune*, Webber's articles were written for the black middle class who lived in North Philadelphia's segregated communities west of Broad Street and away from the poor and working-class African Americans of Blood Hill. West of Broad Street was known as "Little Harlem" because it was a community of eighty-seven thousand black residents with "glittering" cafés, theaters, and nightclubs frequented by upper-class, interracial clientele while politicians went there to win "black votes."[17] In fact, the area surrounding Columbia Avenue from Broad Street to 18th Street—not far from landmarks like the famed Pearl Theatre in Little Harlem—was referred to as the "Gold Coast," reflecting the wealthy white and black business owners and gangsters who established themselves there.[18] Although Webber's articles were about issues involving African Americans and written for a black audience, his series reflected two major concerns that black *and* white middle-class residents of North Philadelphia had about the influx of working-class black migrants to their area: the drop in their home's real estate value and rise in neighborhood crime. Nevertheless, Webber's series informed the public about the looming threat of black migrants whose working-class status and possibly rural Southern backgrounds threatened to bring blight and crime that could spill over into their community. Webber held the sentiment that the black poor were disadvantaged, misguided, and susceptible to criminal activity. However, other journalists in the city who viewed race and class segregation as the proper order of society used crime narratives, particularly those about juvenile gangs, to warn middle-class Philadelphians to remain vigilant and resist demographic change in their neighborhoods as desegregation took place throughout the city.

From the 1930s through the 1950s, Southern black migrants who settled in the impoverished and underdeveloped areas of Philadelphia like North Central were associated with the stigmas of poverty, slum residency, and criminality. As white flight intensified in Philadelphia's neighborhoods, the communities where these migrants lived became stigmatized when police and journalists used news media to disseminate crime narratives to the public about black neighborhood slums with juvenile gangs. These gang narratives encouraged white *and* black middle-class families to maintain racial and class segregation in their communities or face blight and crime. While community activists from North Central sought to redeem the reputation of delinquent black youth and reform them through poverty alleviation and antigang programs located at settlement houses like the Wharton Centre, the police department used Police Athletic League centers and incarceration to curb juvenile crime. Nevertheless, from 1935 to 1957, police and journalists in Philadelphia cultivated the stereotype of "the jungle"—a poor, crime-ridden, gang-filled black neighborhood in North Philadelphia and beyond—which inspired white residents to resist desegregation, stay contained in white neighborhoods, and advocate for tough-on-crime policing to prevent the spillage of black crime into their communities.

The "Gang Problem" in North Philadelphia

In the 1930s, North Central, known to police and journalists as Blood Hill, epitomized middle-class fears of crime because its black migrants, slum housing, and crime threatened to spill over into neighboring North

Philadelphia communities like Strawberry Mansion and Brewerytown. As Webber explained in his 1935 article "In Philadelphia—Third Largest City: Housing Cancer Is Undermining City," communities like North Central were stigmatized as slums because they were places where black tenants and homeowners were forced to pay inflated prices for unworthy homes that often lacked heat, hot water, bathrooms, and other elements necessary for maintaining a healthy and sanitary lifestyle.[19] Real estate agents redlined working-class neighborhoods like North Central, Yorktown, and Sharswood as risky for financial investment because the people who resided there were believed to be criminals by nature.[20] The white people who lived there prior to black migration refused to remain in the area as it desegregated, resorted to panic selling, and engaged in white flight to other residential communities. Additionally, exposés like Webber's also argued that neighborhoods like North Central were not desirable places for law-abiding citizens to start families because there were many "child criminals" who "infested" the area.[21] Nevertheless, journalists who focused on black juvenile criminals made white and black middle-class residents in North Philadelphia fearful of black crime spilling over into their neighborhoods when children walked the streets unsupervised by parents and teachers.

In the midst of the "housing cancer" Webber described in neighborhoods like North Central, community activists in North Philadelphia sought to fix the core issues of those communities that made them colloquially known as black slums. These activists wanted to not only assist black families in finding affordable housing and decent employment in segregated Philadelphia but also provide recreational facilities for youth who had no outlet for play at home or in their community. African American teens who loitered on city streets were stereotyped as delinquents. Furthermore, the goal activists had in mind was to solve the real issue of inadequate play areas and disprove the myth that black youth were inherently delinquent and criminal.

In April 1930, Quaker and local human rights activist Helen H. Corson published a full-page article in the *Friends' Intelligencer* requesting that the journal's readers donate funds to establish a settlement house in North Philadelphia (for $30,000) that would steer black youth away from gangs and crime to prevent incarceration:

A Few of the Future Patrons

The Susan Parrish Wharton Memorial

Readers of the INTELLIGENCER, I am sure, will be interested in the proposed Settlement House in a congested Negro section of North Central Philadelphia. It is to be named for that devoted friend of the colored people, Susan Parrish Wharton, and is in charge of Whittier Centre, an agency organized by her in 1912 for social work among Negroes.

The plan, however, was not originated by Whittier Centre but by the Welfare Federation of Philadelphia. Their attention was repeatedly called to the lack of recreational facilities in North Central Philadelphia and to the large amount of juvenile delinquency which invariably accompanies such a situation. A very careful survey was made which fully bore out these complaints. The situation is particularly serious because in so many homes both mother and father go out to work, so that when school is out the children must either go back to a cheerless empty house with no care or supervision, or are locked out because their parents fear to have them stay in the house alone.

Convinced by the survey of the appalling need, the Welfare Federation approved organizing a Settlement House and through their Promotion Committee they asked Whittier Centre to take up and push the project.

The plan is to raise $36,000, purchase two adjacent dwellings, throw them together and equip as a settlement house, with two full-time and several volunteer and part-time workers. Of course all the usual activities will be carried on, classes and clubs in health, cooking, sewing, manual training, games, dramatics, etc.

The campaign for funds began last Sixth month and $21,486 has already been subscribed. The remaining $8,514 must be in hand by Sixth month 1st, 1930.

The plan is enthusiastically endorsed by the joint Race Relations Committee of Race Street and Arch Street Yearly Meetings, several members of which are serving on the Board of Directors.

Buck Hill friends of Susan P. Wharton are much interested and a committee consisting of Caroline Roberts, Mary T. L. Gannett, Marie C. Jenkins, Cornelia Coale, Annie Hillborn and Harriet McDowell are raising a fund of $1,000 which will entitle them to name a room "Buck Hill."

We hear much of crime among Negroes. But what can we expect when thousands of Southern rural Negroes pour into a congested section of a great city and find that practically the only recreational facilities open to them are commercialized pool rooms, speakeasies, lottery establishments and a low type of movie and vaudeville house?

It costs society at least $500 a year to maintain a boy for a year in a modern reformatory. To keep a boy in a boys' club costs nine to ten dollars of society's money, and his parents maintain him. Boys' clubs do not completely eliminate delinquency but they very greatly decrease it. *Can we afford to waste society's resources, not only in money but in the far graver aspect of warped characters and misspent lives?*

Contributions in any amount will be most gratefully received and should be sent *now*, while you are still thinking of it. Checks should be drawn to order of Whittier Centre and mailed to its Treasurer, Samuel H. Carpenter, care of Pennsylvania Company for Insurances on Lives and Granting Annuities, Fifteenth and Chestnut Streets, Philadelphia, Pa.   HELEN H. CORSON.

Helen H. Corson's article in the *Friends' Intelligencer*. April 12, 1930, Special Collections Research Center, Temple University Libraries, Philadelphia, PA / *Friends' Intelligencer*.

> We hear much of crime among Negroes. But what can we expect when thousands of Southern rural Negroes pour into a congested section of a great city and find that practically the only recreational facilities open to them are commercialized pool rooms, speakeasies, lottery establishments and a low type of movie and vaudeville house? It costs society at least $500 a year to maintain a boy for a year in a modern reformatory. To keep a boy in a boy's club costs nine to ten dollars of society's money, and his parents maintain him. Boys' clubs do not completely eliminate delinquency but they very greatly decrease it.[22]

Corson's plea for a settlement house to rehabilitate and provide community resources for black youth was based on the common knowledge and daily observations made by social workers that "gang groups" were known to hang out on street corners and at movie theaters, taprooms, candy stores, liquor stores, and poolrooms in the community.[23] Oftentimes, these locations became sites for gang violence that affected not only gang members but also innocent bystanders, residents, and business owners. For example, the Vogueteers were a group of ten boys between the ages of seventeen and twenty who were known to frequent the "colored" Vogue Theater at 19th Street and Columbia Avenue and often fight rivals like the Mohawks and Swans.[24] By 1931, the Susan Parrish Wharton Memorial Settlement House, or Wharton Centre, opened at 22nd Street and Columbia Avenue in North Philadelphia as a social uplift organization for African Americans. Similar to the Whittier Centre in South Philadelphia, the Wharton Centre (named in honor of philanthropist Susan Parrish Wharton, who died three years prior) operated in collaboration with white and black donors, social workers, residents, and city officials to improve the lives of African Americans living in the slums of neighborhoods like North Central Philadelphia.[25]

Social workers from the Wharton Centre noticed the existence of youth gangs in North Central once the settlement house was up and running, and they began to investigate the factors that created the phenomenon. According to the black social workers who conducted sociological studies on black families in North Philadelphia, the reason for the rise of youth gangs in this section of the city was because of the "social problems and neighborhood conditions" of generational unemployment, crime, and family instability that nurtured some youth into

The Wharton Centre community, circa 1929, Special Collections Research Center, Temple University Libraries, Philadelphia, PA / The Photo Illustrators.

delinquency.[26] Slum housing offered to African Americans at exorbitant rates forced employed black parents to often work lengthy hours to pay for inadequate living conditions while their children remained unsupervised and susceptible to delinquency outside of school hours.[27] Nevertheless, the Wharton Centre's social workers combatted the myth of inherently criminal black youth by demonstrating through community activism that the social conditions of racial segregation, poverty, and slums created a dangerous society where some black youths in North Central happened to engage in gang activity.

Throughout the 1930s, the Wharton Centre responded to the gang problem in North Central by offering recreational programs for youth and sponsored community service projects to benefit teenagers and adults. The Wharton Centre sought to uplift black families facing the disadvantaging effects of racial segregation and financial woes by offering classes in health and cooking along with clubs focused on domestic skills and creative arts like sewing and dramatics.[28] In regards to recreation, the settlement house offered art classes and shows, citywide youth concerts, a gymnasium for sports and tabletop games, and summer camps for black children in North Philadelphia.[29] Social workers and college-aged volunteers even initiated community street-cleaning projects to convert vacant lots into playgrounds for neighborhood children.[30] Nevertheless, the goal of these activists was to not only improve the social conditions of these residents but also change the narrative that journalists cultivated in news articles about black residents, slums, and juvenile gang activity.

Postwar Desegregation, Race Rioting, and the Police's Influence on Black Youth

The United States' involvement in World War II (1941–45) sparked the Second Great Migration (1940–70) of approximately five million Southern blacks to Northern and West Coast cities looking for homes and jobs. As approximately 180,000 Philadelphians served in the armed forces, thousands of black migrants arrived in the city, often settling in hypersegregated black areas like North Central.[31] Although black migrants during this period tested the strength of segregation in Philadelphia's residential communities, it was not until after World War II that many neighborhoods desegregated.

During World War II, over seventy-five thousand manufacturing jobs opened in Philadelphia where laborers of any race and gender (due to the federal government pressuring local companies to be equal opportunity employers) were able to produce wartime goods for the nation. Laborers who were hired to fill wartime jobs found work at textile and apparel companies like Stetson that produced hats, coats, blankets, uniforms, and parachutes; worksites at the Navy Yard and Frankford Arsenal that built ships and weapons; and manufacturing firms like Budd Company, which made aircraft parts, or the Baldwin Plant, which built diesel engines, tanks, and locomotives. Furthermore, as historian Roger D. Simon explained, World War II effectively ended the Great Depression and "restored" the nation's "prosperity" and "self-confidence."[32]

On the home front, US soldiers returned from the war with numerous opportunities available to them. The 1944 Servicemen's Readjustment Act (GI Bill) enabled military veterans with honorable discharge and at least 120 days of service to purchase new houses with low-cost mortgages, receive cash payments from the government for tuition and living costs to attend vocational school or college, and collect up to a year of unemployment compensation.[33] The GI Bill helped some African American veterans buy homes in decent neighborhoods and obtain industrial jobs at factories.[34] However, as historian Lizabeth Cohen explained in her 2004 book *Consumer's Republic: The Politics of Mass Consumption in Postwar America*, few African Americans achieved middle-class status from the GI Bill. The Federal Housing Administration (FHA) redlined residential neighborhoods to maintain segregation and regularly denied African Americans mortgage loans for homes in nonwhite communities labeled as "high-risk" investments. Additionally, African American veterans were excluded from the GI Bill's educational benefits for pursuing a postsecondary education that would lead to a well-paying, skilled profession because the law only funded accredited institutions, which, because of segregation, were virtually all white.[35]

Between 1946 and 1953, housing options for African Americans were bleak, since *only* 347 of 120,000 new homes built in Philadelphia were for black people. Many of the preexisting homes available to African Americans were not only crammed and overpriced but formerly occupied by working-class whites who migrated to Northeast Philadelphia and suburban towns like Levittown seeking affordable housing in "racially homogenous" communities.[36] African Americans' desire to live in all-white neighborhoods was not an act of provocation against white people. Black people simply wanted quality housing, schools, jobs, and recreational facilities in their neighborhoods. Since these amenities were available in *segregated* white communities, black families were persistent in achieving a better quality of life for not only themselves but also their children.[37]

In regard to education in Philadelphia, schools were not segregated by law, as in the Jim Crow South, but school district administrators found implicit ways to implement de facto segregation well into the postwar era. Prior to World War II, black and white children attended integrated public schools, with African American students composing as low as 8.1 percent of the school district population in 1920. As the Great Migration brought thousands of Southern black families to Philadelphia, the school district's demographics drastically changed, and administrators attempted to "steer" white children away from integrated schools with gerrymandering and promises of building new schools to accommodate the increase in student enrollment.[38] Additionally, the school district even cultivated racial segregation among teaching staff when administrators intentionally assigned black teachers to predominantly black schools to educate youth. Even black educators who received college training in middle- and high-school-level instruction were often restricted to teaching in elementary schools where there were larger percentages of black youth, while white teachers, regardless of their academic training, were sent to all-white and integrated middle and high schools. Furthermore, as education scholar John P. Spencer explains, the major consequences of this citywide practice were high turnover rates among white teachers who refused to educate black students, low achievement rates for black youth who received a subpar-quality education, and the "destructive psychological effects of separate education" black youth faced when white teachers verbally insulted their intelligence in a noticeably segregated classroom.[39]

Following World War I, administrators and teachers used intelligence tests to segregate black and white children in the same school and place them in one of the following two curriculum tracks: a low-track education for students who should enter vocational professions after graduation *or* a high-track education for pupils who should attend college for mathematics, science, or liberal arts and acquire careers as white-collar professionals. During this era, IQ tests not only were racially and class biased in favor of white middle- and upper-class English-speaking students who had access to quality academic instruction but also offered no leeway for students like Southern rural black migrant children whose prior educational opportunities were inadequate in comparison to those found in the North. Moreover, the school district successfully utilized several methods to keep black and white children segregated whether they were educated in separate schools or in the same building.[40]

For one Philadelphia school in particular, school officials utilized gerrymandering, the creation of a new building, academic track systems, and IQ testing to keep white children separated from black and later Puerto Rican youth: Northeast Manual Training School.[41] In 1890, Northeast Manual Training School was established in an old schoolhouse in Northeast Philadelphia for the white sons of working-class families.

These boys could not afford a private education, but they desired training in industrial skills necessary for men who would occupy railway, steamship, manufacturing, and textile jobs in the city's urban centers.[42] By 1903, the school moved to a massive three-story edifice located at 8th Street and Lehigh Avenue in North Philadelphia's Fairhill neighborhood. Much care and effort went into designing this institution of learning for working-class boys. The building, designed by well-known architect Llyod Titus, was created as a luxurious symbol of bridging equal opportunity between the rich and the poor—the $400,000 structure occupied a full city block, was made of limestone and silver granite, and was accented with stained-glass windows, gargoyles, stone lions, and bas-reliefs on the exterior of the building. Essentially, this building was a castle in comparison to other Philadelphia schools that were housed in churches, homes, and farmhouses. The new location of the building was also strategic, in that the school was surrounded by potential employers: textile companies such as Quaker Lace Company and Stetson Hat Company and locomotive manufacturers like Baldwin Works. Further prestige was added to this school when dignitaries such as then president of Princeton University Woodrow Wilson, Pennsylvania governor Samuel Whitaker Pennypacker, and several CEOs of railway companies attended the grand opening of the building.[43]

Following the increase in racial diversity and the demand for industrial labor in Philadelphia during World War II, much had changed at Northeast academically and demographically. During the 1940s and 1950s, the school was required to serve all boys regardless of their race, class, and skill level. Since the school had to accommodate boys with different capabilities, the institution developed a tracking system in which IQ tests determined which boys would follow a low-track curriculum and which boys would follow an honors-level high-track curriculum.[44] Additionally, the school also changed racially. As African American enrollment in the School District of Philadelphia increased to 30 percent by 1950 during the Second Great Migration, Northeast's student population gradually became 50 percent black and 50 percent white.[45]

By 1952, Northeast's Alumni Association—composed of white businessmen, lawyers, doctors, scientists, clergymen, soldiers, and politicians—secretly met to propose a building change for the white students to attend Northeast in a white neighborhood.[46] Despite the fact that urban schools were in decline, the alumni were primarily angered by the fact that more and more African Americans (and a few Puerto Ricans) were moving into their predominantly white neighborhoods and schools.[47] Many white residents had already moved to the suburbs to escape their black and Latino neighbors, but for the alumni, this solution would not suffice. Furthermore, the alumni petitioned city officials and the members of the Board of Education to permit the school to relocate to Northeast Philadelphia. The Alumni Association truthfully argued that Northeast's building was old and deteriorating; however, it simultaneously lied to the board, stating that the school's population had outgrown the edifice when, in actuality, the student body was shrinking.[48] The Alumni Association inevitably convinced city officials and members of the Board of Education (many of whom were Northeast graduates themselves) to grant them permission to relocate the school.[49] In May 1953, the new building site at Cottman and Algon Avenues was purchased for $500,000, and in 1954, the school board granted Northeast $6 million for construction. By 1956, construction of the new school building was complete, and Northeast reopened at the new location for the 1957–58 academic year.

In Philadelphia, the school district traditionally encourages pupils to transfer to their school's new location if the building is still located in their neighborhood. But in Northeast's case, the Alumni Association sought to keep white students and bar African American youth from attending the school, so they created a "grandfather clause" stating that only students who lived near 8th and Lehigh and had a grandfather who was a Northeast graduate could enroll at the new location.[50] As a result of this "grandfather clause," all the black students (and a few white students) who were first-generation Northeast attendees were excluded from enrolling in the new school. Although the successful 1954 Supreme Court ruling in the *Brown v. Board of Education* case prohibited racial segregation in schools, the Alumni Association escaped reproach because it manipulated the school board's rule that students attending nonmagnet schools must go to a school in their neighborhood. As a result, the "grandfather clause" re-created Northeast into a prestigious and luxurious school for white children.[51]

Back in Fairhill, the school board kept the 8th and Lehigh school building open and renamed it Thomas Edison High School. However,

the Alumni Association and the school board's financial and social efforts went into the new Northeast school and not Edison.[52] Instead
of the school board allocating money for Edison's deteriorating
fifty-two-year-old building to be repaired, the board sanctioned $1 mil-
lion of the $6 million given to Northeast to be spent on several athletic
fields for hockey, soccer, football, and baseball; four tennis courts; a
quarter-mile track, grandstand seating for 6,700 people; and three parking lots. Additionally, the school board authorized Northeast to transfer
its "name, traditions and specialized courses" to the new location. Along
with those remnants of Northeast, the stained-glass windows, basketball trophies, and World War II veterans' dedication plaque also went to
the new Northeast. Even the leadership staff of the pre-1957 Northeast
High School left Edison: the principal, five department heads, and the
athletic director.[53] This practice reflected a citywide district approach
of curtailing integration in the postwar era. By the early 1960s, school
administrators were so successful in limiting Philadelphia's integrated
public schools to 16 percent of all district institutions that, as historian
Lisa Levenstein explains, 85 percent of black students and 93 percent
of black teachers were in schools that were at least 80 percent black.[54]
Nevertheless, rampant racism in the school district left black youth in
schools like the former Northeast High School not only academically
disadvantaged but also stigmatized by the myth that black children were
racially inferior to their white peers and therefore undeserving of a quality education.

As schools and neighborhoods desegregated, many white people
continued to rebel against the migration of African Americans to neighborhoods that had been all-white before World War II. From 1944 to
1964, the School District of Philadelphia witnessed its black student enrollment increase from 24 to 53 percent, and in response, many white
families avoided integrated public schools by sending their children to
exam-based admission (magnet), parochial, and private schools in the
metropolitan area.[55] White residents also rebelled through violent harassment outside the homes of black families and by provoking violent
attacks against them in schools. According to historian Karl E. Johnson, the desegregation of Philadelphia's residential neighborhoods in
the 1940s sparked high incarceration rates for black men and boys in the
city.[56] As neighborhoods desegregated, many white Americans rebelled

against the migration of African Americans to neighborhoods that were all white before World War II by holding mass riots outside the homes of black families and provoking violent attacks against them in public spaces like schools. In these instances, whites in Philadelphia fought to keep their neighborhoods segregated because they believed in several racist stereotypes that made them unwilling to have black people as neighbors, such as African Americans being "prone to poverty, crime, and sexual promiscuity."[57] Furthermore, throughout the 1940s, police often arrested blacks but not whites for rioting. In 1947, social scientist G. Gordon Brown elaborated on the issue of police bias in his published survey "Law Administration and Negro-White Relations," which investigated the racial tension between black citizens and white police. The survey exposed the "strong racial prejudices" white law enforcement officers had toward African Americans.[58] In Brown's interviews with white policemen, he discovered that many officers (of different ranks) were simply racist or held animosity toward African Americans who acquired homes and jobs in all-white communities. This anger resulted in countless white police not only embracing racist stereotypes that labeled black people as prone to criminal behavior but also justifying the use of excessive force against African Americans.

In one interview, a patrolman reacted to the 1944 Philadelphia transit strike in which white workers halted public transportation to protest the hiring of black streetcar conductors with vengeful sentiment: "Next time they [African Americans] try [something like that], we'll get them good."[59] In another interview, a detective described how black people were innately unprincipled: "They are not bad people, but they seem instinctively to be more likely to commit certain kinds of crime than whites are. Maybe it is their African ancestry." Additionally, Brown had overheard a conversation between a detective and investigators in which the detective suggested that African Americans be *contained* and content within their given station in life of poverty and denied civil rights: "You don't have too much trouble with the Negroes if you keep them in their place."[60]

When Brown interviewed African Americans about their opinions of white policemen, he learned that while some respected the police, many black people (particularly the working class) thought poorly of them. Several black Philadelphians told Brown they mistrusted white police because many used excessive force; falsely arrested African Americans; refused to thoroughly investigate crimes where black people were the victims; received bribes, gifts, merchandise, meals, and "services" from operators of illegal drug dealing, prostitution, and numbers racketeering in black neighborhoods; and were openly racist and disrespectful in their interactions with upstanding black citizens.[61] In one of Brown's interviews, an assistant to a molder's helper acknowledged the racial bias white police had toward alleged black suspects: "The police treat the colored rougher than the whites because they think that all the crimes are committed by colored." In another interview, a black official stated that many black residents mistrusted police and judges because they felt they were incompetent and harbored racial prejudices that influenced them to unfairly arrest and prosecute African Americans: "Police are dominated, first, by Irishmen who live in a racial no-man's land, and, second, by Southerners who have drifted in, and who got a job with the police because they could not do anything else."

Brown's research also uncovered the sentiments of a black newspaper editor who was also particularly critical of Irish American officers who (in his opinion) purposely arrested more African Americans than Irish: "The police definitely discriminate against Negroes. The police have all the prejudices of their class, and these are intensified by their service. . . . The police would not pick up an Irishman, except for a major crime."[62] The fact that African Americans during the 1940s constantly recounted their confrontations with specifically Irish American police harkens back to the racial tension that occurred when black families first moved into predominantly Irish all-white neighborhoods during the 1920s. Furthermore, some of the racist white adults and teens who resisted African Americans in their neighborhoods, schools, and workplaces with racial violence continued their discriminatory abuse as police officers out of self-interest and neighborhood solidarity, knowing that their authoritative position enabled them to get away with police misconduct. Moreover, white police officers often acted as "dirty workers" who fought to maintain an "informal apartheid" of white supremacy in desegregated neighborhoods by disproportionately arresting and incarcerating African Americans during race riots.[63]

While the Philadelphia Police Department did engage in racially biased policing against African Americans in black and desegregated neighborhoods, the police department and the city's police union, the Fraternal Order of Police (FOP), made superficial efforts to build positive police-community relations with youth in crime hotspots to prevent them from engaging in potentially criminal behavior. During the 1940s, the Dawn Patrol, a subdivision of the Juvenile Division, instructed plainclothes male and female police officers to patrol transportation centers, bowling alleys, dance halls, and other public hangouts in the city from 8:00 p.m. to 4:00 a.m. The goal of the Dawn Patrol was to intercept underage youth on the streets after curfew who engaged in drinking, gambling, or prostitution.[64]

By 1946, Philadelphia police officers, under the initiative of Sergeant August "Gus" Rangnow (1892–1972), established the Police Athletic League (PAL) following World War II to deter youth of underprivileged communities from engaging in street crime and drug use.[65] Rangnow knew what it was like to be poor and underprivileged because he was a textile laborer during his childhood. Rangnow even joined labor activist "Mother" Mary Harris Jones in her 1903 "Children's Army" march from a Kensington mill in North Philadelphia to President Theodore Roosevelt's summer home in Oyster Bay, New York, in protest of the exploitative labor laws that subjected youth to dangerous working conditions and unfair wages and made them unable to attend school.[66] Furthermore, once Rangnow witnessed youth playing handball in a busy police parking lot, he spent three years organizing the Thirty-Sixth Police District's PAL center in North Philadelphia and furnishing it with recreational equipment with the help of policemen and private business owners in the area.[67]

The main goal of PAL centers was to connect police officers with neighborhood children through mentorship, friendship, and sportsmanship in athletic games of boxing, baseball, basketball, table tennis, and marching band.[68] PAL centers in North Philadelphia and other working-class communities in the city offered free after-school programs for tens of thousands of children from ages six to eighteen and even granted college scholarships from private organizations like the Christian Schmidt Foundation to a select number of youth from 1950 onward.[69] Active police officers and city officials participated in events sponsored at its centers to encourage youth to not only be familiar with law enforcement officers but also develop respect for them as authority figures in the community. One activity PAL centers offered to instill this value was "Commissioner

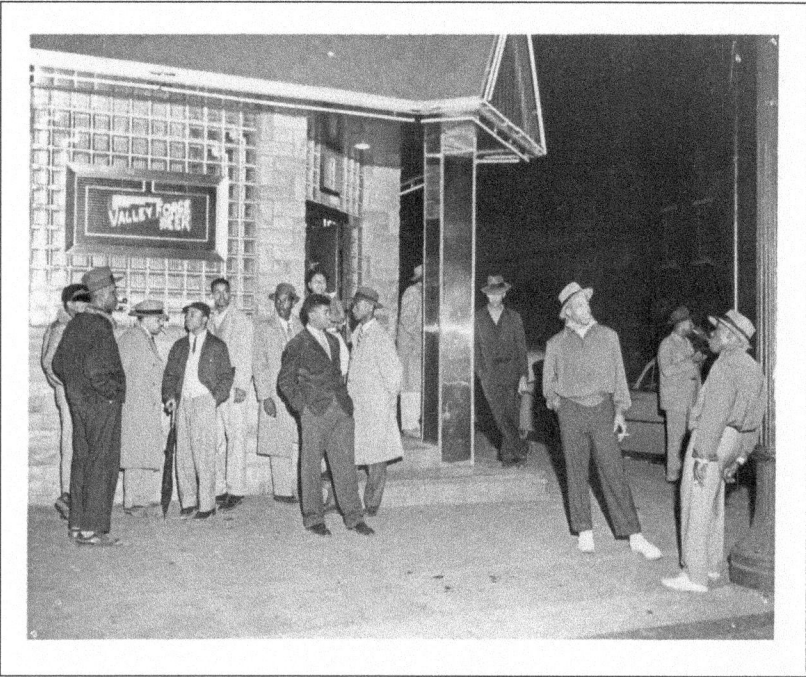

Young black men socializing in front of Valley Forge Beer in North Philadelphia. Date unknown, Special Collections Research Center, Temple University Libraries, Philadelphia, PA / Wharton Centre.

for a Day," in which the police commissioner gave teenagers assignments at police headquarters and educated them about the work police officers did on a daily basis.[70] Additionally, officers, coaches, and mentors at PAL centers also promoted American patriotism by encouraging children to say the pledge of allegiance and sign oaths of allegiance that were sent to the mayor and other state and national politicians.[71] Nevertheless, PAL's patriotic activities were meant to not only steer children from crime but also indoctrinate them into being loyal citizens. Moreover, the overall mission of PAL was, in part, a superficial attempt to mentor youth. Although the FOP knew that crime often occurred in impoverished areas, the organization refused to acknowledge the sociological argument that social workers at institutions like the Wharton Centre defended, which was that poverty begot crime. The organization did not initiate poverty alleviation programs that would tackle issues of racial inequality, housing

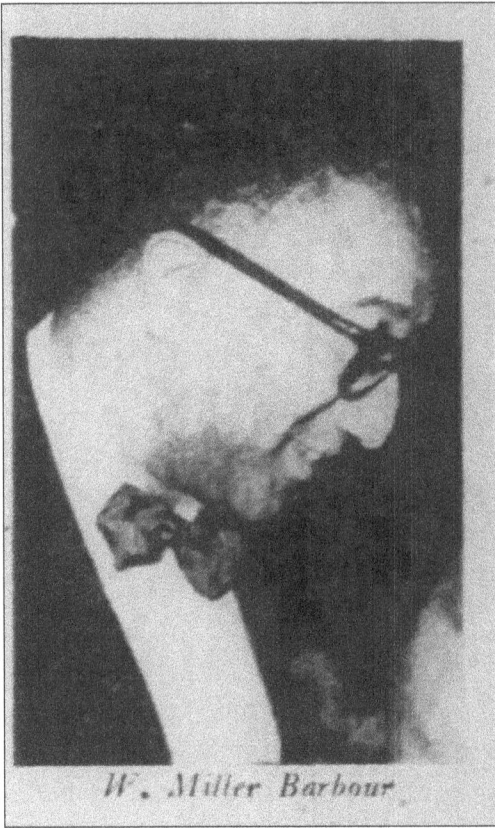

A 1957 newspaper graphic of W. Miller Barbour. *California Eagle*.

discrimination, and unemployment in working-class and poor neighborhoods but attempted to lessen the suffering children faced from those hardships with recreation and career-oriented opportunities. Instead, the FOP operated under the premise that some people, particularly poor white ethnic immigrants and African Americans, were by nature prone to engaging in criminal behavior and it was the police's duty to intervene through either recreation or incarceration.

"Cultivating Potential": The Wharton Centre's Operation Street Corner

While PAL offered recreational facilities for children in the slums as a form of crime prevention, the Wharton Centre offered nurture-based, teen-centric programs for youth in North Philadelphia to demonstrate to black children that although their neighborhood may have been a "tough" place to live, they didn't need to join a gang to survive. Unlike PAL, the Wharton Centre operated under the belief that poverty begot crime and children, including the black poor, were not inherently criminal. Nevertheless, the organization's social workers and gang workers offered neighborhood children recreational activities that would shape them into positive, law-abiding citizens and shelter them from the negative influences of drugs and crime present in the slums.

Settlement houses like the Wharton Centre often relied on college-educated social workers trained in the latest research to organize social welfare programs centered around disadvantaged youth in communities like North Central. In the 1880s, the Whittier Centre operated social welfare programs for youth under the direction of the Vassar College–educated social worker Susan Parrish Wharton. In the 1940s, the Wharton Centre, an offshoot of the Whittier Centre, operated recreational antigang programs under the guidance of Temple University–educated social worker W. Miller Barbour.[72] Social workers believed that poverty, social ostracism, and the desire for social belonging were influential factors in the formation of juvenile gangs because of the research they read from sociologists like Frederic Thrasher and William Foote Whyte.

In Thrasher's 1927 monograph *The Gang: A Study of 1,313 Gangs in Chicago*, he argued that a gang was an "interstitial group" whose members united through conflict like animosity from outsiders who opposed them.[73] Based on Thrasher's observation of over one thousand gangs in Chicago from 1923 to 1926, he argued that all childhood playgroups (including social and athletic clubs) were potential gangs, since members met face-to-face, were attached to a territory (like the neighborhood playground, a school, or a city block), and were *inclined* toward but not necessarily involved in delinquency.[74] Additionally, juvenile gangs were often shaped by "neighborhoods in flux," "urban geography," and "codes of honor and glory."[75] One of the final conclusions Thrasher's book made was that the solution to gang activity is the creation not of additional recreation centers for juveniles but inclusive institutions with positive and influential mentors to steer children away from antisocial and criminal activity.

Although Thrasher's research on youth gangs was widely accepted throughout academia as a fair assessment of the "gang problem" in urban cities during the 1920s and 1930s, his monograph lacked an in-depth discussion of gang formation based on ethnicity, race, and gender. His study also neglected to strongly investigate the existence of black gangs. Instead, *The Gang* implied the cultural bias that non–Anglo Saxon families had an inferior culture that made them more prone to crime. He described the early integration of European immigrants into "old-stock" (Anglo-Saxon or German) American communities as "transitioning" neighborhoods that were experiencing a change in population based on class and ethnicity.[76] According to Thrasher, discrimination and excommunication from the dominant culture enticed immigrant children to join gangs to have a place of belonging and protection from police and street violence. Although Thrasher acknowledged that American-born juveniles made it difficult for immigrant children to assimilate to American customs and social mores, he often stereotyped immigrants as having a flawed culture and family upbringing that hindered their progress toward Americanization and social inclusion.[77] Furthermore, while Thrasher's monograph was foundational, it contained biases against immigrant children of Irish, Italian, and Jewish descent that coincided with the white supremacist ideology of Anglo-Saxonism typical of the era.[78]

While Thrasher's research suggested that social ostracism played a role in the development of juvenile gangs, sociologist William Foote Whyte explained how poverty influenced juvenile gang formation. In Whyte's 1943 ethnocentric gang study *Street Corner Society: The Social Structure of an Italian Slum*, he supported Thrasher in identifying social exclusion, foreignness, and the need for protection as the rationale for the creation of gangs. However, Whyte also added new research explaining how financial need enticed youth into gang activity. In Whyte's monograph, he explained how he used participant observation to investigate why some male juveniles chose to be "corner boys" who were involved in gangs versus "college boys" who pursued postsecondary education to achieve wealth and social acceptance.[79] After Whyte spent eighteen out of forty-two months of research living with an Italian family in the North End neighborhood of Boston, he learned that some young men found it easier, quicker, and more profitable to achieve financial sustainability by joining a gang that engaged in an underground economy (like racketeering, gambling, alcohol, and prostitution) than attend college and hope to acquire a job offering middle-class wages and status.[80] Despite the limitations in Thrasher's work and Whyte's exclusive focus on one ethnic gang, their theories on gangs provided insight and strategies for social workers like Barbour to use participant observation to study, interact with, and attempt to rehabilitate gang members in North Central.

From 1943 to 1958, gang workers from the Wharton Centre established the antigang initiative Operation Street Corner to engage black gang members on street corners and attempt to reform "groups" of potential juvenile delinquents within a four-block radius of the center.[81] In the campaign, gang workers like Barbour observed, documented, interacted with, and directed teenagers from "gang groups" like the Warders, North Coasters, and Tophatters to the settlement house where they could receive mentorship and access to recreation as alternatives to delinquency.[82] As the chairman of the Wharton Centre Robert Rosenbaum would testify before the US Senate Committee to Investigate Juvenile Delinquency in April 1954, gang workers like Barbour used a long-term strategy based on building a rapport with youth to convince them to dissolve the "groups" they established on the street corner:

> He [the gang worker] studies the neighborhood and its influences and its facilities. He becomes a loiterer. Casually he leans against a lamp post. He may kibitz a crap game, although he never joins one. He may admire the swell tie the guy is wearing. And he may open with, "Well what do you think of the Phillies this year? I wonder how the big fight is doing tonight?" At first his overtures to friendship will inspire little or no response, gloomy look or half-hearted reply. The man from Wharton Centre moves on. Periodically, he will return to a particular corner. There are always several corners under his observation. Gradually, the boys realize that he is not a dick. The cops don't come during or after his passing. They find that he is from Wharton which has won the respect and trust of all neighborhood factions. It may take several weeks, but eventually the man from Wharton Centre is tolerated as a straight guy.[83]

After gang workers were able to successfully direct gang members away from schoolyards, drugstores, and saloons and into the center, they

A ping pong game and dance held at the Wharton Centre. Date unknown, Special Collections Research Center, Temple University Libraries, Philadelphia, PA / John W. Mosley / Ruben E. Hall.

offered youth access to approximately fifteen clubs supervised by two staff members and an assistant.[84]

By the 1950s, the Wharton Centre was serving over three hundred former gang boys and girls between the ages of twelve and eighteen years old with athletics, weekly dances, trips, social clubs, and educational programs where they learned life skills like hygiene, money management, job training, teamwork, and leadership.[85] In addition to the Wharton Centre managing black juvenile crime in North Philadelphia under Operation Street Corner, its staff also partnered with community residents, police, churches, schools, affiliates from the Raymond Rosen housing project, and PAL on outreach programs like all-city art and music shows and neighborhood parades. Gang workers even maintained detailed records of their interactions with black and white gangs, residents, churches, schools, and business owners in the neighborhood and recruited leaders and operators of local institutions to participate in fundraisers and community service projects to benefit gang-prone youth and the neighborhood at large.[86]

In 1958, the Wharton Centre ended Operation Street Corner due to "insufficient funds" to maintain specialized staff and the board's belief that a lack of neighborhood support for youth living in an "antisocial"

A newspaper article about the juvenile gang problem in Philadelphia. December 13, 1956, *Philadelphia Inquirer*.

environment would cause a regression into delinquency once they left the center.[87] The Wharton Centre's ability to identify the major root causes of juvenile delinquency was not a new revelation. In Rosenbaum's 1954 testimony about the importance of Operation Street Corner at the US Senate Committee to Investigate Juvenile Delinquency, he explained why many youth in North Philadelphia resorted to gangs:

> Our Operation Street Corner realizes that the bonds between the members of street corner groups are frequently stronger than their family ties. . . . Well the family in many instances, in these over-crowded areas is a broken family. The pressures of work, their working mothers and working fathers, frequently mean an empty household. When father and mother do come home from work, they are tired. They want to listen to Jack Benny, or some other favorite program and the child is asked to leave, get out in the street and shift for himself. It finds itself naturally in association with others of the same age. And having common activities and common interests there is frequently this loyalty to that group rather than to the family group. . . . We desire to cultivate the potentials for constructive efforts in such cases. . . . The gang, instead of being a chaotic group must be helped to become an organized club.[88]

Unlike PAL, the Wharton Centre specifically acknowledged that havens like theirs were necessary because of racial segregation and economic exploitation in the housing and job markets. Juvenile delinquency and crime arose from how children were poorly nurtured and neglected, not from the nature of their being. Poverty affected not only parents who worked constantly to pay bills but also children who felt abandoned when they received limited parental interaction and guidance at home. Additionally, gang crimes like robbery temporarily solved issues of financial need. Similar to the sociological research Thrasher and Whyte reported, social workers at the Wharton Centre believed some youth joined gangs because they desired social interaction, belonging, and mentorship from someone in their community who could cultivate an ethos of hope for a better future in their lives. Although the Wharton Centre made great strides toward curbing juvenile gang activity, as black migration and racial tension increased in Philadelphia through the 1950s, some police and citizens began to accept the idea that race and class determined a person's nature, especially when residents—black and white, middle class and poor—lived in segregated spaces where life was dramatically different based on one's identity.

"Kid Gloves Won't End Gang Wars"

As black migration to Philadelphia continued in the 1950s, police and journalists continued to report crime narratives about black gang violence to the public, which suggested that tough-on-crime policing and incarceration were necessary for criminal black youth. From 1950 to 1960, 153,000 blacks migrated to Philadelphia, while 225,000 whites moved out of the city. It was also during this period that 700,000 whites took up residence in many of Philadelphia's suburbs.[89] Racism encouraged many whites to believe the presence of African American neighbors stigmatized their communities, causing filth, crime, and the property values of their homes to decrease.[90] Job flight and white flight from city neighborhoods left these spaces racially and economically imbalanced, especially when an already struggling city tax base slowly began to underfund local schools, streets, and public housing.[91] Therefore, the racist assumption that poor African Americans brought financial destruction and crime had many middle-class Philadelphians resisting desegregation with the help of police power or leaving Philadelphia with the sentiment that safety and prosperity resided in an all-white community.

As white flight exacerbated racial tension between whites and blacks during this decade, the police department instructed beat officers to take a "pro crime fighter" stance of placing less emphasis on "emergency services and maintaining order" and focusing more on "serious crimes" like rape, murder, robbery, and burglary. Police officers carried out this order by "relying on motorized patrol, rapidly responding to calls for services, and using forensic science to investigate crimes."[92] This focus on "serious crimes" often resulted in excessive force because forcible felonies permitted police to invoke legal deadly force against a suspect when an individual's life was threatened.[93] Additionally, discriminatory policing led to the overrepresentation of African Americans in prisons and their underrepresentation in law enforcement. On January 10, 1950, the *Philadelphia Tribune* published an article stating that 40 percent of the city's prison population was African American, even though black people were only 18 percent of Philadelphia's population.[94] The article also pointed out that several black leaders were upset that in segregated facilities like Holmesburg Prison, Eastern Penitentiary, and Moyamensing Prison, where numerous black people were placed in overcrowded cells before they received a trial or were found guilty, there were no black prison guards or administrators.[95] Other black Philadelphians complained that there were few African Americans in the police force because of corrupt police who administered "farce" civil service examinations and Republican ward leaders (city councilmen) who chose the policemen they wanted in their districts.[96] In fact, in 1950, only 195 of the 4,500 officers in the police department were black.[97] With such a clear racial bias in the incarceration of individuals and a nearly all-white police force operating in the city, black crime became a greater cause of concern than white crime.

During the 1950s, police were concerned about juvenile delinquency, particularly gang activity, which rose sharply in major cities like Philadelphia.[98] From 1951 to 1956, the Juvenile Aid Bureau (officially established in 1952) tracked black and white youth gangs throughout Philadelphia and documented the growing number of gang-related crimes and arrests among teenagers.[99] Although city officials and welfare agencies estimated that only 2 percent of teenagers in the city were gang affiliated, the rising arrest rates for teenagers made gang violence an alarming issue.[100] In 1951, Philadelphia police arrested 5,397 boys and girls for gang activity that included weapons use, intoxication, arson, robbery, burglary, and homicide. From 1952 to 1955, the amount of gang-related youth arrests increased each year at a rate fluctuating between 11 percent and 14 percent.[101] During that time period, the Juvenile Aid Bureau identified the existence of nearly thirty prominent youth gangs, particularly in North, South, and West Philadelphia. While there were gangs like the Five Points in Northeast Philadelphia, the police focused more on black, white, and multiracial gangs near middle-class neighborhoods and major commercial centers, including Center City, because gang activity threatened to increase job flight from the area.[102] Additionally, girl gangs like the Torcheretts and the Demarcarretts were also a concern for police. Girl gang members composed approximately 18 percent of juvenile arrests annually until 1953, when the number dropped to 14 percent.

By 1954, the Juvenile Aid Bureau established the Morals and Gang Control Unit, which focused on youth engaged in gang activity and violent crime on city streets. When police arrested youth between the ages of six and seventeen for serious crimes, juveniles awaited their criminal trials at the newly established Youth Study Center (YSC) at 21st and Benjamin Franklin Parkway.[103] Throughout the 1950s and 1960s, the YSC often experienced overcrowding and soon only accepted youth up to age sixteen. Children who could not gain entrance to the YSC were sent to another juvenile institution outside the city limits or an adult prison. That same year, Philadelphia witnessed seventeen gang-related homicides, and less than two years later, the number climbed when there were forty murders by September 1956. Much of this deadly violence was due to teenagers gaining illegal access to razors, knives, pistols, and shotguns.[104] Gangs like the DeMarcos, Valley, and Tenderloins were even engaging in warfare with improvisational weaponry constructed from everyday items, as Edward "Butch" Anthony, a former gang member who lived at 27th and Gordon Streets in Strawberry Mansion, recalled:

> We were into making zip guns and tack guns. We were taught by an old man, an army veteran. He even gave us gunpowder so we could protect our turf from other neighborhood gangs. All we really needed was wood, a car antenna, and a door latch. . . . We would obtain the wood in wood shop at FitzSimons Junior High School, steal the antennas off of parked cars, and grab simple door latches whenever we spotted one in someone's house. At school we'd cut a block of wood in the shape of a handgun and carve a narrow path along the top where the barrel would be placed. The bottom section of an antenna worked perfectly as a barrel of a gun. Twenty-two caliber bullets passed through it perfectly. The screw would then be put in place as the trigger mechanism. Thick rubber bands were used as the trigger. . . . A tack or nail would be placed at the front end of the gun and we'd hold a match to the back end until it ignited. There would be a loud bang and the nail would be propelled out of the barrel. . . . It could cause a great deal of pain, break the skin or cause the loss of an eye if it caught you there.[105]

Nevertheless, journalists reported that police had a difficult time trying to hamper street violence because juvenile gang members could create functioning weapons from almost anything they found at home, at school, or in their neighborhood.

By December 1956, journalists like Harry J. Karafin of the *Philadelphia Inquirer* were expressing their concern, outrage, and vulnerability to the rise in violent gangs with statements like "Twenty-nine armed teen-age gangs are waging constant deadly warfare among themselves and upon a virtually defenseless Philadelphia public, committing crimes ranging from simple assault to murder."[106] That year, there were approximately ten thousand arrests of youth under eighteen years old for gang activity. In 1956, within the police department's 103-officer Juvenile Aid Bureau, the Gang Unit had twelve members who monitored youth gangs throughout the city, mapped their turf, and "periodically" raided gang hangouts for weapons. Although the police department was meticulous in its investigation of juvenile gangs in the city, Police Commissioner Thomas J. Gibbons, Councilman and Chairman of the Public Safety Committee Paul D'Ortona, and Commander of the Juvenile Aid Bureau Captain Harry G. Fox argued that the Gang Unit needed more officers.[107] According to Captain Fox, more officers were needed to fight gang violence because youth gangs were so volatile that a minor "provocation," such as opposing gang members brushing past one another, could trigger a "flare up" of gang warfare. Other city officials believed that the city was "hampered" in its use of effective gang prevention or law enforcement because of the city's financial constraints. In Karafin's article, he reported that the juvenile court was backlogged with cases because its staff was "undermanned and underpaid."[108] Additionally, the YSC was full, and youth unable to enter the YSC were sent to the adult institution, Moyamensing Prison, where they would be negatively exposed to and possibly influenced by "hardened criminals" like "narcotics addicts" and "sex offenders."[109] Although gang violence existed throughout the city regardless of race, police and media gradually focused more on gang activity in certain neighborhoods that were defined by their race and class stratification, in part due to segregation. One gang-related criminal case that exemplified the growing criminalization (and fear) of poor black youth who lived in the slums was the 1956 murder of Chris Schauer in North Philadelphia.

Just after 9:00 p.m. on December 6, 1956, the operator of Silver Dollar Check Cashing, fifty-three-year-old Chris Schauer, was going toward the night depository at Broad Street Trust Co. (located at Broad Street and Fairmount Avenue) when he got caught in the cross fire of a gang shoot-out.[110] Youth gangs the Tenderloins and the Spaniels were engaging in warfare when Schauer was shot once between the eyes as he stepped out of his 1956 Cadillac parked on the curb. Although Schauer was im-mediately taken to Hahnemann Hospital in a police emergency car, he died of his injury minutes later. When Police Commissioner Gibbons (from 1952 to 1960) heard about the crime over his police car radio, he ordered a search of every "taproom and dive" in the area, joined the manhunt, and reportedly stated, "He [Schauer] never had a chance. . . . We are living in a jungle. This is the one time the courts are going to have to do something about it. They've been letting these people off with three-month sentences. If they don't do something now, whether the Civil Liberties Union likes it or not, I'm not going to have everybody brought in who's found carrying a gun. It's time the courts woke up to

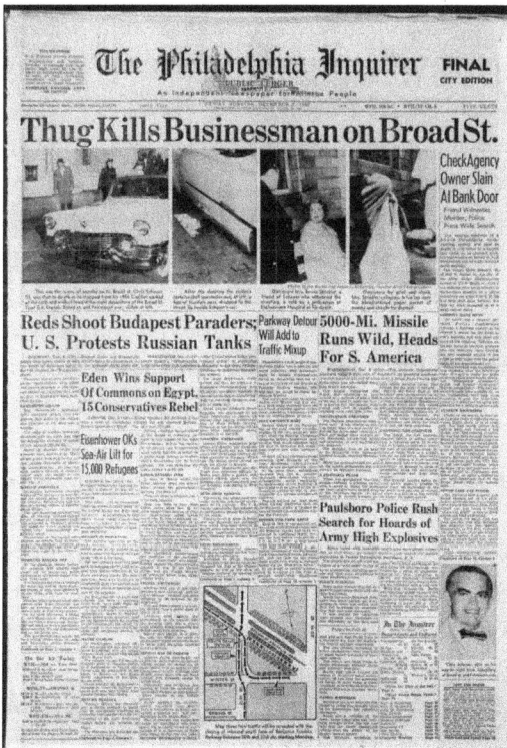

The front-page story about the murder of Christopher Schauer by a teenage black gang member in North Phil-adelphia. December 7, 1956, *Philadelphia Inquirer*.

this danger."[111] That year, prior to Schauer's death, Gibbons expressed his disdain and hopelessness for this area of the city when he referred to North Central (and other predominantly black neighborhoods in North Philadelphia) as "the jungle" because it was an impoverished, trash-strewn community with the highest crime rate in the city.[112] Gibbons, an Irish Catholic who grew up and lived most of his young adult life in the largely blue-collar and all-white Southwest Philadelphia neighborhood of Kingsessing from the 1910s through 1930s, did not believe class status alone was a strong determinant of the character of a community but believed race played a role. In fact, after rising through the ranks to police captain by 1950, Gibbons moved with his wife, children, and parents to the all-white yet mixed-income Northeast Philadelphia neighborhood of Mayfair—before Kingsessing even had the chance to desegregate during the Great Migration.[113] Moreover, the proliferation of troubling crime statistics and Gibbons's reputation as the "Lone Wolf" twenty-seven-year veteran officer who Mayor Joseph S. Clark Jr. named police commissioner over several high-ranking officers in an age of mass departmental corruption made his view of the neighborhood and his stance for tougher criminal sentencing influential in how officers, city officials, and citizens perceived North Philadelphia as well.[114]

The next morning, Schauer's murder was a front-page news story in the *Philadelphia Inquirer*. In the article entitled "Thug Kills Businessman on Broad St.," the unknown author described the tragedy with sympathy laced in middle-class consciousness, a scourging anger for urban youth crime, and a conflation of stereotypes where black gang members were not just violent but also potential thieves. In the article, the journalist mentioned how Schauer was an innocent victim of a "thug" and "bandit" who shot him on the street as his friend Bessie Strickler witnessed the event.[115] Strickler told police that she and Schauer were stepping out of the car when she heard the sound of a "cap pistol" as three youths came from the corner of Fairmount Avenue. Then a "young Negro" between the ages of fifteen and sixteen—"heavily built" and standing at approximately five feet, seven inches tall, wearing a "tan jacket and light-colored trousers"—aimed a gun at Schauer and shot him. From the author's viewpoint, Strickler's account of the murder was reputable not only because she was with Schauer when he was shot but because her socioeconomic status as the widow of highly esteemed University of Pennsylvania dermatologist Dr. Albert Strickler, who died with a $709,925 estate, certified her as a "decent citizen."[116] Additionally, the article featured not only sound bites from the journalist's interview with Strickler but also crime scene photos that photographically demonstrated Strickler being reportedly "overcome by grief and shock" as she held a "blood-stained paper packet of money and checks for deposit." Among the photographs of the murder scene were images of Schauer's *new* 1956 Cadillac along with his "tortoise-shell spectacles" and "box of fountain pens" that fell in the street as he collapsed from taking a bullet to the head.[117] The author's emphasis on Schauer's car, glasses, and fountain pens reflected a middle-class consciousness that not only reaffirmed his status as an "upstanding citizen" but also indirectly suggested that the section of the city where he was murdered, Francisville, was a dangerous place where he and others like him (middle-class and white Philadelphians) did not belong. The author's stereotyping of Schauer's murderer as a "thug" and "bandit" labeled black gang members as capable of committing violence and robbery against middle-class whites. Furthermore, Schauer's death was not the only gang-related crime that cultivated public sentiment that poor black neighborhoods in North Philadelphia were irredeemable and off-limits to white and middle-class citizens.

In 1956, there were numerous reports of innocent bystanders and gang members killed by illegal firearms on city streets and in public housing projects.[118] Police and judicial response to gang violence in "crime hotspot" areas was often immediate, punitive, and racially stigmatizing for the youth involved. For police and journalists, black youth crime in hypersegregated neighborhoods was a sign that police and city officials needed to implement more tough-on-crime policies to control what they believed to be a rising tide of uncontrollable black crime. In February 1956, twenty-year-old truck driver Gilbert Davis was shot to death at Bouvier and Master Streets when he attempted to break up a shootout between the Moroccans and the Cabot Streeters. Following the murder of the husband and father of three, police from the Juvenile Aid Bureau brought three hundred black youth into custody and questioned them over the span of thirty-six hours until they found their murder suspects: seventeen-year-old Norman DeLoatche and sixteen-year-old Charles Talbert.[119] In April 1956, fifteen-year-old Village gang member James

Midgett was shot and killed by members of a rival "project" gang at a house near 25th and Norris Streets in the James Weldon Johnson Homes over an unpaid debt for a torn jacket. By February 1957, sixteen-year-olds Frederick Woods, Robert Carroll, and LeRoy Brinkley were tried in court and sent to jail for murdering Midgett.[120] By December 16, 1956, twenty-six youths were brought into court on criminal charges of homicide and juvenile delinquency. Judge Victor DiNuble later charged nine teenagers with the gang-related murder of Schauer.[121] Although there were many gang-related homicides that triggered anger, outrage, and public demand for tough-on-crime policing of juvenile gangs, one *Philadelphia Inquirer* article detailing the Schauer case captured the law-and-order sentiment police, city officials, and some citizens adopted into the 1960s on the growing issue of juvenile gangs in black neighborhoods making "their streets unsafe for decent people": "Kid Gloves Won't End Gang Wars."[122]

On November 9, 1957, *Human Events* published journalist Morley Cassidy's article "The Most Explosive Race Problem Is in the North: 'Tyrannosaurus' Stalks in the City of Brotherly Love." In this piece, he argued that black gang violence was a result of the "invasion" of Southern black migrants in Philadelphia.[123] Cassidy's fearmongering piece equated Southern black migrants to a "Tyrannosaurus" stomping into Northern cities like Philadelphia and bringing crime and blight to the city's middle-class neighborhoods. In the article, Cassidy stated that from 1950 to 1957, the black population increased by over 113,000 at a rate seven times that of whites in Philadelphia. With 489,900 African Americans living in Philadelphia, they were already 22 percent of the city's population and expected to exceed that number in the years to come.[124] Cassidy also emphasized how neighborhoods in Philadelphia changed for the worse because black migrants were allegedly collecting welfare benefits instead of seeking employment, sending their "retarded" children with "disciplinary" problems to good schools like Benjamin Franklin High School, and electorally transforming the city's historically Republican government into a Democratic stronghold. Additionally, Cassidy connected the "invasion" of black migrants to the rise of slums, black gangs, and blighted communities in West Philadelphia, where many African Americans were choosing to settle when housing options were unavailable in North Philadelphia:

Police Sergeant David Brown maps out rival teenage gang territory at the Juvenile Aid Bureau's headquarters in the Board of Education Administration Building at 21st and the Parkway. April 1, 1954, Special Collections Research Center, Temple University Libraries, Philadelphia, PA / Dominic Pasquarella.

The first Negro is the portent of wholesale invasion. Much of West Philadelphia, thus, has been transformed from an area of solid middle-class respectability into a heavily colored area where trouble is spreading rapidly. Huge sections along Lancaster Avenue have been downgraded into the meanest kind of slums, noisy with barrooms, brawls, juke boxes and hoagie shops, where even the police walk warily, in pairs. The once fashionable Strawberry Mansion section is now a domain divided among juvenile Negro fighting gangs, waging war among themselves. The meaning of all this, in loss of property values, is something Philadelphians with the best good will cannot ignore.[125]

Furthermore, Cassidy not only scapegoated Southern black migrants for transforming good neighborhoods into slums but also declared that the middle-class fear of the spillage of black crime was now a reality. He argued that the black gangs Police Commissioner Gibbons reported on in North Philadelphia's "jungle" were now threatening the law-abiding white communities of West Philadelphia while black leaders were allowing black crime to thrive by spewing "hate-mongering" accusations of police brutality against the police.[126] Nevertheless, Cassidy suggested that criminal activity spread throughout the city as black migration expanded across Philadelphia.

Cassidy's article was published in *Human Events*, a news outlet similar to the *Philadelphia Bulletin* that catered to a white readership.[127] However, the article was also republished in the black middle-class newspaper the *Philadelphia Tribune*. The editors of the *Philadelphia Tribune* republished the article twice in February 1958 as a "public service" without any disclaimers about the racist and classist undertones present in Cassidy's piece.[128] Moreover, white middle-class Philadelphians were not the only residents who accepted the "jungle" trope associated with black migrants and their working-class communities. Many middle-class African Americans who lived away from the "black slums" believed in the "jungle" trope too and chose class solidarity over racial solidarity in the postwar era of residential desegregation.

Conclusion

As historian Timothy Lombardo explains in his 2018 book *Blue-Collar Conservatism: Frank Rizzo's Philadelphia and Populist Politics*, police and journalists had an authoritative role in shaping the perception average citizens and city officials had of *where* crime occurred and *who* were the perpetrators of offenses like gang violence.[129] When officials like Police Commissioner Gibbons used the term "jungle" in 1956 to describe North Philadelphia, that label embodied the racist connotation that a black-inhabited working-class community struggling with home maintenance and high levels of poverty and crime was a threat to the safety of "hardworking" middle-class citizens. Gibbons's term "jungle" influenced journalists like the *Philadelphia Evening Bulletin*'s Charles Shaw to pen the February 1957 article "The Jungle: Seven Square Miles that Shame—and Menace—Our City," describing Lower North Philadelphia, beyond its black neighborhoods, as marked by "blighted housing, a troublingly high crime rate, and a shamed population" where the poor were impoverished because of their supposed moral failings as "drunks, thieves, and transients searching for instant gratification."[130] However, journalists like Anne E. Hellyer reinvestigated Shaw's news story by conducting interviews with white residents of North Philadelphia, and from her research, she indirectly learned that the "jungle" was indeed a racialized term that referred not to the white ethnic neighborhoods of North Philadelphia—such as Port Richmond, Kensington, Fishtown, and Brewerytown—but the black areas within the North Central Police Division's patrolling boundaries.[131] White residents in North Philadelphia who viewed the black communities adjacent to their neighborhoods as "jungles" clung to racist tropes of black inferiority because they chose to see only the "filth and crime" present in black areas and turn a blind eye to the generations of white discrimination in housing, employment, education, recreation, and policing that consequently created those racially distinct neighborhood conditions. White residents who bottled up their feelings of white guilt over racial discrimination against African Americans assessed the socioeconomic landscape of their city and determined that from their viewpoint, racial solidarity was more profitable than class solidarity in a racist and capitalist society that viewed the poor as lazy, dirty, and undeserving of social welfare. These white residents subscribed to the racist ideology that black people had moral and cultural deficiencies, along with criminal inclinations, as an excuse to not protest or challenge the racist status quo that gave blue-collar white people racial innocence and privilege regardless of their economic status. Nevertheless, if working-class black migrants were going to be scapegoated for crime based on their race, then blue-collar white residents could capitalize on black criminalization by climbing the social ladder and finally being seen as equals to the white middle and upper classes who were firmly stereotyped as "hard-working, clean, decent, 'God-fearing'" people.[132]

News stories of black gang violence in "blighted" and impoverished neighborhoods, like the 1956 murder of Christopher Schauer in North Philadelphia, cemented the public's belief in the trope of threatening black gangs from the "urban jungle" who needed to be policed and contained in "black spaces" away from Philadelphia's "proud, blue-collar neighborhoods" deemed as "white spaces" where violent crimes were not supposed to happen.[133] Nevertheless, the term "jungle" was based on race and class stigmas that created a unique self-fulfilling prophecy where, over several generations following the Great Migration, white segregationists (with assistance from the police) resisted African Americans in their community so strongly with segregation, economic exploitation, social disadvantage, and violence that they helped create what their stereotypical minds feared: a "ghetto" composed of black communities filled with poverty, despair, crime, and eventually gang violence.[134] In 1958, police and journalists facilitated the publicity of a new threat to the ideal society: the spillage of black gang violence into white neighborhoods of middle-class status. Nevertheless, "gang" murders like that of a University of Pennsylvania graduate student in West Philadelphia, In-Ho Oh, sparked government support and citizen consent for the tough-on-crime policing of black youth from the late 1950s through the 1970s.

3

Tough on Crime

Policing or Rehabilitation?

On Friday, April 25, 1958, twenty-six-year-old graduate student In-Ho Oh decided to mail a letter to his parents in Korea. Oh was in his first year studying political science at the University of Pennsylvania, where he enrolled after working as a US Army interpreter during the Korean War.[1] Around 9:00 p.m., Oh left the apartment at 3610 Hamilton Street that he shared with his Uncle Ki Hang and Aunt Za Yung Oh to walk to the mailbox at the corner of 36th and Hamilton. Oh's apartment was in Powelton Village, a quiet, integrated West Philadelphia neighborhood near the University of Pennsylvania and Drexel University. It was filled with single and twin homes for middle-class families and college students, red-brick sidewalks, and heavily shaded, treelined streets.

One block from the mailbox, eleven African American teenage boys had just left St. Andrew's Episcopal Church on Baring Street after officials turned them away from a society club's dance. The boys, who ranged in age from fifteen to nineteen, lived roughly a half-mile away in and around the working-class black neighborhood of Mantua, north of Powelton Village. In fact, Hamilton Street was the dividing line between Powelton Village and Mantua, whose three-story rowhomes, brown brick apartment complexes, and lack of trees and green spaces distinguished it from Powelton Village. The teenagers were angered that society officials denied them entry because they did not have the thirty-five cents admission fee and were dressed in "improper attire."[2] Gathering together, they decided to "roll [rob] somebody."[3]

As Oh returned to his apartment, the boys were strolling up 36th Street to the same corner. They approached Oh and attempted to rob him. As a few boys watched, the remaining teenagers scuffled with Oh, who fought back in self-defense. As some of the boys pinned Oh down, others rifled through his pockets for money.[4] Then they punched,

University of Pennsylvania graduate student In-Ho Oh, Special Collections Research Center, Temple University Libraries, Philadelphia, PA.

kicked, and beat him with bottles and a blackjack before fleeing. Witnesses later told police that nearly a dozen boys ran from the scene. At 9:20 p.m., neighbors spotted Oh lying on the sidewalk. His face was beaten beyond recognition. Taken by ambulance to Presbyterian Hospital, he died in transit ten minutes later.[5]

Police began investigating immediately and within forty hours had "rounded up," arrested, and interrogated the eleven boys.[6] Days later, the community held a town hall meeting on gang violence at St. Andrew's while police dispatched an additional 125 officers to patrol Powelton Village on Thursday, Friday, and Saturday nights to prevent future gang crimes.[7] When Oh's parents learned about their son's murder, they wrote city officials to express their sorrow and hopes for juvenile reform for the boys. Oh's parents were devout Presbyterians, and they developed empathy for others through the human suffering they experienced and witnessed during World War II and the Korean War.[8] Oh's family requested that the teens who murdered him not receive the death penalty and that the city accept their $500 donation to assist in reforming the lives of the boys involved in the crime.[9] Oh's parents even hired locally renowned black undertaker William A. Cuffee to oversee the funeral rites of their son as a demonstration of how they held no racial hatred against African Americans for the crime committed by the black teenagers.[10] Mayor Richardson Dilworth (1956–62) was so shocked and embarrassed by Oh's murder that he campaigned to raise a $6,000 college scholarship in Oh's honor at the University of Pennsylvania to appease and complement the Oh family's demonstration of forgiveness and charity.[11] At Oh's funeral, Dilworth further expressed guilt and penance for the "gang murder" under his watch. With tears in his eyes, he told the fifty mourners at the West Philadelphia funeral that "it is a horrible thing that this could happen in our city."[12] Amid the talk of forgiveness, however, many Philadelphians viewed the incident as a cautionary story about the dangers of integration and black gangs.

In-Ho Oh's murder quickly became national news. In publications like the *Philadelphia Inquirer*, the *Philadelphia Evening Bulletin*, and *LIFE*, Oh's murder was described as a "slaying" committed by "thugs," "hoodlums," and a "gang of boy street thieves."[13] *Time* described the aggressive police response to Oh's murder in graphic, racialized terms, referring to patrolmen "swarming" the "integrated area" around Penn's campus to "collar all eleven of the junior-grade thugs" suspected of involvement in the crime.[14] Given Philadelphia's hypersegregation, interracial murder was a rarity, making up less than 10 percent of homicide cases in the 1950s. But it was front-page news when it happened.[15] The media portrayed Oh's murder as the tragic annihilation of an ideal integrated

Mr. and Mrs. Ko-Phung Oh visit the grave of their son, In-Ho Oh, at Old Pine Presbyterian Church. Special Collections Research Center, Temple University Libraries, Philadelphia, PA / Nelson.

community secure in middle-class values and public safety. It also falsely labeled it a "gang murder" because a group of black teenage boys committed the crime.[16] Oh's murder thus sparked local concern about "gang violence" and "black criminality" in integrated urban spaces.

As Philadelphians reckoned with the city's purported "gang problem," members from the black community and school activists, on the one hand, and city officials and police, on the other, offered divergent responses to the issue. Community groups such as Herman Wrice's Young Greats Society sought to eliminate black gang violence through education, recreation, social welfare, and job training.[17] Police and public officials, however, responded to Oh's murder with a full-fledged tough-on-crime program. From 1958 to 1969, they became more concerned about "roving black gangs" in integrated neighborhoods than in all-black neighborhoods. Fears about white flight and white middle-class disinvestment from the inner-city institutions that fed Philadelphia's tax base fueled these concerns.[18] Viewing black gang crime as a "threat" to integrated middle-class neighborhoods, police and city officials sought to eliminate black crime through policing and mass incarceration. Ultimately, this tough-on-crime approach prevailed over black Philadelphians' deeply rooted tradition of community-based rehabilitative social welfare.

The municipal government targeted real and imagined black gangs to convince the white middle class to stay in the inner city. Job flight, white flight, and depopulation had been major fears for city officials since 1939, when a budget deficit meant the city needed additional tax revenue to finance services like water, sewage, street paving, street cleaning (including snow removal), street lighting, police, and firefighters.[19] Over time, City Council did not want anything to provoke Philadelphians into leaving the city for suburban life, especially violent crime. Under Mayor Bernard Samuel's administration (1941–52), the city implemented a wage tax to supplement its insufficient real estate tax. Although "postwar prosperity" bolstered city coffers during the 1950s, by 1961, a 3.3 percent population decline forced city officials to annually increase the real estate and wage taxes to finance necessities like schools.[20] These challenges left municipal policymakers wary of anything that might provoke white Philadelphians to leave the city, especially violent crime.

Throughout the 1950s and 1960s, city officials, including Mayors Joseph S. Clark Jr., Richardson Dilworth, and James H. J. Tate, lobbied the federal and state governments for grants to finance improvements to health and welfare programs, public housing, highways, the airport, and the subway. But these efforts yielded limited results. Furthermore, City Council's inability to increase the tax base and its concerns about debt and depopulation encouraged it to massively invest in policing and incarceration in hopes of controlling violent crime—particularly gang violence—to retain middle-class taxpayers.[21]

Different factions in Philadelphia used In-Ho Oh's murder to bolster their social and political views. For white residents who feared integration and viewed black Southerners as backward and violent, the incident demonstrated the danger that rural working-class black migrants posed for Northern middle-class white communities.[22] They believed if police maintained neighborhood segregation through tough-on-crime policing (like surveillance, manhandling, arrests, incarceration, and deadly force), then white residents would feel safe in their communities and keep their residences and tax dollars there. Meanwhile, politicians like Dilworth knew an international student's death would make foreign students highly concerned about public safety in America.[23] For this reason, city officials permitted universities to gentrify historic black communities near their campuses and provide private housing for students in neighborhoods dotted with emergency call boxes and patrolled by university police.[24]

Black community activists sought a different path. For them, Oh's murder was an opportunity for African Americans to preemptively provide "guardianship" to black youth to keep them out of the prison system and promote a positive reputation for black citizens.[25] Black guardianship over gang-involved youth was essential in reaffirming delinquent black children's humanity and demanding effective solutions to racialized poverty, social inequality, and violent crime. This tradition of black guardianship of juvenile gang members fostered by organizations like the Wharton Centre set a precedent for future Philadelphia activists to utilize rehabilitative social welfare programs rather than tough-on-crime policing in response to gang violence. Policymakers, however, rejected rehabilitative social welfare in favor of punitive policies intended to slow white flight.

A "Noose" around Philadelphia: Fighting Black Gangs to Stop White Flight

The public outcry against the "gang attack" of In-Ho Oh involved disbelief, anger, and regret about the failed experiment of residential integration. In the mid-1950s, city planners, religious institutions, and community organizations nationally established multiracial social clubs and sponsored recreational events to transform all-white middle-class neighborhoods from what historian Abigail Perkiss describes as communities advocating racial homogeneity to ones promoting "class-based exclusivity."[26] In Philadelphia, some community members believed religious and cultural centers that offered activities such as movie nights and dances could promote positive race relations between black and white people as middle-class African Americans attained upward social mobility and moved into formerly all-white middle-class neighborhoods.

These efforts faced challenges given Philadelphia's history of residential segregation. In West Philadelphia, pre-1965 Korean immigrants like In-Ho Oh were often middle-class individuals who were students at nearby colleges, white-collar professionals, the spouses of Korean War veterans, or aspiring entrepreneurs. Although Koreans were considered nonwhite and therefore at risk of facing racism and xenophobia, their class status, educational attainment, and the American-imposed stereotype of Asians being a "model minority" enabled Asians like Oh to live in predominantly white communities like Powelton Village.[27] Significantly, as Philadelphia's racial demographics diversified, its neighborhoods remained largely segregated.

Some white residents in Northwest and West Philadelphia supported residential integration and promoted multiracial organizations like the West Mount Airy Neighbors (WMAN). These residents encouraged their black and white neighbors to build community around recreational events at social institutions like the Germantown Jewish Centre and the Unitarian Church. However, these white prointegration community activists were not entirely altruistic. They also sought to prevent their fellow white neighbors from moving to Northeast Philadelphia or the city's suburbs to escape incoming black residents. They did so by urging neighbors to reject realtors who financially profited from segregation and blockbusting by engaging in panic selling. Their goal was to create a stable multiracial community that would discourage white flight and inspire white residents to accept their black neighbors.[28]

Many white middle-class residents who favored racial inclusivity wanted to be racially progressive while also deterring blight and crime in their community. Many of these white residents who feared blight and black crime also wanted to remain in their neighborhoods to retain their ethnic and communal ties and access to good schools and recreation centers.[29] They assumed that black middle-class residents would possess similar values and would therefore maintain the reputation of their new neighborhood.

Like the residents of Mount Airy, many white Philadelphians in middle-class neighborhoods like Powelton Village preferred middle-class black families as their neighbors due to the race- and class-based stigmatization of working-class African Americans as unrefined and criminal. In 1952, police captain of the Sixteenth District Frank L. Rizzo gave residents in Powelton Village reasons to fear having black neighbors when he told members of the citizen's group Young Independent Political Action Committee and the press that "the crime rate in West Philadelphia is the worst in the city." Rizzo, an Italian American from South Philadelphia who began his career as a North Philadelphia foot patrolman in 1943, claimed that there were four hundred speakeasies in the majority-black area that were not only selling illegal liquor but also spewing out men and women in "various stages of intoxication," which later led to some patrons engaging in violent crimes like stabbings.[30] That year, Rizzo's police district made a record of at least six hundred arrests per month, but the conviction rate was much lower, suggesting that most criminal cases may have involved trumped-up charges or false arrests. Although Rizzo argued that he was not "racially prejudiced" and did not "run roughshod over the citizens in the district," over time, many black citizens, business owners, and community activists—like Cecil B. Moore of the National Association for the Advancement of Colored People (NAACP), Spencer Coxe of the American Civil Liberties Union (ACLU), and Gregory M. Harvey of the Americans for Democratic Action (ADA)—across the city would file complaints about Rizzo authorizing intrusive surveillance and illegal raids of homes, businesses, and organizations without warrants along with committing police brutality against alleged criminal suspects.[31] Many white residents throughout Philadelphia believed Rizzo was a credible witness to crime in the city because throughout his police career, he gained notoriety from achieving eighty-nine citations and awards from various city and social organizations while local newspapers like the *Philadelphia Daily News* heroized his police work for years, praising him as the "Cisco Kid": a "cowboy on the streets" who could apprehend a suspect without handcuffs or a gun.[32]

Furthermore, these white middle-class residents wanted to feel "safe" in their communities while also protecting their homes from devaluation based on the "racial theory of property value."[33] However, when the news media revealed that Oh's murderers were in Powelton Village to attend a church-sponsored neighborhood dance promoting racial integration, some white Philadelphians questioned whether residential integration was a long-term social good.[34] Some also openly speculated whether criminality was an inherent trait among African Americans, especially the black poor. For many white citizens, the Oh murder supposedly traumatized them into believing that the influx of black migrants into their communities would inevitably result in violent crime.

Following the media blitz surrounding Oh's murder, West Philadelphians vented their anger and concern about public safety. Many white Philadelphians used racist "jungle and animal analogies" to describe the black teenagers who murdered Oh.[35] For example, an unsigned May 1958 editorial in the *Philadelphia Bulletin* castigated the teenagers, stating they were "not human enough" to experience emotion, fear, or remorse given their capacity to commit a murder "as wantonly fierce as ever stained a jungle thicket." They were, the editorialist maintained, as "insensitive" as "a pack of hyenas regards a carcass."[36] At the teenagers' arraignment, Judge J. Stanley Hoffman ordered that the boys be tried as adults and face the death penalty after describing them as "vermin" whose "barbaric piece of savagery brought undeserved shame to a decent, law-abiding segment of our population."[37] Additionally, Dilworth, a Democratic politician concerned about both racialized poverty and the rise of violent crime, received three boxes of letters from residents who described incidents in which they or their family members were "assaulted, held up, burgled, or harassed" by predominantly black teenagers. Some of these writers demanded tough-on-crime punishments for the youth, while others expressed their desire to leave the city.[38]

These reactions pushed Mayor Dilworth and Police Commissioner Thomas J. Gibbons to embrace tough-on-crime policing to control the spillage of black gang violence into integrated middle-class neighborhoods. Nine days after Oh's murder, on May 4, 1958, Dilworth responded to all the letters he had received during a televised news conference. He began by discussing how race relations between blacks and whites were marred by segregation, racial discrimination, and economic exploitation in homeownership. Dilworth then explained that black crime in Philadelphia was high because "there are so many low income Negro districts." From his viewpoint, tough-on-crime policing was not the best approach because crime rates could drop if there were more social services, youth recreational facilities, and "specialized institutions" for juvenile offenders. Furthermore, Dilworth argued that Philadelphians could only "solve the problem" of violent interracial crime if they worked as a "community." For Dilworth, that meant whites had to stop practicing racial discrimination and blacks had to exert more leadership in tackling social problems in their community.[39]

In October 1958, months after Dilworth gave his televised address about the In-Ho Oh murder, Philadelphians sent him over a dozen letters after local newspapers reported that another University of Pennsylvania student was beaten with an iron pipe by two assailants at 42nd Street and Osage Avenue.[40] The thirty-eight-year-old international student, Manmatha Kumar Das from Calcutta, India, reportedly survived the attempted robbery but required treatment in the hospital for a fractured skull.[41] In these October letters, residents recalled the Oh murder and offered their solutions for how violent crime committed by black youth should be handled. Richard P. Brown, a businessman from the Girard Trust Company, wrote a letter to Dilworth laced with racist tropes about Indians and African Americans, stating that the "jungles of Philadelphia are far more dangerous" than "the jungles of India where poisonous snakes exist" because during his recent trip to India, he was able to walk the streets of "Bombay, Jaipur, Delhi, Agra and Banaras" at night without the fear of being "slugged from behind without warning" from a robber. Brown ultimately argued that the National Guard be called in to "help patrol our city streets" and then sent a copy of his letter to the *Philadelphia Inquirer* and the *Philadelphia Evening Bulletin* to publish in their respective editorial columns.[42]

Although many Philadelphians advocated for immediate action against crime while openly expressing their racist and classist prejudices against African Americans, a few residents wrote letters to Dilworth that were sympathetic to the victims of violent crime and their attackers. Their suggestion to use government funds to rehabilitate delinquent youth reflected the psychosocial belief that poverty begot crime. Mrs. D. German of 883 North 23rd Street wrote to Dilworth requesting that criminal youth be sent to work camps, and he responded to her suggestion with agreement. However, Dilworth also explained that while Governor George M. Leader also supported the idea of establishing camps similar to the Civilian Conservation Corps (CCC) camps created for unemployed urban men during the Great Depression to do conservation work in fields, parks, and forests, it had been a four-year uphill battle trying to get the State Legislature to expand its funds for the project beyond support for one hundred juveniles.[43] Jacob Copman, the owner of Bevan Manufacturing Company, wrote a letter explaining how young men need "pocket money" and money for "clothing and board," but oftentimes there are no jobs available to keep them "out of trouble," so they resort to violence to get what they need. Furthermore, Copman argued that there were more sustainable solutions to violent juvenile crime than "adding to the police force and building detention homes," and he recommended that, just like "President F.D. Roosevelt pulled this country out of the worst depression by providing jobs," City Council should create jobs for youth, even if it meant increasing local taxes to fund the project.[44] Dilworth later responded to Copman's letter with thanks and said that the idea would be considered by his administration.

In other letters, some residents suggested that Dilworth implement extreme measures to deal with violent crime. Cereta M. Shockley, a registered nurse at the Graduate Hospital of the University of Pennsylvania, explained in her letter to Dilworth how reformatories and prisons were ineffective and called for more police along with a "whipping post" near City Hall where "every citizen can witness their [the criminals'] punishment."[45] In fact, several residents argued for the implementation of the whipping post, which, given the racist animal and jungle tropes many journalists and citizens were using to describe criminal black youth at the time, indirectly referenced a racialized punishment administered to enslaved black people before 1865. In response to this proposed offensive punishment, Dilworth wrote to Joseph T. Clancy of Rittenhouse Square a charged and defensive reply in which he advocated for nonviolent solutions to juvenile crime rather than violent punishments that involved public humiliation:

> I have your letter concerning the recent wave of violence in the City of Philadelphia. I can only say I think our police are doing an excellent job in that they are arresting the criminals in nearly every case, and that in itself is a tremendous task. Undoubtedly, the Courts have permitted themselves to get behind in their trial calendars, and some few of the Courts have not administered fair or reasonable sentences. However, by and large I think the Courts are doing a constructive job. We do suffer from a very serious lack of correctional facilities for juveniles, and so in many cases the Judges are not at fault in permitting probation . . . I was

a District Attorney and am a Marine Corps veteran of both World Wars, but I am convinced that extreme punishment defeats its own ends, and violence merely begets further violence . . . when England had a great wave of crime in the early 1700's, there was a whipping post in London and pick-pocketing was a hanging offense. However, all this served as no deterrent. In fact, the public hangings were the pick-pockets' favorite spots as the public's attention was so fascinated by the hangings that it was easy to pick their pockets.[46]

Nevertheless, Dilworth wanted an end to crime in Philadelphia, but he did not want to intensify the racial conflict, poverty, and criminalization of black youth already present in the city and its justice system. Dilworth's letters in response to his critics demonstrated how he had contempt for people like Clancy who wanted tough-on-crime policing and violent punishment while also maintaining "no sympathy" for residents like Benjamin Cohen who threatened to "flee the city just because it has problems." Dilworth wanted all Philadelphians to be invested in addressing poverty, racism, and inequality as the root causes of crime. As Dilworth explained in his response to Cohen, he was not a "do-gooder or Social Service worker" but someone who believed in discipline and the potential of people in a "big city" like Philadelphia to be unified in solving "challenging problems" without "cruel punishments" and "counter-violence."[47]

Although Dilworth asserted in his replies to residents' letters that he was not worried about people who chose to leave Philadelphia, he was still concerned about letters he received from residents like Marilyn Steinberg who considered flight to the suburbs. "I've always loved living in the City of Philadelphia," Steinberg wrote. "But during the past year I've thought more than once of moving as far out as possible." As historian Eric Schneider explained, Dilworth recognized that urban integration and crime deterred whites from remaining in the city while the allure of "modern housing" and racial homogeneity in the suburbs enticed them to flee. In fact, Dilworth once referred to suburbanization as a "white noose" strangling Philadelphia, which relied on the white middle class to feed its tax base. While Dilworth initially opposed the tough-on-crime policing of poor African Americans, he supported urban renewal projects that would benefit—and retain—the middle class. These projects included revitalizing Center City as a commercial district and building new roadways to connect Philadelphia to other metropolitan areas.[48] By clearing and gentrifying low-income black neighborhoods like West Philadelphia's Black Bottom, those plans displaced African American residents, established the middle-class University City community, and elevated racial tension between blacks and whites.[49]

In contrast to Dilworth, Police Commissioner Gibbons—who a year earlier had referred to "blighted," impoverished, and black-inhabited neighborhoods as crime-ridden "jungle[s]"—instructed the police department to implement tough-on-crime initiatives following Oh's murder. Gibbons received forty-six letters from citizens expressing their outrage over the West Philadelphia homicide. In addition to complaining about the criminal justice system's leniency toward juvenile delinquency, many letter writers expressed their desire to move to a "safer area."[50] By 1965, Gibbons (while in retirement from the police force) would oversee the gradual expansion of the police department's Gang Unit, the use of the police's K-9 unit on public transportation, and motorized police patrols to "curb the crime wave" of gang violence that tough-on-crime supporters feared. Furthermore, while only one of the eleven African American teens who murdered Oh was allegedly a member of an active gang, this "gang murder" triggered tough-on-crime policies that included less detention of juvenile delinquents in youth facilities and more imprisonment of "criminal youth" in adult penitentiaries.

Black Gangs, Interracial Violence, and Tough-on-Crime Policing

After news coverage of Oh's murder sensationalized Philadelphia's "gang" problem, from 1958 to 1969, police focused on black gangs and closely investigated their names, turf, reputations for violence, and crimes.[51] Public concern about black gangs also spurred black journalists and social activists to investigate the sociological explanations and rehabilitative solutions for juvenile gang activity. Historically, West Philadelphia was distinctly segregated by race and class. During the 1940s, newspaper crime narratives describing "murders and a number of stabbings, burglaries, larcenies, petty thieving and gang warfare," along with stereotypes and stigmas about black residential areas in the "Tops" and

A group of boys near 34th and Haverford in West Philadelphia. February 9, 1968, Special Collections Research Center, Temple University Libraries, Philadelphia, PA / Joseph Wasko.

"Bottoms" that were in proximity to white residential spaces sparked white and middle-class fear and derision of the black people who lived in those areas.[52] The "Tops" (bounded by Lancaster Avenue to the north, Market Street to the south, 52nd Street to the east, and 59th Street to the west) was known as a neighborhood where "some of the best Negro residential areas" in the city existed, and over 19 percent of black residents there were homeowners. The "Bottoms" (bounded by Lancaster Avenue to the north, Market Street to the south, the "freight cars of Pennsylvania Railroad" at 30th Street Station to the east, and 42nd Street to the west), on the other hand, was known as an "older" and "run-down" section of the city where over 90 percent of black residents were renters instead of homeowners. Despite the class difference between black people in the Tops and Bottoms, both areas experienced gang activity from groups like the Zephyrs, Haverfords, and Toastie Tops that hung out at playgrounds, drugstores, candy stores, luncheonettes, and poolrooms.[53]

During this decade, sociologist John J. Kane became inspired by the "lurid accounts" of black gang violence featured in Philadelphia newspapers to investigate the causes of gang activity among black youth in West Philadelphia. Kane toured the area in a police patrol car, acquired statistical and informational data from Philadelphia's municipal court and Saint Ignatius of Loyola Catholic Church, respectively, and interviewed social workers, police, and "boy residents of the area" to "study the locale, origin, structure and behavior patterns" of the gangs and offer a sociological explanation for the phenomenon. By 1948, Kane completed his research, and although exuding some racial bias in referring to the Great Migration of thousands of African Americans to Philadelphia as a "Negro 'invasion,'" his article vividly recalled and aligned with the sociological research and theories of Frederic Thrasher and William Foote Whyte.[54] In the article, "The Tops and Bottoms: The Study of Negro Gangs in West Philadelphia," Kane argued that black gangs like the El Doradoes and Noble Dukes existed because issues like a lack of accessible recreational facilities (in part due to racial discrimination), poverty, decreased "home supervision" due to parents constantly working, poor housing, truancy, and negative experiences with "dissatisfied teachers and [racial] conflict" encouraged youth to find community, solace, and emotional relief by joining a "delinquent gang."[55] His conclusions confirmed not only Thrasher and Whyte's findings about juvenile gang activity arising from experiences with social exclusion but also the work of social activists like Helen H. Corson and W. Miller Barbour from the Wharton Centre, who outlined similar issues among the gang-prone black children they rehabilitated at their institution in North Philadelphia.

Although Kane's sociological research from the 1940s offered an explanation for gang activity and poverty-induced crime among urban African American youth, countless journalists from mainstream newspapers like the *Philadelphia Inquirer* and *Philadelphia Evening Bulletin* chose to ignore it following Oh's murder. However, staff writers from the black-owned newspaper the *Philadelphia Tribune* sought to reinvestigate the issue of black gang crime in May 1958. On May 3, staff writers Theodore W. Graham, Art Peters, J. Donald Porter, and Charles Thomas released their report about the living conditions and family lives of the teenage boys who killed Oh to offer readers an empathetic view into the lives of the young men charged with murder.[56] Upon walking through the boys' West Philadelphia neighborhood, Graham, Peters, Porter, and Thomas noted that some city blocks reflected the "oppressiveness of a drab neighborhood" because vacant lots, homes in disrepair, empty buildings with "gaping walls," and piles of rubble and debris in lots and on homeowners' properties clashed with "clean and newly painted" porch-front residences that sat parallel to railroad tracks or a coal and lumber yard. However, when the *Tribune* journalists visited the homes of Lonnie Collins, Harold Johnson, Leonard Johnson, Harry and Edward McCloud, Franklin Marshall, James Wright, and Percy Johnson, they often found the homes of the youths' parents or guardians clean, furnished, decent, and livable to varying degrees. At each of the residences, the staff writers listened as the boys' relatives expressed how ashamed, shocked, and saddened they were by their children's involvement in Oh's murder. Leonard Johnson's middle-aged adopted mother told the journalists she was "sick at the stomach" over the criminal case, while Franklin Marshall's mother hid in her home, exclaiming that she also was sick and did not want to see the "*Tribune* or anyone else." Nevertheless, the *Tribune* reporters received a unanimous sentiment of hope that the children were innocent and a declaration that justice be served if they were guilty from each household, summed up best by Leonard Johnson's mother: "I don't know what happened. Just what I've heard in court. . . . If my boy did this, if he helped kill that man . . . he'll have to pay the price."[57]

Based on the interviews Graham, Peters, Porter, and Thomas conducted, the potential causes for the boys' crime were complex. All the youths appeared to have come from decent homes, and their relatives often characterized them as well-mannered, occupied with school and sports, and willing to work to have money in their pockets. However, there were some internal and external socioeconomic factors that made their personal lives unstable. Harry and Edward McCloud came from a two-parent household they shared with their three younger sisters in a six-bedroom rowhome, but their father was unemployed. James Wright, who lived with his mother and four younger brothers, received a "church upbringing" in his household and had dreams of becoming a professional football player. However, Wright's parents had separated three years prior, his family was on welfare because his mother was unable to work, and he recently failed several courses at Overbrook High School, which jeopardized his opportunity to graduate and become a professional athlete.[58] Lonnie Collins and Harold Johnson came from broken nuclear families with an absent mother and a deceased father, respectively; regularly sought out employment to meet their financial needs; and were known to hang out with the "wrong crowd of boys" despite their parents and guardians' advice to stay away from gangs. Although Collins and Johnson's families explained that the youths had access to money for their "pocket" through employment or a one-time allowance, the *Tribune* alluded that the boys were financially frustrated because Collins had recently been laid off from his job at a grocery store while Johnson had to wait nearly a week to return to his summer job in Atlantic City. Nevertheless, by detailing these accounts of familial and financial turmoil, the *Tribune* journalists provided its readers with the sociological factors that possibly influenced the boys to commit the crime. Overall, the *Tribune* staff writers agreed with the general public that the murder of In-Ho Oh was "brutal" and tragic, but their article sought to humanize the boys amid incessant media reports that focused on the "bestiality" and "viciousness of the crime."[59]

By 1959, leading members of the United Presbyterian Church in the United States were so distraught over the nationally publicized murder of In-Ho Oh that they released a twenty-nine-minute evangelistic film to spark public discussion about poverty-induced crime. *An Epistle from the Koreans* was both a memorialization of Oh's life walking in the Presbyterian faith and a critique of the urban society that nurtured some black youth into delinquency and violent crime.[60] The overall message of the film was to teach its viewers the lesson of forgiveness. However, its filmmakers also wanted to inspire collective sympathy for the African American youth involved in Oh's murder. *An Epistle from the Koreans* included not only a reenactment of the tragedy but also dialogic scenes highlighting the teenagers' jail experience, criminal trial, and the community where they lived. The film's particular focus on the boys' neighborhood was to draw the viewers' attention to how the youths' upbringing in the poor and working-class black communities of West Philadelphia influenced their social behavior.

In a similar vein to Kane's article and the *Philadelphia Tribune* staff writers' exclusive report, one of the most poignant lines of the script in *An Epistle from the Koreans* was an explanation of how a black community shaped by housing discrimination, residential overcrowding, and neighborhood blight created a toxic environment where teenagers were potentially nurtured into a lifestyle of delinquency, violence, and crime:

> They lived in a kind of neighborhood that some people thoughtlessly call a jungle, a cliché like that can obscure important facts about the deteriorated parts of a big city. What's this neighborhood like? For one thing, it's a place where fire escapes and stone steps take the place of grass and rolling hills. It's a population pocket of low-income families swollen by the influx of thousands of newcomers from the South and isolated in an old part of town that had already been given over to crumbling mortar and rotting wood.[61]

For the filmmakers, neighborhood overcrowding, poverty, and blight sparked the mental frustration and anger that motivated the robbery and murder of a complete stranger who appeared to be a picture of privilege without struggle. Furthermore, the filmmakers' goal in portraying the youths' perspective was to argue that the black teenagers were not completely responsible for the crime because they were products of a racist and classist society where they were exposed to the devaluing socioeconomic conditions of slum housing, racial ostracism, and segregation. For the filmmakers, the black youths murdered Oh out of frustration and anger at being rejected by society for being forced to live in a segregated and blighted neighborhood. Moreover, *An Epistle from the Koreans* indirectly identified the boys involved in Oh's murder as products of what would later be known as the "culture of poverty."

Despite the ethics conversations organizations like the United Presbyterian Church initiated to explain violent crime committed by urban youth, the police department sidestepped sociological data and pursued tough-on-crime and public safety initiatives to specifically prevent black gangs from committing interracial crimes in integrated public spaces. Moreover, tough-on-crime policing overshadowed rehabilitative programs run by social activists in Philadelphia because journalists cultivated a fear of black gangs from "the jungle" spilling into other areas of the city. Philadelphians who discussed with their neighbors how Oh's murder was unforgettable and unforgivable also contributed to the mutually reinforcing feedback loop between the press, middle-class white residents, and city officials who promoted the aggressive policing and strict criminal sentencing of black youth.[62]

When local news media reported on black-on-black gang violence, city officials and police were not triggered to respond with tough-on-crime policing. This occurred because the crime neither involved a nonblack victim nor threatened white middle-class residents. For example, on June 17, 1963, six members of the Camac and Norris Street Gang attacked and killed fifteen-year-old Theodore Furman outside of North Philadelphia's John Wanamaker Junior High School.[63] At 3:15 p.m., sixteen-year-old Isaiah McFadden, a pupil of Thomas Edison High School, waited with his friends outside of Wanamaker to retaliate against Furman, a member of the Valley gang, for beating him up three weeks prior.[64] When Furman exited Wanamaker after school, McFadden and his friends immediately attacked him. As several students watched, the boys beat and stabbed Furman four times in the chest with a penknife until he broke away and ran one block to 12th Street and Columbia Avenue, where he collapsed in the gutter. Soon the police arrived at the scene and transported Furman to St. Luke's Children's Medical Center, where he was pronounced dead on arrival at 3:40 p.m.[65]

When the 1963 black gang murder of Theodore Furman occurred, there was public outrage but no media blitz or tough-on-crime reaction similar to the aftermath of In-Ho Oh's 1958 murder. As Schneider explains, black gang stabbings and shootings in all-black neighborhoods and housing projects often failed to generate press coverage or additional police patrols and interventions.[66] Although newspapers like the *Philadelphia Inquirer*, *Lebanon Daily News*, and *Courier-Post* reported Furman's murder, the story never made the front page or reached outside of the mid-Atlantic region of the country.[67] However, the courts responded similarly to Furman's homicide as to Oh's murder. At the criminal trial, county court judge J. Sydney Hoffman, who also oversaw the Oh murder trial, called the youths who killed Furman "teenage gangsters who make it impossible for adults and innocent youths to walk city streets without fear."[68]

Philadelphia city officials and police treated the Oh and Furman murders differently, since they were more concerned about black crime affecting white middle-class people. This prioritization of white middle-class interests explains why police and journalists accelerated their consideration of tough-on-crime policing in black neighborhoods after African Americans in North Philadelphia engaged in a 1964 uprising and riot against white business owners and police. By 1963, formerly desegregated North Philadelphia neighborhoods like North Central had become predominantly black due to white flight. The majority of businesses, however, remained under white ownership. That meant that black people in areas like North Philadelphia, where two-thirds of the city's six hundred thousand black residents lived, often had to patronize white businesses in order to get necessary food, clothes, and household items.[69] White businessmen sometimes cheated African Americans, and high prices often prevented black families from affording certain goods. Furthermore, racial tensions simmered between black and white Americans as black people faced inequality and economic disparity in their neighborhoods. The early 1960s were a time when black people, in addition to having issues with white businessmen, were on edge about police brutality.

In 1964, the *Philadelphia Tribune* published many articles on police brutality, which resulted in several Philadelphia officers facing criminal trials that ended in acquittals.[70] While police brutality was not a new problem in the city, heightened racial tensions led to a race riot on Columbia Avenue on August 28, 1964.[71] That day's riot began at 8:30 p.m.

when an African American married couple, Odessa and Rush Bradford, stopped their car at the busy intersection of 22nd Street and Columbia Avenue to argue and physically fight in the middle of the street. Two police officers, African American officer Robert Wells and white officer John J. Hoff, arrived at the scene, approached the couple, and ordered them to move their car. Wells soon got into a confrontation with Odessa Bradford, who refused to move the vehicle. Odessa then slapped Wells, and he slapped her in return. Eventually, Wells chased Odessa around the car until he and Hoff were able to arrest her and place her in a police wagon.[72]

Then forty-one-year-old James Mettles appeared among the officers and punched Hoff to protect Odessa from what he believed to be police brutality. Someone else then threw a brick and a bottle toward the officers, and the uprising and riot against the police began. The uprising and riot became widespread when twenty-five-year-old Raymond Hall, a known "neighborhood agitator," spread the false rumor that a white policeman beat a pregnant black woman to death.[73] During the uprising and riot, which lasted two days, African American residents burned cars, destroyed and looted more than two hundred white businesses, and fought with police.

When Police Commissioner Howard R. Leary (1962–65) heard about the uprising, he immediately ended his weekend vacation at the South Jersey shore and drove back to the city while about 1,800 police officers responded to stop the riot and restore order under the temporary command of Deputy Police Commissioner Frank Rizzo. When Leary arrived on the scene, he ordered the officers to stand down and not engage in any physical confrontation or shooting of protestors, rioters, or looters—to Rizzo and Mayor James H. J. Tate's (1962–72) chagrin. As *Philadelphia Daily News* journalist Fred Hamilton explained, Leary was concerned about the safety of the residents along with his officers, who were potentially outnumbered, lacked crucial equipment like hard hats, and were vulnerable to snipers who could have been hiding on the roofs and upper floors of the buildings that lined Columbia Avenue. Therefore, the police commissioner chose not to escalate the situation with force unless it was absolutely necessary.[74] As a result of Leary's decision, the only person to die in the riot was twenty-one-year-old Robert Green, whom police fatally shot when he attacked an officer with a knife.

After the riot, almost all white business owners permanently left North Philadelphia to reopen their restaurants, furniture stores, grocery stores, and other businesses outside the black community.[75]

Following the events on Columbia Avenue, police and journalists began to conflate "mobs" with "gangs" and used the terms interchangeably to refer to African Americans who committed violent interracial crimes in groups of three or more.[76] When police and journalists likened black gangs to mobs, they suggested that gangs were inherently violent and capable of theft and destruction similar to the individuals who stole from and destroyed white businesses during the Columbia Avenue riot. For example, on March 6, 1965, six black teenage boys jumped a Broad Street subway turnstile at the Race-Vine station near Center City, grabbed a fifteen-year-old white girl from the platform, pulled her onto the train bed, and attempted to rape her. Although there were several people on the platform, a twenty-three-year-old white naval airman, James R. George, was the only person to intervene. George fought the teens, rescued the girl, and although badly beaten, reached the cashier cage to tell the operator to call the police.[77]

From March 7 to March 15, 1965, journalists wrote *heroic* accounts—reminiscent of the white supremacist film *The Birth of a Nation*—detailing how George saved the fifteen-year-old white girl from a "mob" of black boys. In one article, *Philadelphia Inquirer* journalists described how George was visiting Philadelphia from Chamblee, Georgia, for two weeks to complete naval training at Willow Grove Air Station.[78] George was traveling by subway on March 6 to sightsee while on his break from training when he saw the group of boys attack the girl. The reporters then explained how George unsuccessfully "plead" for six "Negro adults" on the subway platform to help him rescue the girl.[79] When George's request went unanswered, he "waded into the mob of 15 to 20 youths surrounding the girl" and rescued her. Although the journalists suggested that the six black adults stood "idle" while the attack happened, other news reports proposed that given the violent reputation "black gangs" had in the city, they were too afraid to assist George in the rescue. The article also mentioned how the very next day, a fifteen-year-old black girl was walking alone at night when five black teenage boys grabbed her near 56th and Pine Streets, dragged her into a vacant house, and raped her a half a block away from her home.[80] Despite the shocking nature of the crime, the six-paragraph report of the rape was brief and over-looked compared to the nearly thirty-paragraph article focused on the attempted rape and rescue of the white teenage girl.

The *Philadelphia Inquirer*'s depiction of George, a white Southerner, saving a white girl from being raped by "black brutes" used a racist trope from the Civil War, Reconstruction, and Jim Crow eras.[81] As historian Stephen Berry explains, post–Civil War Southern apologists depicted Confederate soldiers as having fought "honorably" in the Civil War to protect both white womanhood from black brute rapists and the safe, pure, and powerful white society their bodies symbolically repre-sented.[82] Later, Hollywood revived the trope through D. W. Griffith's 1915 film adaptation of a 1905 Thomas Dixon novel where the Ku Klux Klan protected white women from interracial sex and violence.[83] Like Griffith and Dixon, the *Philadelphia Inquirer* intended to tell a heroic story of a "black gang attack" that reinforced racist ideas about "black male brutes" who needed to be controlled to maintain a safe white society.

The attempted rape spurred Philadelphia's police and city officials to expand tough-on-crime policing and surveillance at major public transportation stations citywide.[84] On March 9, 1965, Police Commis-sioner Leary announced that police would implement a "program of increased protection." The program involved police dog patrols and ci-vilian emergency call boxes at "strategic locations" on subway platforms and concourses and "public address speakers" notifying police officers of nearby crime. Later that day, Mayor Tate held an emergency session with police officials to plan for improving citizen protection. Those attend-ing Tate's "crime conference" were Police Commissioner Leary, Deputy Commissioners Frank L. Rizzo and Edward Bell, Chief Inspector Harry Fox, Inspector Frank Nolan, Captain Anthony Wong, Captain Thomas Hannigan, and Lieutenant Joseph Larkin.[85]

During the meeting, Tate expressed his anger with the Philadelphia Transportation Company (PTC) for its ineffective and time-wasting pro-tocol directing employees to contact PTC dispatchers regarding criminal acts before calling police.[86] He then proposed to "halt crimes of violence" by shutting down subway stations from City Hall in Center City to Girard Avenue in North Philadelphia during the "critical hours" beyond mid-night. As the meeting ended, Tate ordered police to increase their patrols on the transit concourses and train cars of the Broad Street subway and

Judge Juanita Kidd Stout (left) takes the oath at municipal court. October 23, 1959, Charles L. Blockson Afro-American Collection, Temple University Libraries, Philadelphia, PA / John W. Mosley.

Market-Frankford el, which served racially and socioeconomically diverse riders. Tate also informed the police officials that he would consider the "possibility of hiring additional police" to patrol the subway systems.[87]

Tate and Leary's new police patrol designed to combat black gang crime in the transit system went into effect at 1:00 p.m. on March 10,

1965. Leary issued twenty-four-hour police patrols where members of the K-9 Corps rode subway trains and patrolled subway stations with police dogs along the Broad Street subway and Market-Frankford el lines within the city's limits.[88] The K-9 Corps more than doubled its number of working dogs from eleven to twenty-five, while thirty officers were added to the seventy-five-man patrol, equipped with walkie-talkies. Officers not assigned to the interior of the subway system were ordered to patrol transit stations every half hour along Broad Street in "jeep patrols."[89] Notably, police and city officials implemented more crime prevention tactics against black gangs following the attempted rape of a white teenage girl than they had following the *gang* rape of a black girl or the murders of an Asian man like In-Ho Oh and a black boy like Theodore Furman. Moreover, Philadelphia's city and police officials did not target public transportation to advance their tough-on-crime policing initiatives simply because the survivor of the March 6 attempted rape was white. They also did so because the transit system was the most desegregated public space in the city, therefore increasing the opportunity for interracial crime.

Black Community Activists and "Guardianship" over Black Youth

Although city officials, police, and journalists often accused the African American community of not taking leadership to solve black gang violence in Philadelphia, black leaders in fact attempted to combat black gang violence through punitive and rehabilitative guardianship. In the juvenile court system, black judges like Juanita Kidd Stout pursued tough-on-crime sentencing to reform black youth who engaged in violent crime.[90] When Judge Stout received the March 7th rape case involving the fifteen-year-old black girl, journalists described her as "visibly angry" in court when she stated, "If it's rape today, it's jail tomorrow." During the criminal trial, Judge Stout promised to "swiftly" carry justice "for any rapist who came before her." She then charged the five teens with rape, statutory rape, assault with intent to ravish, indecent assault, assault and battery, and conspiracy. Stout later sentenced the three "ringleaders" to indeterminate terms at the State Correctional Institution at Camp Hill and gave the two others six months in a juvenile correctional facility.[91]

When Judge Stout took on the attempted rape case involving the fifteen-year-old white girl, she gave the black boys involved a similar sentence. Among the eight teenagers arrested as participants and on-lookers of the assault, Judge Stout sentenced five boys to Camp Hill until they turned twenty-one years old, two boys to indeterminate terms in Youth Development Centers, and one boy to probation. Additionally, she publicly commended sixteen-year-old Alfonso Dunlap for being the only "gang" member who tried to persuade the "mob" to leave the teen-age girl alone.[92]

While Stout used incarceration to curb violent crime among black youth believed to be gang-affiliated, community activist Herman Wrice used social welfare programs to rehabilitate black children before they could commit gang crimes. In April 1965, twenty-six-year-old drug labo-ratory technician Herman Wrice established the antigang program the Young Greats Society (YGS) in Mantua with his friend and neighbor, twenty-nine-year-old accountant Andrew Jenkins. Wrice created the or-ganization in West Philadelphia because he was concerned about the rise of black juvenile gang violence.[93] He knew what gang life was like because when he was fifteen years old, he was a member of the West Philadelphia gang the Flames, headed by gang leader "Poppy Tate."[94] As a gang member, Wrice took beatings, witnessed gang fights, and of-fered to do "nearly anything for Poppy" because he wanted to be part of a group that offered him protection, mentorship, and belonging.[95] By 1962, Wrice left the gang, graduated from Overbrook High School, and earned a Bachelor's degree from Temple University.[96] However, his con-cern for juvenile gang members provoked him to create a community organization to end gang violence when he witnessed a gang attack on April 3, 1965.

That night, Wrice was sitting on Jenkins's porch in Mantua when they heard a shotgun blast through the window of a grocery store located at 36th and Aspen Streets. A juvenile gang member was aiming at two rival gang members who refused to leave the store, but the bullet missed them. Wrice and Jenkins were upset about the violent act, especially because their wives were on their way to that store when the shoot-ing happened. By April 5, Wrice and Jenkins established the antigang program YGS with $3.20 and a plan to rehabilitate black gang mem-bers. According to Wrice and Jenkins, their goal was to foster "closer

Youth from the Young Greats Society exercising at a football camp near Brandywine (above) and members of the YGS Giants football team displaying their jerseys, 1972–73. Special Collections Research Center, Temple University Libraries, Philadelphia, PA / Michael J. Maicher / Don Camp.

relationships between neighborhood youngsters and to make the streets safe for adults."[97] Wrice and Jenkins first hosted a town hall meeting in the Mantua Hall housing project at 35th Street and Fairmount Avenue for community members. At the meeting, fourteen gang members, including two gang runners and a war chief, told Wrice and Jenkins that they were involved in violent gang activity because they wanted to "blow off steam among themselves" by "hanging on corners and contenting themselves with singing and shadow boxing."[98] Following the meeting, Wrice and Jenkins made plans to rehabilitate youth with recreation and social welfare programs.

By August 1965, the YGS provided over 2,500 black youths from five neighborhood gangs with recreation. Wrice's program offered boxing, singing groups and bands, baseball and basketball teams, drama and art classes, and a Civil Air Patrol chapter that operated from the community room of Mantua Hall. In addition to recreation, the organization also focused on communication and mentorship. Jenkins explained to the *Philadelphia Daily News* in September 1965, "Our tack is never to tell the boys what to do. We ask them. We give them time to express themselves and listen to their problems and suggestions."[99] Mentors at the YGS also mediated between rival gangs to prevent gang wars. Wrice explained, "You have to start at the bottom. Find their interest and gain their confidence. When I know a war is scheduled for a particular night, I pretend I know nothing about it and go around to the gang leaders. I take them to a movie or something and there is no fight."[100] Furthermore, Wrice's slogan—"Stop talking and act"—reflected his technique of talking to gang leaders, settling disputes between rival gangs, conducting a neighborhood watch, and even confiscating weapons from gang members to protect youth and adults from gang violence.

Since the YGS was a private nonprofit organization, Wrice and Jenkins earned the funds they needed to operate by showing movies, conducting raffles, and selling chicken dinners that professional cook Ralin Gordon from La Salle College prepared.[101] From 1968 to 1979, the YGS expanded their programs in Mantua. It recruited youth to participate in science projects, football camps, and a "camp work program" that involved clearing trash and junk from and repairing and painting houses in the community.[102] The YGS also provided resources for working parents. In 1968, Wrice purchased five vacant homes at 32nd and Wallace

Members of the Young Great Society repair houses. July 25, 1973, Special Collections Research Center, Temple University Libraries, Philadelphia, PA / Frederick A. Meyer.

Streets for use as daycare centers to enable working mothers to attend night school.[103] By June 1970, the YGS was even able to sponsor a one-week trip to Puerto Rico, where juvenile gang leaders learned about the island's gang problems.[104] Although Wrice's Young Greats Society had a major impact on black youth in neighborhoods, it did not completely eliminate black gangs in the city or deter all children from joining gangs.

Wrice, however, was hardly the only black Philadelphian seeking community-based approaches to rehabilitative social welfare. During the 1960s, Philadelphia-area educator M. Phineas Anderson researched the formation, prevalence, and impact of black gangs in Philadelphia. In his 1969 teacher's manual on managing gang activity in the classroom, *The Gang Unit*, Anderson explained that African American gangs were the most common in Philadelphia because of racial discrimination:

> My belief—formed after widespread reading as well as discussions with gang members, teachers, and other knowledgeable adults—[is] that racial discrimination is a fundamental cause of gang violence. There are, of course, other causes. But why, I asked, is membership in Philadelphia's violent gangs overwhelmingly black? Because, the answer came over and over again, discrimination forces so many black children to grow up under exactly those community conditions which have been shown to produce violent gangs among people of any race.[105]

Anderson's argument was based on research he gathered from the local newspaper the *Evening Bulletin*, the Philadelphia Police Department's Gang Unit, the juvenile court, and the Pennsylvania Crime Commission. From these sources, he learned that black children who lived in poor and working-class communities in North and West Philadelphia participated in gangs because they sought a place where they belonged, protection from neighborhood rivals *and* police, and income to overcome poverty.

Using policing data he believed to be objective, Anderson discovered the Philadelphia Police Department identified approximately three thousand youths between the ages of twelve and twenty-three as gang members. Anderson's teacher's guide explicitly focused on black children because Philadelphia's Gang Unit reported that approximately 90 percent of gang members were black. Even though 1.5 percent of all youth in the city were involved in gang activity, the percentage among black youth was the highest at approximately 3.2 percent. Additionally, in 1968, the Pennsylvania Crime Commission reported approximately fourteen thousand juvenile arrests and eighty-three thousand gang members in Philadelphia, with "core" gang members being repeat

Juvenile gang leaders, under the sponsorship of the Young Greats Society (YGS), prepare to board an Eastern Airlines jet from Philadelphia International Airport to Puerto Rico to study gang problems there in a week-long program. June 26, 1970, Special Collections Research Center, Temple University Libraries, Philadelphia, PA / Salvatore C. DiMarco Jr.

offenders of violent crime.[106] While Anderson's reliance on police data did not offer concrete evidence that the "gang problem" was increasing in Philadelphia, police, city officials, and community activists gradually considered working together to solve black gang violence instead of tackling the issue on their own.

Lewis Yablonsky's 1962 book *The Violent Gang* strongly influenced Anderson's sociological research and recommended solutions for Philadelphia's juvenile gang activity.[107] Yablonsky's theories on social, delinquent, and violent gangs were based on the research sociologists like Frederic Thrasher and William Foote Whyte completed in the 1920s through the 1940s. According to Yablonsky, "social gangs" formed around an interest in a "socially constructive" goal, "delinquent gangs" formed to engage in illegal behavior like robbery or assault, and "violent gangs" formed to commit "spontaneous prestige-seeking violent activities" for "psychic gratification" or thrills.[108] In *The Gang Unit*, Anderson bolstered Yablonsky's argument that youth gangs of the 1950s and 1960s were unlike pre–World War II gangs, which were mostly "friendship organizations." Modern gangs were different, Anderson maintained, because they "provided gang youths the opportunity to channel [the] aggressions and hostilities" they had about "school, family, the neighborhood, prejudice, or any other problems" into gang wars or random attacks on innocent people.[109] Moreover, Anderson agreed with Yablonsky's sociological position that although gang activity was a choice, black youth—black males in particular—often joined gangs because they felt ostracized in their society and desired to be accepted in some sort of community.

Depending on the gang, boys and young men were inducted into the organization if they voiced their desire to be a member, proved their potential by stealing a designated item, or fought one or more gang members. As one teenage gang member explained, "You have to fight about ten guys to join. You don't have to beat them all up, but you must show that you can defend yourself and that you have guts."[110] The initiation process was simpler if the individual was related to a current gang member or possessed a gun. It was a rare occurrence for individuals to be "drafted" or forced to join a gang against their will. According to Police Sergeant Joseph E. Rich, supervisor of the Gang Unit, the only time youth were coerced to join was when a gang lacked "troops" in the middle of "warfare" with a rival. He observed, "The only time a kid is drafted into a gang is when the gang is over-extended militarily—that is, fighting two or three fights at once. The 'runners' [leaders of the gang] are pretty smart; they know that draftees don't make such good fighters."[111]

Once in a gang, members were organized into different levels: the "Old Heads" (members eighteen to twenty-three years old), the "Young Boys" (ages fourteen to seventeen), the "Midgets" (twelve to fourteen years old), and the recruits-in-waiting known as "Pygmies" or "Swiggetts" (twelve and younger).[112] Among the "Old Heads," the "runner" or "warlord" was the gang's leader. Some gangs had a "runner" who held total responsibility for the gang and a "warlord" who was in charge of "military" affairs. The "second runner" was next in command when the "runner" was not present. Lastly, the "checkholder" was responsible for overseeing the lowest rank of gang members (the "corner boys") and reporting those "troops'" activities to the "runners."[113]

The names gang members selected were based on the neighborhood of their headquarters or one or more of their group's personal characteristics.

For example, the 8th and Diamond Streeters referred to the North Philadelphia intersection where the group lived. Zulu Nation reflected the gang's racial pride in being black. And the Moon Gang signified how its gang members were "active" when the moon appeared at night.

In times of "warfare" or "protection," gangs carried a multitude of weapons: rods, shotguns, pistols, zip guns, switchblades, razors, car antennas, chains, pipes, and leather straps.[114] Gangs purchased guns either illegally in their neighborhood or legally through older members. In Philadelphia, there were no well-established gangs composed of girls and young women. Oftentimes, the girlfriends of gang members participated in gang activities such as spying on rivals, carrying weapons, or fighting a girl affiliated with another gang.[115]

Anderson concluded his research with lesson plans teachers could use when educating black students in areas with gang activity.[116] Anderson recommended that teachers coordinate both open class discussions about gangs in their community and recreational activities to build

Author's photo of a mural dedicated to Herman Wrice at 33rd and Haverford Avenue in Mantua.

character. According to Anderson, black students could learn responsibility by organizing their own dances, develop confidence through "free discussions on current political thought," and cultivate self-respect by participating in crafts and library programs centered around African and African American art and history.[117] Moreover, African American community activists like Anderson focused on curbing black gang activity in black *and* white neighborhoods because they wanted to not only fight racial stereotypes and end violence but also provide much-needed social welfare programs to disadvantaged black youth.

Philadelphia: The "Gang Capital" of America

In 1969, the *New York Times* named Philadelphia the "gang capital" of America, since the city had the highest rates of gang-related murders and violent attacks in the country: forty-five murders, 267 injuries, and numerous incidents of "burglary and purse snatching" that affected gang members and innocent bystanders, including children.[118] That July, the Pennsylvania Crime Commission released a report on Philadelphia's gang violence stating there were seventy-five active, sporadic, or dormant gangs, each composed of anywhere from 25 to 250 black, white, or Puerto Rican members for a total of 3,000 gang members known by police. About 84 percent of gang members were over sixteen, though some were as young as twelve.[119] That same year, the Philadelphia Police Department's Gang Unit reported that approximately 20 percent of the city's gang violence involved individuals who were shot, stabbed, or beaten despite being unaffiliated with a gang.[120] Nevertheless, as gang violence appeared to increase in 1969, Mayor Tate told the *New York Times*, "Gang violence is giving Philadelphia a bad name."[121]

Sociologists and criminologists of the postwar era accepted the theory that concentrated poverty along with poor housing and education—not race—were to blame for the formation of juvenile gangs.[122] They also knew that gang violence was an issue in many major cities with histories of racial segregation and concentrated poverty, including New York, Los Angeles, and Chicago. When national news outlets identified Philadelphia as America's "gang capital" in 1969, the city's poorest neighborhoods were suffering from a poverty rate of 25.3 percent, approximately thirteen points above the national average.[123]

Despite criminologists, activists, and public officials' shared under-standing that poverty was the root of crime in Philadelphia, local and state lawmakers prioritized municipal and white middle-class eco-nomic interests above black poverty. Pennsylvania State attorney general William C. Sennett, for instance, ignored Philadelphia's above-average poverty rates by arguing, "You have the same poverty situations in other cities but you don't have the high incidence of killing."[124] Given Sennett's willingness to reject the assessment of criminologists, Republican gover-nor Raymond P. Shafer assigned him to chair a crime commission that promised to discover the roots of juvenile gang activity.[125]

In June 1969, Sennett led Pennsylvania Crime Commission hearings on gang warfare in Philadelphia. At the hearings, three witnesses made significant proposals on the issue: recently appointed Police Commis-sioner Rizzo, antigang activist Herman Wrice, and black police officer and Baptist minister Melvin Floyd.[126] Rizzo rejected theories of poverty-induced crime and institutional racism, arguing that juvenile criminals deserved incarceration and maximum penalties for felony crimes be-cause they were "sick," "lacked education and intelligence," and used vio-lence "to get even with those more competent" than them.[127] He then proposed that Philadelphia not only eliminate bail for repeat offenders but also increase police funding and juvenile detention centers to curb crime. Wrice and Floyd proposed slightly different approaches to solving gang violence. Drawing upon his experience with YGS, Wrice argued that poverty alleviation programs, jobs, and positive mentors were re-quired to rehabilitate gang members and dissuade them from crime.[128] Floyd, the supervisor of the North Philadelphia antigang missionary or-ganization Teen Haven, suggested that gang-control workers from the community be assigned to youth, while "hard core delinquents" should face long-term incarceration.[129] Despite the various recommendations presented at the hearings, Rizzo's proposal ultimately won approval when Philadelphia allotted $88.6 million of its 1970 budgetary spending for police and prisons.[130] With this outcome from the hearings, Rizzo, who rose through the ranks of the police force from beat cop to police commissioner over the span of twenty-four years, demonstrated how influential he had become in the city. Rizzo's vast experience policing districts in North, South, Northeast, West, and Center City Philadel-phia; celebrated arrest record; numerous awards for civic service; and

tactical planning and expansion in the Stakeout, Intelligence, Civil Dis-
obedience, and Labor Squads encouraged city officials, especially Mayor
Tate, to view him as the most credible official in assessing how to handle
crime and juvenile gang activity.[131] Additionally, Rizzo's constant presence in the city in which he was consistently available to do police work
and refused to "take weekends off" gave officers under his command the
gall to say what journalist Fred Hamilton quoted from a ten-year veteran
of the force: "They'd walk barefoot over broken glass for him" because
they loved, respected, and trusted Rizzo so much.[132] This prestige Rizzo
won as a policeman throughout the 1960s would inspire the majority
of Philadelphians to elect him as mayor in the next decade.

Conclusion

In post-1958 Philadelphia, the "gang" murder of In-Ho Oh was one of
many cautionary narratives policymakers used to justify aggressive
policing of black youth to maintain the safety of white and middle-class
Philadelphians. From 1958 to 1969, police and journalists' reports of
interracial crime committed by black "gangs" and "mobs" reaffirmed the
stereotype that poor black people were inherently criminal and had to
be policed, incarcerated, and sentenced like adults. City officials and
police viewed black gang crimes as threats to both white residents who
contemplated flight to the suburbs and the city's steadily declining tax
base. Ultimately, the government found it more profitable to finance
tough-on-crime policing while divesting from social welfare programs
that could preemptively halt poverty-induced crime. In fact, community activists like Andy Jenkins, the president of the Mantua Community
Planners and cofounder of the Young Greats Society, responded to the
city's proposal to fund the police department and prisons with over
$88 million in 1970 with anger. In a July 1969 statement Jenkins made
to the *Philadelphia Tribune*, he explained how city and state officials
make moral arguments like suggesting alcohol consumption causes high
crime rates and gang warfare, but they actually "encourage the existence
of this crime" when they allow "bars and State Stores in the black ghettos" to thrive instead of closing them down. Jenkins further implied that
political figures benefited from black alcohol consumption because the
owners of those tax-yielding institutions were individuals with political

power in local and state government. Jenkins then concluded the interview by arguing that greed, willful ignorance, racial bias, and neglect defined the approach local and state governments often took to curb crime in black communities:

> We talk about the high rate of crime in black communities and we pay a fortune for police protection while the city and state continue to allow more bars and State Stores to flood our communities. . . . At the rate we are going, crime will only get worse and then maybe we'll have a police state. In fact, many black people think we have one already. It's quite obvious that if there were white gang members being killed or white gangs fighting black gangs, teenage gang wars would have been analyzed and resolved many months ago.[133]

Nevertheless, this economic trade-off was devastating to black youth and a sign that community activists concerned about black gang violence would continue to face an uphill battle in trying to convince government officials that structural inequality, not racial inferiority, was the root cause of elevated rates of black crime.

The robbery and murder of Oh by eleven black teenagers was an unprovoked tragedy deeply rooted in a history of social rejection and exclusion. It was an incident of rage and rebellion birthed from socioeconomic ostracism and stigma based on race, class, and residency.[134] Philadelphia's history of segregation, poverty, slum housing, job discrimination, and racially biased policing partially created the social conditions that enabled the murder to occur. These were the issues black activists like Herman Wrice and M. Phineas Anderson understood and tried to rectify with social welfare programs involving mentorship, recreation, education, and social resources for the black community. Their guardianship of black youth humanized delinquent children and demonstrated to city officials that rehabilitation and a communal commitment to social equality could decrease poverty-induced crime, incarceration, unemployment, and recidivism.[135] Yet policymakers rejected this approach.

Fortunately, from 1969 to 1976, the rise of gang murders in the all-black neighborhoods of North and West Philadelphia encouraged city officials, police, and community activists to set aside their differences, reassess the issue, and try working together on implementing a rehabilitative antigang program rooted in sociological research. Moreover, city officials like District Attorney Arlen Specter would propose the bipartisan antigang program Safe Streets, Inc., as an alternative to tough-on-crime policing. However, like other community-based programs focused on rehabilitation over incarceration, Safe Streets, Inc., had to compete with the Philadelphia Police Department for financial aid and public approval as Police Commissioner Frank Rizzo, a rising figure in government, vigorously argued for tough-on-crime initiatives as mayor.

PART II

Black Struggle, Isolation, and Criminalization (1970–79)

The inclination to violence springs from the circumstances of life among the ghetto poor—the lack of jobs that pay a living wage, limited basic public services, the stigma of race, the fallout from rampant drug use and drug trafficking, and the resulting alienation and absence of hope for the future.

—Elijah Anderson, *Code of the Street*

4

Safe Streets, Inc.

The "Hustle" to End Black Gang Violence

In the early 1960s, many community activists and politicians viewed North and West Philadelphia as blighted neighborhoods that were in free fall as poverty, inequality, and gang violence exacerbated the stresses of urban life for residents in these communities. From 1962 to 1968, gang-related homicides jumped from one to thirty per year.[1] From 1967 to 1969, over 50 percent of those gang-related homicides occurred in North Philadelphia. On June 23, 1969, Democratic state senator Herbert Arlene, who represented North Philadelphia, was so unnerved by the high rates of gang-related deaths that he told the press, "I am disturbed by the rash of gang killings. Most of these killings have occurred in the black communities."[2] Additionally, he vowed to unite in racial solidarity with other black community leaders to end gang wars affecting African American youth. Although African American leaders like Arlene were interested in taking guardianship over the black community and solving black gang violence on their own, Philadelphians of different racial, class, and social backgrounds also wanted to use their knowledge, platform, and concern for youth as city officials, police officers, and former gang members to detract from tough-on-crime policing and invest time and money in community-based antigang programs.

After the shocking 1958 murder of twenty-six-year-old international student In-Ho Oh by eleven black teenagers in Powelton Village, a progressive, middle-class, and desegregated neighborhood in West Philadelphia, the murders of young, innocent victims continued to provoke citizens and politicians alike to take action against gang violence in Philadelphia. Residents of North and West Philadelphia who witnessed juvenile gang violence in their communities petitioned the city to financially invest in social reform programs instead of tough-on-crime policing because they believed that limited recreation centers, poor education, and unemployment were the reasons for youth joining gangs like Valley and Dogtown. As black police officer Heywood Matthews put it, "the city just isn't doing its job. So long as we have slums and no recreation, we'll have gangs. These kids want . . . a decent education, a decent home, a steady job . . . but they'll never get it so long as the power structure remains apathetic."[3] In 1969, Matthews himself became one of the few police officers who worked with former gang members in the antigang program Safe Streets, Inc., which Philadelphia district attorney Arlen Specter founded that year.

From 1969 to 1976, Safe Streets, Inc., operated as a bipartisan community organization that recruited police officers and gang workers from juvenile gangs like Zulu Nation and the 8th and Diamond Streeters. The goal of Safe Streets, Inc., was to interact with youth through mentorship, education, recreation, community service, and therapy to stop juvenile gang violence. Murder was the impetus and continual force driving community members of diverse backgrounds to unite under this antigang program launched in North and West Philadelphia. On April 27, 1970, twenty-one-year-old Temple University graduate student David Fineman was targeted and killed by five members of the Gamma Phi United "club" near 13th and Diamond Streets as he was entering his car to go home from his Monday night class.[4] On June 13, 1970, seven-year-old Antoinette Williams was killed by a stray bullet that struck her in the face as she sat on her stoop at 1904 North Franklin Street, occupied with her coloring book.[5] And on April 20, 1971, nine-year-old Rafael Santiago Jr. was fatally hit in the back by a stray bullet when two rival gangs, Zulu Nation and the 8th and Diamond Streeters, began a shoot-out outside his father's grocery store at 532 West Susquehanna Avenue. Furthermore, the deaths of innocent young people like Fineman, Williams, and Santiago inspired city officials, police, and community activists to solve gang violence through community-led peaceful initiatives like Safe Streets, Inc., instead of brute police force. Moreover, although Safe Streets, Inc., was a successful, experimental antigang program that united community activists, city officials, and the police in rehabilitating black gang members, it failed in its "hustle" to convince City Council and the Philadelphia Police Department to make long-term financial investments in the organization because it didn't swiftly lower the rate of violent crime, effectively eradicate juvenile gang activity, or erase the

Gang member, "Country," enters the North Philadelphia location of Safe Streets, Inc., at 2236 Ridge Avenue. August 21, 1973, Special Collections Research Center, Temple University Libraries, Philadelphia, PA / Don Camp.

stigma of black gang violence pegged on the African American communities of North and West Philadelphia.

The Formation of Safe Streets, Inc.

In summer 1968, a series of incidents in North Philadelphia encouraged community residents and politicians to invest in a program to end gang violence. When news spread that a boy was shot and killed in a gang fight and gang rivals Zulu Nation and the 8th and Diamond Streeters had declared war, Yorktown residents sent a message to the district attorney's office asking for help. On Independence Day, residents and staff from the DA's office met with leaders of both gangs on a North Philadelphia street corner to end the violence. Following this series of incidents, politicians became more interested in finding remedial solutions outside of policing to address gang activity in the city.[6] Philadelphia DA Arlen Specter, a liberal-minded politician who was a Republican in name only, contacted President Richard M. Nixon to propose his project, Safe Streets, Inc., after taking into consideration the statistics on gang violence, advice from family court judge Paul A. Dandridge, and the community's pleas for solutions. President Nixon responded with the suggestion that Specter apply for a Law Enforcement Assistance Administration (LEAA) grant to fund the nonprofit organization. Specter applied for an LEAA grant in May 1968 to fund the pilot antigang program designed to lower the rate of teenage gang homicides and "*encourage gangs into constructive programs.*"[7] In the LEAA application, Specter stated, "Gang violence has reached proportions which threaten the entire law enforcement process of the community," highlighting the urgency of a program that would curb gang violence and juvenile delinquency in the city. Among the proposed activities Specter pitched were four-day retreats at hostels or in rural settings where gang members could gain free counseling from group therapists, an idea inspired by the New York City drug addiction treatment organization Daytop Village, founded in 1963 by psychiatrist Daniel Casriel and Roman Catholic priest Monsignor William B. O'Brien.[8]

In spring 1969, Specter formally established the organization to lower juvenile delinquency and crime while also ensuring there was proper procedural action in criminal cases. By June 1969, Safe Streets received

The Safe Streets, Inc., Board speaks to West Philadelphia residents and gang members about their newly established antigang program, January 12, 1970. From left to right: Arlen Specter, Philadelphia DA; Preston Edwards, assistant director of Safe Streets; William H. Wilcox, executive director of the Greater Philadelphia Movement; Walter W. Cohen, Philadelphia ADA; and Heywood Matthews, executive director of Safe Streets. Special Collections Research Center, Temple University Libraries, Philadelphia, PA / Charles J. Tinney.

a $80,267 LEAA grant for youth gang control in North and West Philadelphia.[9] The LEAA program granted $215 million to state and local governments to improve police forces, courts, and correction systems. One of the conditions for LEAA-approved organizations was that state and local agencies had to fund between 40 and 50 percent of the organization's budget. If an LEAA-approved organization did not meet local and state standards, those agencies could deny it funding. The Pennsylvania Crime Commission disbursed discretionary funding to Safe Streets approximately every six months. As a federally approved organization, Safe Streets received a list of priorities from the local government, but its LEAA grant status could not be revoked by local or state agencies when it did not meet its goals. In 1969, approximately 75 percent of Safe Streets's funding came from the LEAA grant, while the remaining 25 percent ($25,000) came from a grant given by affiliates of the Greater Philadelphia Movement.[10]

In August 1969, Safe Streets was in operation with a mixture of politicians, police officers, and community activists from the neighborhood surrounding the two centers. At each center, there was a unit director who planned and supervised activities, an assistant director who worked directly with gangs on the street, eight youth workers who worked with gang members, two teachers for tutoring, and a community organizer who facilitated parental and community support for the center's activities.[11] In 1969, the organization's board consisted of Specter as the program chairman, Police Detective Heywood Matthews as executive director, Clarence Fowler as unit director of the North Philadelphia center, Assistant District Attorney Walter W. Cohen as the project administrator of federal funds, and assistants Dave Johnson and Bernard Rhodes. The staff at Safe Streets were often men like Bennie Swans, a former gang member turned community activist, who were paid to facilitate recreational and community service activities with youth involved in and/or vulnerable to gang activity near its two locations.[12]

From its inception, the mission of Safe Streets was to be a *"one-stop juvenile center"* where police officers, former gang members, and community activists worked together to teach at-risk teenagers "responsibility and concern for themselves and society" so that they did not end up dead or incarcerated.[13] North and West Philadelphia were chosen as locations for the centers because gang activity was most entrenched in those poor and working-class black neighborhoods.[14] In its early stages, Safe Streets saw thirty-five to fifty juveniles enter each center daily, with youth workers attempting to develop one-on-one relationships with attendees. Among the activities offered to hundreds of teenage visitors were academic tutoring, job training, neighborhood cleanup projects, sports, newspaper writing, and publishing. Since many youth who were "directed" to the centers were "troubled," lived disadvantaged lives, and/or faced inequality in schools, housing, and employment, Safe Streets provided group therapy sessions (facilitated by residents from the North Philadelphia drug treatment center Gaudenzia House) and annual trips to the theater and the Poconos to

Members of the 8th and Diamond Streeters gang wait outside of Manhattan's Public Theater for the viewing of the play "No Place to Be Somebody." September 7, 1969, Special Collections Research Center, Temple University Libraries, Philadelphia, PA / *Philadelphia Evening Bulletin.*

rehabilitate and provide positive recreation for attendees. According to Specter, events like the four-day retreat to the Poconos for one hundred boys during the summer were great opportunities to reduce gang violence and end turf wars between rival gangs.[15]

The same year that Safe Streets was established, the Philadelphia Police Department, under Police Commissioner Rizzo, petitioned city officials to increase its budget spending on tough-on-crime initiatives. With Rizzo in charge of the police department, violence between black males and white police officers began to spike with the use of police policies and procedures of stop and frisk, quotidian surveillance, illegal house raids, *public* strip searches, false criminal accusations and arrests, and verbal and physical assaults on suspects, average law-abiding citizens, political activists, and protestors at peaceful demonstrations.[16] Nevertheless, City Council still supported the police department by awarding it an LEAA

District Attorney Arlen Specter referees a boxing match between Robert Taylor (left), twenty, and Robert Hariss, nineteen, at the West Philadelphia location of Safe Streets, Inc. January 12, 1970, Special Collections Research Center, Temple University Libraries, Philadelphia, PA / Charles J. Tinney.

grant of $19,733 to create a closed-circuit television system linking the city's police districts.

For Safe Streets, there was always a struggle to convince City Council to disinvest from tough-on-crime spending and increase funding for antigang programs that identified poverty and social inequality as the main cause of crime. Safe Streets's mission was to demonstrate to City Council that social welfare and rehabilitation could eliminate gang activity among youth. Other local Great Society programs like Start Towards Eliminating Past Setbacks (STEPS) and Philadelphia's Leaders of Tomorrow (PLOT) also promoted rehabilitation over incarceration because they believed that therapy sessions, recreation, and employment for youth would eradicate not only gang activity but also police-community tensions.[17] Even community and civil rights organizations like the North City Congress (NCC) and the Congress of Racial Equality (CORE) attempted to curb gang activity and juvenile delinquency by arranging truce meetings between major North Philadelphia gangs, citizens, and police.[18] Unfortunately, politicians like Mayor James H. J. Tate doubted these social programs would lead to major crime reduction. In 1969, the Tate administration attempted to persuade the federal government to allocate only $44,000 to Specter's program and give the Philadelphia Police Department $56,000 for crime-fighting initiatives.[19] Moreover, this was the beginning of a long-term battle between liberals and conservatives over how federal funding would be distributed and spent to combat juvenile delinquency, crime, and rioting.

The Fight for LEAA Grant Funding

In 1970, *Philadelphia Inquirer* journalists William J. Speer and Tom Ferrick reported on their visits to Safe Streets's North Philadelphia center in February and July, respectively, of that year. Their report exposed the organization as a high-stakes program operating on a shoestring budget. When Speer arrived at 2201 West Stewart Street, he saw a three-story, six-room storefront that looked like a "neglected 50-year-old building with a swift paint job."[20] He described Safe Streets as an "experimental program" open six days a week from 9:00 a.m. to 9:00 p.m. where juveniles received help with "scholastic and job difficulties" and rival gangs could "rap out" their differences in intense group therapy instead of resorting to violence with "pipes, cleavers, knives, and guns."[21] For the girls who attended the center, there were "local women" who taught them sewing and other homecrafts, but the organization primarily wanted the girlfriends of gang members as an exploitative measure in which their presence could "win the confidence" of the young men and help them get reformed.[22] Ferrick's description of the contents in the North Philadelphia center demonstrated the financial difficulties the organization had: chairs, a few "ancient desks," a blackboard, a ping pong table, and a record player "that looks too old to play."[23]

In Speer's article, he depicted the centers' economic struggles to provide educational resources by describing how the staff at the West Philadelphia center (sharing a facility with the Christian Young Life organization) were tutoring youth with thirty- and forty-year-old reading and math books as they awaited the arrival of books donated by the Board of Education. The centers offered meager success in employment for gang members because the facilities did not provide adequate job training in vocational skills.[24] Speer noted that while the Philadelphia Tutorial Project offered study help to juveniles, the State Bureau of Employment Security provided job counseling, though its visits to the center were rare.

Speer's report on Safe Streets also cast doubt on the organization's long-term effectiveness when he suggested it had to successfully prove it could solve youth gang violence, since it was "being watched" by civic and law enforcement agencies. Safe Streets was concerned about not only attendee retention at the centers but also possible gang activity at night when the centers were closed.[25] Additionally, the lack of parental, community, and gang member support for the organization troubled not only Speer but also Unit Director Clarence Fowler:

> If the problem doesn't hit them [parents] in their own parlor, they just don't get concerned about it. . . . If you get the [gang] leader on your side, you got the whole gang with you. . . . In many cases, the leader has more power over the gang members than the boys' parents. . . . We want the boys to look beyond their present situation. We want them to see that there is no future in being a gang member.[26]

Nevertheless, the staff at Safe Streets remained committed to their mission to reduce gang violence, as voiced by Project Administrator Walter W.

Program Director Willard Scott (far right) and Auto Mechanics Instructor James Swain award certificates of completion to gang members from Safe Streets, Inc. August 1, 1975, Special Collections Research Center, Temple University Libraries, Philadelphia, PA / Frederick A. Meyer.

Cohen: "Our central aim is to stop killing, but that is not our final aim— our final aim is to enable these kids to see the senselessness of killing and to participate in normal activities."[27] Nine days after Ferrick's article was published, the *Philadelphia Evening Bulletin* reported the LEAA allocated $150,000 for "Philadelphia's emergency juvenile gang control project." Once Specter learned about the allocation, he asked Senate Minority Leader Hugh Scott to expedite the funds, since the organization was in immediate need of them to continue operations.[28] The City of Philadelphia also received an LEAA grant (a month prior) in the amount of $80,267. Despite the brewing competition Safe Streets had with the police department for funds, Specter reiterated the significance of his program in a press release by stating his grant would be used to "increase job opportunities, overcome functional illiteracy, and set up guidance group interaction techniques to instill a more mature socially responsible attitude and behavior pattern in juveniles."[29]

Superintendent of Philadelphia Prisons Edward J. Hendrick gives District Attorney Arlen Specter and Police Commissioner Frank L. Rizzo a tour of Holmesburg Prison, July 7, 1970, Special Collections Research Center, Temple University Libraries, Philadelphia, PA / Higgins.

Despite the financial and political hardships Safe Streets experienced, the organization had many supporters from the community. One supporter was a Philadelphia mechanic who read in the newspaper about the organization and volunteered to fund transportation to his shop so that he could teach youth from the centers his trade.[30] In August 1971, Willard Scott, a sixty-six-year-old black proprietor of an auto repair business (since 1929), heard about Safe Streets's mission and called the DA's office requesting to train gang members to be mechanics.[31] Scott was concerned about what he saw as senseless gang violence in his West Philadelphia neighborhood. But he also thought he knew how to solve the problem: "These black kids need jobs and a challenge. But they keep killing each other and tilling up the jails. I know my own 16-year-old—he's so crazy about hot-rod engines, he can't get into trouble. . . . Send me some of those gang members. I've got a car business and I'll teach them how to work on engines. If it works, maybe we can get some of 'em jobs."[32] According to Safe Streets's executive director, Heywood Matthews, Scott was the first businessman to volunteer a vocational training program for the cash-strapped organization. Scott soon welcomed eight youths to his garage at 1501 North 61st Street and was immediately impressed by their work ethic: "I couldn't believe how nice they were, how hard they'd work. I had 'em tearing down engines eight hours a day, learning the basics. They wouldn't go across the street for cigarettes without asking my permission."[33]

Once Christmas 1971 arrived, attendance decreased, as six youth dropped the program because they could not afford the bus fare and lunch required to participate. Safe Streets tried to procure a forty-dollars-a-week subsistence for the boys' expenses, but the organization struggled to acquire the funds. Instead, Scott, Reverend Marshall Shepard's congregation at Mount Olivet Tabernacle Church, and Reverend Joseph Whearty of Our Lady of Victory Church raised money to cover the costs.[34] By February 1, 1972, Scott accepted a class of ten gang members with the goal of getting them jobs as mechanics after ten weeks of training at one of the fifty garages and service stations in his community. The *Philadelphia Evening Bulletin* journalist covering the story of Scott's partnership with Safe Streets in March 1972 not only demonstrated how appealing and vital vocational training was for gang members but also concluded his article with a sharp critique of the police state in America's major cities:

Herman Smith and Clarence Peterson of the Black Panther Party distribute free lunches to North Philadelphia residents at 2315 Ridge Avenue. August 17, 1971, Special Collections Research Center, Temple University Libraries, Philadelphia, PA / Richard Rosenberg.

solving gang violence this way is a "bargain" in the "era of $100 million police budgets."[35] By 1975, Scott was the program's director and oversaw the granting of certification in auto mechanics to dozens of boys.[36] Moreover, Scott's auto program at Safe Streets, Inc., was evidence of how peaceful, community-centric activities were more appealing and effective in rehabilitating youth than incarceration.

"No Longer a Civilized Neighborhood"

While Safe Streets operated as a community-based organization rehabilitating black juvenile gang members, tensions between the police and black men in Philadelphia were growing as antipolice violence and black radicalism became major concerns for the police department. Nevertheless, a series of events in 1970 led to the reaffirming of black criminality tropes and increasing advocacy for tough-on-crime policing in black communities. In August 1970, Police Commissioner Rizzo conflated black radicals with black criminals and ordered the raid of multiple offices of the Black Panther Party (BPP) following the shootings of four policemen in two days. On August 29, 1970, thirty-nine-year-old Park policeman James Harrington was sitting in his police wagon a hundred yards from the Cobbs Creek guardhouse in West Philadelphia when five black men from the revolutionary group the Black Unity Council shot him at point-blank range.[37] The men then entered the guardhouse and shot forty-three-year-old Fairmount Park Police sergeant Frank Von Colln five times, murdering him as he sat at his desk.[38] On the night of August 30, 1970, twenty-five-year-old Patrolman Thomas J. Gibbons Jr. (the son of former Police Commissioner Gibbons) and his partner, twenty-eight-year-old John J. Nolen, were shot after they stopped two black men in a stolen car in Southwest Philadelphia. After two days of antipolice violence from black men, Rizzo spoke to the media about both incidents. Following Rizzo's visit to Gibbons and Nolen at Misericordia Hospital, he told news reporters, "This is no longer a civilized neighborhood."[39] Rizzo then erroneously announced that the Panthers were responsible for Sergeant Von Colln's murder instead of the Black Unity Council.

Rizzo was already unhappy with the Black Panthers because, since 1966, the BPP's goal for black youth was to take a Marxist, black nationalist view and educate them on how institutional racism, poverty, and police brutality damaged the black community.[40] The Panthers' pamphlet *Ten-Point Program* outlined the goals the organization had for the community, which included demanding the government provide full employment, decent housing, and education for black people. The BPP's pamphlet *Eight Points of Attention* outlined moral principles for its members to follow as role models in the black community, such as "Do not hit or swear at people," "Do not take liberties with women," and "Do not damage property of the oppressed masses." Additionally, the Panthers provided numerous mission programs to alleviate some of the socioeconomic burdens lower-class blacks faced each day.[41] These programs included a community ambulance service, free medical and legal clinics, a police patrol (where Panthers openly carried guns and followed police cars to preemptively prevent police brutality), community centers, and the Free Breakfast for School Children Program.[42] The Panthers provided these free resources to impoverished blacks in the city, and their political propaganda appealed to the black community because it identified institutional racism and the failure of social welfare programs as causes for the struggles of the urban black poor.

In the early morning hours of August 31, 1970, Rizzo assisted one hundred police marksmen on a series of raids on BPP offices in North and Northwest Philadelphia and the organization's main headquarters in West Philadelphia.[43] As they took them away, the officers publicly strip-searched seven Panthers on a residential street, effectively humiliating them in front of onlookers and news media. The image of several bare-chested, barefoot, or completely nude Panthers lined up against a wall was captured by *Daily News* photographer Elwood P. Smith and later distributed around the world by United Press International. In press conferences, Rizzo responded to the incident unabashed:

> This was an excellent job. They can hide weapons, grenades and so forth, in their clothing. . . . We did nothing wrong. . . . Their feelings were hurt. The big Black Panthers with their trousers down. . . . We had information from infiltrators and informers and from the black community that they did have guns in there. . . . Some black leaders spew out. Why did they not speak out before? I didn't hear them speak out when Von Colln was shot. As far as I'm concerned, they can go wash their necks.[44]

Furthermore, this incident demonstrated not only how black activists and criminal suspects were negligently categorized as one threatening entity to police but also how organizations promoting alternative methods to solving the societal problems of urban life would be discredited publicly by city officials who believed government spending on crime-fighting was more useful than social programs meant to uplift citizens.

While police and tough-on-crime politicians like Frank Rizzo spread inflammatory rhetoric criminalizing black youth and young adults, some white residents in Philadelphia continued to believe African Americans threatened the safety and property values of their homes as more and more formerly all-white working-class neighborhoods began to desegregate. However, from 1970 to 1971, the *Philadelphia Inquirer's* news stories about gang warfare in Southwest Philadelphia suggested that a legacy of white vigilantism against black residents was a factor in the rise of black gangs in neighborhoods like Kingsessing. In David J. Umansky and Acel Moore's June 1970 article "Economic, Racial Fears Fan Bartram Row," they described how the white gang the Dirty Annies was responsible for numerous violent and sometimes deadly assaults on black youth near 58th Street and Chester Avenue.[45] The Dirty Annies, named after a former candy store in the area, was made up of a group of blue-collar white teenagers who primarily went to West Catholic High School. According to journalists and police, the Dirty Annies were violent toward African Americans because they were angry about black residents moving into their neighborhoods, attending public schools in their community (like Bartram High School), and occupying the street corners and play areas they frequented, like the Meyers Recreation Center.[46] Furthermore, much of the gang violence between white and black youth was stirred up by white parents, as one recreation center worker explained to reporters: "These kids hear it from their parents—that's why they talk about hating colored people. When there's a fight in the playground nothing happens if it's two white kids or two colored kids, but if it's a black and a white they go home and tell their parents and it's practically a race riot. Kids are kids and they'll fight, and people make too much of it."[47]

Evidently, many white blue-collar parents feared the influx of black residents in their communities and black youth interacting with their children because they believed the stigmas associated with blackness. Even though white and black youth often got into scuffles over minor incidents like rock throwing or the "occupation" of recreational areas in the neighborhood, some white teenagers felt scapegoated for all the juvenile delinquency residents and shop owners blamed on groups like the Dirty Annies and adopted racist views of their black neighbors to justify their use of gang violence against them.[48] When Umansky and Moore interviewed white youths about an incident where, over the span of two weeks between May and June 1970, police and teachers had to intervene in neighborhood clashes after white students from West Catholic High School threw rocks and bottles at black students who took SEPTA's G bus to Bartram High School, one white teenager explained, "What are we supposed to do? Those niggers have been yelling and throwing things out of the buses at us for four years and nobody says anything." Additionally, another white youth, a sixteen-year-old West Catholic High

School student, suggested that there was a racial bias in how crime was policed in their neighborhood that disadvantaged whites and privileged blacks: "You paint on a black face and you've got it made. . . . If that had been white kids [initiating violence] they would have all been hit and they would have locked them up."[49] Through Umansky and Moore's interviews with residents, they also uncovered that serious racial confrontations occurred not between black and white adults but between children. One black Kingsessing woman who was interviewed suggested that there were deeper roots to constant fighting between black and white children: "Those kids don't get that way by themselves. They have to hear it [racist attitudes] from their parents." Another black woman who had personal experiences of "trouble with white youth" suggested to reporters (as she watched a police car go by) that the racial violence in the neighborhood was specifically initiated by white residents who lived in the area for generations: "If I had known what kind of neighborhood this was, I never would have moved here."[50]

Prior to World War II, Southwest Philadelphia neighborhoods like Kingsessing were made up of predominantly Irish, Jewish, and Italian middle-class families headed by businessmen, doctors, and lawyers. By 1938, residents from the professional class began to move to neighborhoods in the Northeast and the suburbs, and tradesmen or semiskilled workers moved into Southwest Philadelphia followed by factory workers and other unskilled laborers.[51] In 1970, real estate agencies noticed that contrary to popular belief, new residents to Southwest Philadelphia were not renters but homebuyers (many of whom were African American) who received FHA mortgages at a rate of 99 percent. Interestingly, while home values remained constant as black people moved into the area, the value of commercial property declined, which coincided with the decline of industrialism in Philadelphia. Nevertheless, real estate agents like Peter McGinnity suggested that the fear-induced violence whites invoked on blacks in Kingsessing was based on myth and self-interest: "The white people are frightened and want to get away. Many can't afford to move, but the economic factor cannot overcome the fear of integration in many cases."[52] Furthermore, white blue-collar residents resisted their black neighbors by sending their children to predominantly white public and private schools in other neighborhoods or the suburbs while also encouraging their children to not play with black

Mrs. Betty Bradley hosts gang members and residents in her Wynnefield home in West Philadelphia to discuss solutions to gang activity and violence in the neighborhood. October 31, 1974, Special Collections Research Center, Temple University Libraries, Philadelphia, PA / Joseph McLaughlin.

children. They eventually formed gang groups based on race to protect themselves from violence, and when major fights broke out on street corners, playgrounds, and schoolyards, hundreds of police in riot gear often assembled and arrived at the location by the busload to deescalate the incident.[53] Moreover, racial violence in residential neighborhoods, panic selling of homes in formerly all-white neighborhoods, white flight, and black criminalization were phenomena impacting not just middle-class areas but also blue-collar neighborhoods. As historian Alex Elkins explained, police and the state operated to maintain a "white racial order tailored to middle-class values and tastes" in all types of neighborhoods throughout the 1960s and beyond, to the detriment of black citizens.[54]

Mayor Rizzo Cracks Down on Black Gangs with Tough-on-Crime Initiatives

Since 1969, Rizzo argued that to combat gang violence, city budget spending should go to tough-on-crime initiatives like adding more police officers to city streets and building more detention facilities for juvenile offenders.[55] When Rizzo appeared at the Pennsylvania Crime Commission's June 1969 hearing on gang warfare in Philadelphia, he told State Attorney General William Sennett that the city needed stronger gun control laws, the elimination of bail for juvenile gang members, and adult criminal trials for youth sixteen and older. Additionally, he "called" for "massive federal and state funds" to combat juvenile gang members who were often "half-bombed by wine." In Rizzo's opinion, Philadelphians had two choices for solving gang violence: "Do you wish unwarranted cries of police brutality, or safe streets and an elimination of this needless loss of life?"[56]

When Rizzo became mayor on January 3, 1972, he immediately began a crackdown on gangs in the city. In 1972, there were approximately two hundred gangs in operation (with 96 percent of members being black males), and citizens and politicians alike were concerned that gang violence was interfering with the everyday lives of Philadelphians.[57] In communities deemed gang territory, merchants had to close their businesses early, parents had to transport their children to and from school, and residents often feared turf wars between rival gangs. There were even news reports of innocent bystanders getting caught in the middle of gang cross fire, like forty-two-year-old Pearl Cooper, who was shot in the chest and arm as she traveled home from the grocery store.[58] Ultimately, the goal of the crackdown was to enforce Pennsylvania's law on the prohibition of concealed deadly weapons while also invoking the city ordinance requiring citizens to register if they wanted to carry a weapon in a public place.

Beginning on January 30, 1972, the city ran a two-week moratorium on the prosecution of gang members who turned in their weapons at neighborhood firehouses with no questions asked. Although some gang members refused to turn in their weapons for fear they would be disarmed and vulnerable to rival gangs, the city recovered a total of fifty-eight rifles and revolvers.[59] Following the moratorium, the city proposed mass arrests of gang members to expeditiously eliminate gang activity. In reference to the police policy of "stop and frisk" for weapons, City Managing Director Hillel S. Levinson was quoted as confirming the procedure as a necessary action: "The city is looking very seriously at gang activities. It is not going to accept them any longer."[60] Rizzo himself was also quoted by the press for his "tough-on-crime" approach as mayor:

"We know who they are. They're going to be stopped on the street by the police and we're going to talk to them. They had better hope they don't have weapons on them. We are going to move against gangs and we are not going to take any stuff from them. If they want to fight hand-to-hand, we'll take them on. That's the challenge."[61]

After the moratorium, the Confederation for the Conservation of Our City asked churches and synagogues to be open twenty-four hours a day on the weekend of February 12–13, 1972, as sanctuaries for gang members if mass arrests occurred. While the city proposed mass arrests, local antigang organizations similar to Safe Streets—such as the West Philadelphia organization Umoja, Inc., run by Falaka and David Fattah—arranged peace talks with about five hundred gang members to avoid the crackdown.[62] According to journalists, organizations like this were in agreement with sociologists and gang members that the solution to gang activity was adequate job-training programs and jobs for unemployed, unskilled high school dropouts.

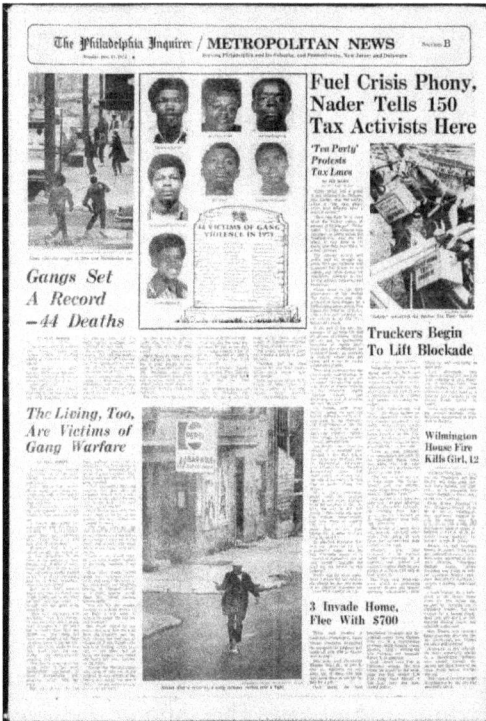

The *Philadelphia Inquirer* spotlights the issues of gang violence and murder with a Section B headliner. December 17, 1973, *Philadelphia Inquirer*.

From 1973 to 1974, gang violence decreased, but there remained a visible presence of gangs in Philadelphia. In summer 1973, newspapers like the *Philadelphia Inquirer* and *Philadelphia Daily News* pegged the progress of antigang programs like Safe Streets, Inc., as disappointing when twenty-seven-year-old gang worker Harvey Wearing was murdered in Southwest Philadelphia.[63] Wearing spent two years with the Department of Welfare's Youth Conservation Corps before working with Safe Streets, Inc., alongside two other gang workers assigned to Southwest Philadelphia: twenty-four-year-old Diane Scurry and thirty-nine-year-old Robert Malone.[64] As gang workers, Wearing, Scurry, and Malone talked with youth on street corners and participated in recreational activities in the community to foster trust with "gang-prone" youth. Wearing himself worked an eight-hour shift until 10:00 p.m. and volunteered as the basketball team's coach at Meyers Recreation Center, located at 58th and Kingsessing Avenue.[65]

Although Wearing had no college education, his peers and mentees viewed him as "having a genuine understanding of young people and an instinctive ability to reach them."[66] The night Wearing was killed, he was reportedly talking "peace" and then "rapping" about boxer Bennie Briscoe with gang members ninety minutes after his work shift ended. Antigang programs sponsored by the city instructed youth workers to wear "dress clothes" so they would be easily identified as social workers while they interacted with gang-involved youth.[67] According to Scurry, the gang-control workers refused and chose to wear "open-collared shirts, turtlenecks, and blue jeans" instead to avoid being perceived as pretentious and paternalistic: "We could have worn the clothes, but they (gangs) would be turned off. They might feel we were trying to be better than they are." The dedication the gang workers demonstrated to the youth who received them gave Malone the impression that the gang members "dug" them.[68] Nevertheless, when gang workers like Wearing and Malone realized that the gang members accepted them, they believed that they earned the youths' trust.

On June 27, 1973, at approximately 11:30 p.m., Wearing was talking to four members of the gang Mongo Nation three doors away from his home at 5506 Warrington Avenue when a "youth" appeared across the street.[69] The "youth" took out a gun wrapped under his jacket and fired one shot, striking Wearing in the head. The shooter, believed to be a rival of Mongo Nation, then dropped his weapon, picked it up, and fled around the corner. Following Wearing's murder, gang members—including twenty-three-year-old Edward "Boo" Benn, a "runner" (leader) of Mongo Nation—vowed an oath of peace in Wearing's memory: "Nobody talks about gang warring now. We are trying to get ourselves together. We are trying to carry on in a manner in which Harv would have wanted us to."[70] According to Wearing's supervisor, Michael Hillegass, two other gang workers had been injured while on duty, but Wearing was the first to die on the job. Nevertheless, many individuals were moved by Wearing's murder. The West Philadelphia Parents Group to Eradicate Youth Violence helped sponsor his memorial service, and members of Mongo Nation reportedly collected nearly $1,000 for Wearing's wife and two daughters.[71]

From June to July, both the *Philadelphia Inquirer* and *Daily News* ran several stories and updates about Wearing and his death. On July 15, 1973, reporters released interview-laced stories about residents, community service workers, gang members, and patrolmen who knew, missed, and respected Wearing in honor of his 3:00 p.m. funeral and memorial service at White Rock Baptist Church that day.[72] Mrs. Miles, a resident who helped organize the memorial service, described the community's collective sentiment over Wearing's death: "Everybody in the community was deeply touched by his death. He gave so much to the community and his death has brought a lot of attention to the gang problem."[73] Seventeen-year-old Fred Ransom, a basketball player on the team Wearing coached at Meyers Recreation Center, detailed the respect many youth had for him: "He was a real cool guy and had a lot of check [influence] around here."[74] Following the memorial, many believed gangs like Mongo Nation, Woodland Avenue, and Market Street would stop "warring" and embrace "peace," but August news reports helped cultivate a renewed sentiment of hopelessness when another gang murder occurred less than a mile from where Wearing died.[75]

From August 13 to August 14, 1973, journalists from the *Philadelphia Daily News* and *Inquirer* reported how the twenty-sixth gang-related shooting of the year occurred when Mongo Nation's Edward Benn used a zip gun to shoot and kill twenty-two-year-old rival gang member Lawrence Drummond.[76] The incident occurred around 1:00 a.m. on August 12th when Benn and his fellow gang members attempted to "crash" a birthday party hosted by members of the Market Street gang at 5822 Ashland Avenue and a confrontation ensued outside. *Daily News* reporter Tyree Johnson's article "Gang Slaying Kills Peace Dream" recalled how the gang killing occurred nearly a month after Wearing's memorial, where Benn stated, "We now want to be productive members of society. That is what Harvey worked for. That was his dream."[77] Johnson's article emphasized how members of Mongo Nation felt pressured to war again because there were rival gangs surrounding their turf and they believed the community only cared about peace after someone was "bumped off" because gang members weren't invited to town hall meetings to discuss the issues that caused the violence.[78] Gang members like Benn argued that they agreed with community members that gang violence had to end in Philadelphia, but they were skeptical of the motives police officers and social workers had to reform them out of gang activity. Gang members only trusted a few mediators like Wearing who could navigate and unite both worlds to establish peace. Moreover, when effective gang workers like Wearing were killed, both gang members and community residents lost hope in eradicating gang violence in the city.

"Too Much for Too Many": Safe Streets, Inc., Becomes at Risk of Closure

By 1974, the Philadelphia Police Department estimated that there were approximately 250 youth gangs in Philadelphia alone, with membership for each gang ranging from eighteen to two hundred individuals between the ages of ten to twenty-two years old. According to police, gang activity was strongly active within the black communities of North and West Philadelphia, leading city officials to concentrate more on curbing crime in those neighborhoods.[79] With these statistics, City Council put pressure on Safe Streets to demonstrate that its efforts were lowering gang-related crime rates. City Council decided to conduct a six-month evaluation of Safe Streets, and if the organization failed to meet the officials' expectations, the Philadelphia Regional Planning Council planned to "discontinue" its disbursement of funds on December 31, 1974. Furthermore, if Safe Streets could not reduce gang violence rapidly, the program would be shut down. Progress reports were regularly sent to the Governor's Justice Commission, where they were transferred to Keith Miles at the Office of Evaluation, LEAA-NILECJ, within the Department of Justice.[80]

In July 1974, Philadelphia's city officials invited an evaluation team from the historically black college Lincoln University to visit Safe Streets's centers, conduct interviews with staff and juvenile attendees, review the program's components, and request records of operation to determine whether the organization was successful at ending gang violence in the city.[81] Once their evaluation was complete, the team determined that Safe Streets "tried to do too much for too many," and given its difficulties with maintaining efficient recordkeeping, employing sufficient and highly experienced staff, and having proper coordination with the Youth Service Commission (YSC) that arranged training programs for juveniles, the nonprofit should close its doors and allow the program to "go on where it can until the new plan is developed."[82]

According to the Lincoln evaluation team, one of the main reasons for Safe Streets's "failures" was financial support. The organization had poor recordkeeping because data on juveniles and program affairs were often handwritten and these documents were only accessible to evaluators when staff had the time and means to produce typewritten copies.[83] The staff who ran the centers were often former gang members who had neither a college education nor formal training in vocational skills or group therapy; therefore, the organization had to hire or solicit volunteers who were trained in the fields necessary to meet the needs of juveniles. Additionally, staff at the centers were often paid low wages and pressured to work long hours so that juveniles could remain at the centers all day instead of spending time on the streets, where gang activity occurred.[84] Lastly, poor recordkeeping and low morale among overworked staff members made program partnerships with the YSC an extra burden.[85] Although evaluators from Lincoln University believed the sports and recreation programs for youth were sound, they "lacked coordination and were weak in social service referral and follow up."[86] Nevertheless, the Lincoln evaluation team concluded that while Safe Streets ideally wanted to end gang violence with the resources it provided, the organization did not have enough manpower or finances to achieve its goals.

In November 1974, the Philadelphia Regional Planning Council rejected Safe Streets's funding application because they received poor evaluations from Lincoln University, and therefore, the Planning Council saw no comprehensive plan to reduce gang activity in the organization's current efforts. Director of the Philadelphia Regional Planning Council, Yvonne Haskins, later stated in a press release the disapproval was because "funding for ineffective programs was wrong" and before additional federal funds are spent, the city's Youth Services Commission must "devise an overall plan aimed at curbing gang violence."[87] Even though Safe Streets was scheduled to close that December, city officials like Arlen Specter attempted to win more funding for the program by petitioning multiple politicians.[88]

On January 6, 1975, the Governor's Justice Commission met in Harrisburg to consider funding Safe Streets and two other social programs City Council identified as "low-performing": the Intensive Area Youth Workers and Youth Development, operated by the Philadelphia Public Welfare Department. At the conclusion of the meeting, Safe Streets, having already received $942,165 in LEAA funds over the years, was granted two more months to operate, with $30,000 in federal subsidies. Initial responses to the news of unexpected funding were mixed. The executive director of Safe Streets, Lewis Taylor Jr., responded with elation, stating that the added funds would safeguard the organization's basketball, job counseling, vocational training, and educational programs for four hundred youth because twenty-seven staff workers would be retained. City Managing Director Hillel Levinson responded with a cautious sense of relief, since the three programs were crucial to curbing gang activity on the community level because they were the only municipal entities outside of the police department that directly tackled gang issues: "To discontinue them would severely restrict our ability to handle gangs other than by police action."[89] Unfortunately, the Intensive Area Youth Workers and Youth Development were denied additional funding, a fate Safe Streets hoped to avoid after its two-month extension ended.

Less than six months after Safe Streets won additional funding from the Governor's Justice Commission, the organization was in jeopardy again when the city's budget for social programs and the police department were under consideration by the Philadelphia Regional Planning Council. On the evening of June 19, 1975, the council met at Midtown Holiday Inn to review Safe Streets's application for $217,496 in federal funds.[90] The council criticized the organization for continuously relying on LEAA grants and not searching for other financial supporters. The council then denied Safe Streets's application with an 8-7 vote, leaving the final decision on funding to the Governor's Justice Commission.[91]

At the same meeting, the council reviewed the city's application for $1.04 million to install a computerized police radio dispatching system for the police department. As early as August 1974, the city noticed a 16 percent increase in police calls and argued that this rise in police requests left the department "overtaxed and unable to respond quickly."[92] Believing rising crime rates required advanced policing techniques to remedy the issue, city officials hired an independent consultant who recommended the police department use a computer system to keep logs of 911 calls, the precise locations of callers, and the availability of police cars to arrive at crime scenes or emergency situations. State criminal justice planner Ted Shoemaker praised the approach, stating that if Philadelphia carried out this plan, it would be the "first in the country" to do so, especially since the city preferred to use a private consultant to set up the system rather than rely on computer firms to simply supply the necessary equipment.[93] Ultimately, the council approved the city's request to spend additional funds on policing. Moreover, City Council largely gave up on rehabilitative social welfare programs and chose tough-on-crime policing to combat black gangs.

Since June 1975, Safe Streets was repeatedly granted additional funding by the Governor's Justice Commission to stay open "temporarily," but the organization always existed with the threat of closure, as it survived on an insufficient budget. Although city officials knew Safe Streets was a financial failure, they believed the organization had a quasi-effective approach to remedying gang activity, rising crime rates, and juvenile delinquency. Additionally, it remained clear that gangs continued to be an issue in the city when Philadelphia was one of the locales analyzed at Harvard Law School's Center for Criminal Justice by Philadelphia-born anthropologist Walter B. Miller.

In Miller's 1975 monograph *Violence by Youth Gangs and Youth Groups as a Crime Problem in Major American Cities*—written after several years of studying the gang situation in twelve cities nationwide based on statistical data and observations he received from 450 representatives from police departments, courts, and youth service agencies—he explained, "Youth gang violence is more lethal today than ever before."

Miller identified Philadelphia and five other cities as having "high levels" of gang violence—greater than the gang activity of the 1950s because youth in gangs were less formally organized, more likely to use guns, and more active in schools. In New York, Los Angeles, Philadelphia, Detroit, Chicago, and San Francisco alone, there were 760 gangs and 28,500 gang members. Philadelphia had the highest estimated rate of youth affiliated with gangs or involved in law-violating groups of the six "gang problem cities," ranging from 59.1 to 88.6 percent. From 1973 to 1975, Philadelphia was reported to have between eighty-eight and four hundred gangs and 4,700–15,000 gang members, and approximately one out of ten juveniles (between the ages of eight and twenty-two) was in a gang.[94] According to Miller, gang activity was "concentrated in low-income ghettos" and schools, where neighborhood buildings were marked as gang turf, and teachers and children could fall victim to intimidation, shootings, killings, and extortion of "protection money."

When Miller's research identified "low-income ghettos" as havens for gang violence, he suggested that poverty begot crime but also argued that youth of color were more prone to criminal activity than their white counterparts. In his study, Miller argued that throughout American history, ethnic populations with recent migrants and low-skilled laborers "produced" gangs. Miller claimed that in the 1880s through 1920s, "white ethnics" from Irish, Italian, Jewish, and Slavic backgrounds dominated gangs during a period of mass immigration from Eastern and Southern Europe.[95] In the 1970s, youth from "recently migrated groups"—like African Americans from the South, Latinos from "Puerto Rico, Mexico, and Cuba," and Asians from "Hong Kong and the Philippine Islands"— were "most heavily represented" in the gang populations of major cities like Philadelphia and Los Angeles. Since Miller's statistical data portrayed "classic white ethnics" of British, German, and Scandinavian descent as "underrepresented in contemporary urban gangs," he came to the conclusion that "ethnic and social class status" were valid indicators of future gang activity among certain groups.[96] Moreover, Miller's research triggered fear among city officials who wanted to curb gang violence to prevent white flight from neighborhoods adjacent to all-black communities. His report of neighborhoods and schools filled with gang shootings, robberies, rapes, and murders in areas like North and West Philadelphia convinced City Council that the best way to retain the white and middle-class taxpayers of Philadelphia was to fortify the police department's budget and divest from antigang programs benefiting black youth like Safe Streets, Inc.

In late August 1976, the Board of Managers of the Philadelphia Youth Study Center wanted to send "troubled and cast-off children" between the ages of nine and seventeen to temporary foster and group homes while they awaited their hearings in juvenile court for minor criminal offenses.[97] City officials, believing that jail was an inappropriate institution for low-risk youth to await trial, considered Safe Streets a potential facility to lodge at least six juveniles at each center overnight, since its mission was to rehabilitate and steer children from violence and crime.[98] However, by December 1976, the organization was finally forced to shutter its doors when its grants from the city and federal governments were discontinued.

Tough-on-Crime Spending Reigns

From 1970 to 1976, Philadelphia gradually spent more money funding the police, prisons, and courts than it did on juvenile commitment and the Youth Study Center.[99] In 1976, approximately 89 percent of Philadelphia's $236 million budget for fighting crime went to the police

Author's photo of the North Philly Peace Park, 2019. Today, there is also a West Philly Peace Park in the Cathedral Park neighborhood of the city.

department, prisons, and the courts. Programs committed to rehabilitating juvenile delinquents received only 3.7 percent of budgetary
spending.[100] City Council believed that curbing black juvenile gang violence through tough-on-crime initiatives was best because the city was
in financial debt and its tax base was dropping because of white flight.
To curb citizens' fears of gang violence and white flight, city officials and
the police department supported tough-on-crime initiatives focused on
incarceration because it was an immediate solution to the gang problem
in the city.

During summer 1970, Philadelphia's population declined further
by 3.7 percent, and its surrounding suburban counties grew by 30 percent.[101] As city depopulation worsened, the city struggled to reduce
crime, with seven hundred police vacancies, limited judges and district
attorneys, and inadequate rehabilitation of prisoners and repeat criminal offenders despite the municipal budget's increase from $100,720,633
in 1947 to $535,361,000 in 1970. In fact, Mayor Tate was so concerned
about financing core municipal services that year that he rejected City
Council's appropriation of $400,000 toward antigang initiatives to pre-
vent gang violence and death.[102]

By summer 1972, Mayor Frank Rizzo contemplated how to fulfill his
campaign pledge to "bring the city together" and not create new taxes
despite the city's issues with racial tension, high unemployment, a bank-
rupt school system, a crumbling mass transit system, and a high crime
rate.[103] Under the Rizzo administration, City Finance Director Lennox L. Moak attempted to balance the budget while Director of Com-
merce Harry Belinger attempted to implement a program to entice new
businesses, industries, and corporate executives to operate and reside in
the city in spite of Philadelphia's 11 percent corporate tax and 3.5 percent
wage tax.[104] In spring 1975, Rizzo wanted to maintain a four-year streak
of no taxes, but Moak discovered that it would be difficult to balance
the 1975–76 budget without an additional $65 million in revenue. Some-
how, Moak was able to fulfill Rizzo's request, but during the next fiscal
year, city taxes increased—particularly the real estate tax, which rose by
30 percent.[105]

In the late 1970s, Philadelphia's economic issues gave government officials like Mayor Rizzo more leeway to argue that unpoliced black crime

contributed to the city's financial difficulties. From 1969 to 1979, approximately 126,000 jobs disappeared from the labor market.[106] Few factories remained in Philadelphia as many companies moved their headquarters and production factories to the suburbs, the Sunbelt, or offshore to reduce business expenses and increase profit margins. As factories left cities, so did jobs. In the summer of 1977, Philadelphia and South Jersey saw the disappearance of more than 11,900 jobs in construction, factories, services, and government, resulting in the region's unemployment rate teetering between 7.1 and 8.8 percent.[107] Although 1,339,400 people were employed and 447,300 new jobs were created in August 1977, the increase in residents quitting the job search made citizens and politicians alike cynical about the city's economic future.

Additionally, Philadelphia suffered from depopulation. According to US Federal Census records, the city's population peaked at 2.1 million in 1950, and twenty years later, it dropped to 1.95 million.[108] Then from 1970 to 1980, Philadelphia lost 10 percent of its population, especially when nearly 250,000 people moved out of the city between 1972 and 1977.[109] With Philadelphia losing business, property, and sales taxes from job flight and white flight, the city's tax base was struggling to finance the public services of water, sewage, street paving, street cleaning (including snow removal), street lighting, police, and fire services.[110] In fact, as former Philadelphia textile worker Jean Seder explained, one visible example of how job flight, unemployment, poverty, and declining public services affected the city was when the largest factory in Kensington, Stetson Hats, closed in the late 1960s, eliminating up to five thousand jobs in the area. By the 1970s, Philadelphians began to characterize the blighted neighborhood as wrought with "high turnover, housing abandonment, dirt, vandalism, decay, and graffiti" in public discourse and the media.[111] Therefore, conservative city officials like Rizzo thought it was more viable to curb crime with massive funding for the police, prisons, and courts to quickly undo the job flight and depopulation issues that plagued Philadelphia. Moreover, City Council's concern about solving the city's issues of financial debt, depopulation, and gang violence would lead to the police department implementing hyperpolicing initiatives like Operation FIND against black gangs and individuals in crime hotspots located in the most stigmatized areas of the city: black-inhabited housing projects.

The Legacy: North Philly Peace Park

Today, if you go to 2201 West Stewart Street, the former location of the North Philadelphia center of Safe Streets, you will find a vacant lot. Throughout the neighborhood of Sharswood, where Safe Streets, Inc., once stood, are signs of desolation and poverty but also hope. There are boarded-up buildings and housing projects, well-kept homes, murals, revitalization projects under construction, and major landmarks— remnants of the demolished and infamous Blumberg housing project, the moderne art deco–styled Vaux High School, and the Free Library dedicated to 1960s civil rights activist Cecil B. Moore. Interestingly, in that vacant area is the North Philly Peace Park, an organization established in 2012 by community activist Tommy Joshua. As in the era of Safe Streets, the North Philly Peace Park is a safe space in the middle of gang territory. Children and adults can enter this large patch of land in Sharswood knowing that weapons, drugs, trash, and violence are prohibited. At the park, there is a community garden, wooden park benches, and brightly painted car tires, used as decoration and recreation for children. The volunteers who work there tend to the garden, distribute free food to community residents in need, and sell trinkets and apparel to raise money for community projects like a vocational school for neighborhood children. Although gang activity there has not dissipated, and Safe Streets, Inc., has been defunct for over forty years, the mission of the organization still lives on in the North Philly Peace Park as community residents and activists work to fulfill the goals that Specter and his board once proposed.

5

"Welcome to the Jungle"

Andre said he was going to get him a cop. A cop shot one of
his brothers. He knew it was a cop who he shot. He picked out
one and he shot him.
—Robert Chambers, suspect in police murder, March 11, 1976

In the 1970s, the Philadelphia Police Department often used excessive force in marginalized black neighborhoods because they believed
the stereotype that criminality and antipolice sentiment were part
of the inherent "nature" of poor and nonwhite people who belonged to
the "culture of poverty." Juvenile criminal court cases and news stories
about crime, "broken black families," and horrible living conditions
at public housing projects provided tough-on-crime advocates, like
former police commissioner Mayor Frank L. Rizzo, the evidence they
needed to justify police tactics that violated the civil rights of African
Americans, such as Operation FIND. Operation FIND was originally
designed in 1968 by Police Commissioner Rizzo as a mass police
search-and-arrest tactic to apprehend groups of criminals involved
in armed robbery and automobile theft. However, the tactic was later
used frequently in all-black neighborhoods and housing projects to
capture suspects who committed violent crimes like murder. When
Operation FIND was ordered, black men and boys faced arrest, interrogation, and abuse whether they were innocent or guilty of a crime.
Moreover, from 1970 to 1976, the Philadelphia Police Department's use
of Operation FIND to fight crime stigmatized poor black communities, terrorized black residents, and criminalized not only black gangs
but also black individuals who were found in hypersegregated environments like housing projects. One case that exemplified the evolution
of this tough-on-crime approach was *Commonwealth of Pennsylvania v.
Andre Martin* (1976).

Newspaper headline about the murder of Police Officer John Trettin. February 26, 1976, *Philadelphia Daily News*.

Officer Down at Wilson Park Project

Around 8:10 p.m. on the night of February 25, 1976, Andre Martin knew his life was over. At fifteen, Martin made the biggest mistake of his life by shooting a police officer, twenty-nine-year-old John Trettin, who was a five-year veteran of the Philadelphia Police Department.[1] The crime would garner a maximum sentence of death by electric chair. Before that, Martin lived a life of dysfunction. His mother, Shirley Munson, was a divorcée struggling with mental health issues as she lived with her five children in public housing for almost a decade.[2] The Wilson Park housing project at 2506 Jackson Street was Martin's home. Life at Wilson Park in the 1970s was one of inequitable isolation. Built in 1953, Wilson Park served as low-income housing for "refugees" of slum clearance from dilapidated and eyesore homes in the city and World War II veterans (who struggled to find employment) and their families.[3] In the 1950s, the low-rise and red-brick high-rise apartments featured 742 sizable units with well-functioning appliances and elevators, clean hallways, efficient laundry and medical facilities, a childcare center, and an outdoor playground.[4]

In 1954, Wilson Park stirred controversy when white *and* black families began to move into the all-white neighborhood surrounding the housing project.[5] Since Wilson Park was bounded by the I-76 expressway to the south and a stream of rowhouses inhabited by Italian families to the east and west, many black children and adults feared racial violence every time they left their "island" of safety to attend school and work.[6] By the 1970s, Wilson Park drastically changed in demographics and living conditions. White flight turned Wilson Park, still surrounded by a "hostile" white neighborhood, into a majority-black community, and diminished federal and local funding for public housing resulted in derelict care for the housing project and its tenants.[7] On any given day at Wilson Park, Martin saw shattered glass on the sidewalk, overgrown weeds, and mud on the grassy lawn, along with trash and graffiti in hallways filled with the stench of urine. Martin witnessed illegal drug and gun sales and heard numerous stories of robberies, random shootings, and children injured and killed because they fell through broken windowpanes or down elevator shafts. Wilson Park in 1976 was (in the words of tenants galore) a "hellhole resort."[8]

Three blocks away from the housing project was Vare Junior High School, the school Martin stopped attending to drink, smoke, and spend time with his friends from the neighborhood. On September 26, 1975, Martin's nineteen-year-old friend Ellis Croft was shot five times by police in an alley after he did an armed robbery at Pantry Pride supermarket, one block away from the housing project. According to Croft, he robbed $4,000 from the supermarket because his family was poor and he was tired of living in public housing with his seven siblings while his mother worked endlessly to pay bills.[9] After Croft was shot by police and taken to the hospital, the news media portrayed Croft as paralyzed from the injuries he sustained when they reported that Croft was taken to Holmesburg Prison in a wheelchair. Following the police shooting, Martin angrily vowed to get revenge on the police for what he believed to be police brutality.[10] Five months later, Martin selected Trettin to be the individual who would pay for all the injustices he experienced in his life.

On the night of February 25, 1976, Martin spent hours smoking marijuana with two friends, sixteen-year-old Robert Chambers and fifteen-year-old Alonzo Shands, in the 4-B apartment of Chambers's

Philadelphia Evening Bulletin photos of the Wilson Park housing project, April 23, 1956. Below, Mrs. Vivian Nicholson serves lunch to her children. Special Collections Research Center, Temple University Libraries, Philadelphia, PA / Frank P. Montone.

grandmother, Catherine Beeme, at the Wilson Park housing project.[11] Soon, Martin and his friends wanted to get "higher," so they left the bedroom of Chambers's sister, Christina "Tina" Lockwood; bought Valium in front of the building at 2506 Jackson Street; and ingested the pills.[12] The teens later smoked more marijuana in Tina's bedroom. Eventually, Chambers reached under his sister's bed and retrieved a 1963 .22 caliber Winchester rifle (covered in Christmas wrapping paper) that he and his friends bought earlier from their twenty-five-year-old neighbor "Kitt" and loaded it.[13] Although the boys were unaffiliated with a gang, they decided to take turns shooting out the window at three boys who appeared to be from the Passyunk Gang behind building 2508.[14] As Shands would later testify in common pleas court, there was "confusion," and Housing Authority guards arrived in the courtyard.[15]

Around 7:33 p.m., Officer Trettin and his partner were among several officers called to the Wilson Park housing project to investigate reports of shots fired.[16] Although Trettin was scheduled to be off-duty that day and at the Philadelphia Civic Center playing with his Quaker City band at the *Show of Shows* event, he had to work because the city required extra security while US vice president Nelson Rockefeller was in town for a testimonial dinner at the Sheraton Hotel in Center City.[17] While officers searched the courtyard, Martin told Chambers and Shands he was going to shoot the police for "his brother" Ellis. Shands and Chambers tried to talk him out of it. When that didn't work, Chambers grabbed the rifle and stuck it in the corner, and then he left with Shands.[18] Martin was then left alone in the room with the gun. No one knows what he was thinking at that moment. Did Martin think about how Croft was shot and critically injured by police for stealing money for his family?[19] Did he know and think about how another black teenager, Michael Sherard, was shot and killed by police after he fled two white officers who suspected him of stealing ten days prior in Germantown?[20] What is known is what Martin did next.

As officers searched the courtyard, a "sniper" from the fourth floor of one of the three high-rise buildings suddenly shot Officer Trettin (who was standing in the doorway of one of the buildings near a lamppost) in the head with a .22 caliber rifle, hitting him slightly above his left eye around 8:10 p.m.[21] Officer Malinowski initially had no idea what was wrong with his partner when he "suddenly slumped to the ground," until he noticed a hole just above the visor of Trettin's cap.[22] Although Trettin was wearing a bulletproof vest, the shot to the head left him critically wounded, and he was immediately taken to Methodist Hospital while officers and police helicopters descended on the complex, searching for the shooting suspect. Soon an Operation FIND alert was issued city-wide, and over one hundred police officers, including Trettin's fellow stakeout officers, arrived at the courtyard armed with shotguns to find the "sniper." Police Commissioner Joseph F. O'Neill, Deputy Commissioner Harry Fox, and several police officials set up a "command post" at the housing project's security office, while other police officers searched every unit of two of the twelve-story buildings at the housing project.[23]

According to the *Philadelphia Tribune*, Wilson Park residents were treated poorly by police, who behaved "lawlessly" as they searched for the shooter.[24] When officers went down the corridors of each floor of the housing project, they shot off door locks and broke down apartment doors when no one responded to their knocks. When inside, some police dragged people out of bed for an interview and ransacked apartments. A police helicopter was also used to investigate "movement" on

Youth playing ball at the Wilson Park housing project. February 28, 1976, Special Collections Research Center, Temple University Libraries, Philadelphia, PA / Joseph P. McLaughlin.

the rooftop of building 2506.[25] Several housing project residents, including children, were taken to police headquarters for questioning. Mayor Frank Rizzo soon arrived at the crime scene to get an update on the search for the sniper.[26]

At the hospital, Trettin had no idea where he was as he laid on the operating table, half-dead, with his head shaved for surgery. Emergency room doctors first X-rayed his head and found a .22 caliber bullet lodged in the base of his skull.[27] Then the ER physicians delivered the disappointing news to the surgeons that an operation was useless because Trettin was brain-dead. At the Trettin home on the 1800 block of Wensley Street, Claire Trettin (who had last seen her husband when he left for work at 5:00 p.m.) was personally notified by a policeman that her husband was shot, and she collapsed to the floor.[28] At 9:54 p.m., Claire and Officer Trettin's parents and sister arrived at the hospital with a police escort. Soon Reverend Raymond McHale of the Roman Catholic Church of the Epiphany administered last rites to the Protestant Trettin, and members of the Police Wives and Interested Citizens arrived at the hospital to comfort Trettin's wife.[29] Around 10:00 p.m., Mayor Frank Rizzo and Police Commissioner Joseph O'Neill arrived at the hospital and offered their condolences to Trettin's family.

Back at the housing project, Martin went to the apartment of his aunt Debbie Martin and told her, "One of us shot a cop. I think it was me." At some point, Shirley Munson instructed her son to go with his aunt and turn himself in to police at 22nd and Tasker Streets. Martin took a walk and then followed his mother's directions.[30] Hours later, police took the three black teenagers (Martin, Shands, and Chambers) to the homicide unit of the Police Administration Building at 8th and Race Streets for questioning. The teens gave conflicting statements, but enough of their stories connected, and later, Martin was identified as the sniper.[31] Martin himself confessed to shooting Trettin as revenge for the shooting of his friend Croft, but he also tried to lie by saying he thought Trettin was a boy from the Passyunk Gang, not a police officer. Soon all three teenagers were charged with attempted murder, aggravated assault and battery on a policeman, reckless endangerment of other persons, possession of an instrument of crime, and possession of a prohibitive offensive weapon.[32] Four days later, Trettin's family decided to take him off life support, and he died that Sunday, February 29th, at 3:55 a.m.[33]

Operation FIND

Operation FIND (Fugitive Interception Net Deployment), the police tactic used to arrest Martin, Chambers, and Shands following the shooting death of Patrolman Trettin, was first designed by Police Commissioner Frank Rizzo in spring 1968 as a way to apprehend suspects who committed forcible felonies like armed robbery and murder.[34] Rizzo described the plan as ideal because it made use of the police department's over two hundred foot patrol officers and 1,341 police cars without additional city funds. After four and a half months of planning, the police department implemented the response procedure on September 18, 1968. By January 1969, newspapers across Pennsylvania deemed Operation FIND a success, featuring stories of how two bank robbers who targeted Girard Trust Bank at 3rd and Arch Streets were caught within eight minutes.[35] Additionally, police officials from eleven US cities along with the deputy superintendent of Hong Kong police came to Philadelphia to study Operation FIND, while the FBI lauded the plan as a breakthrough in policing when it published a five-page story about the police tactic in its November 1971 issue of the *Law Enforcement Bulletin*.[36] However, from the 1970s onward, Operation FIND evolved from a tough-on-crime tactic used to capture bank robbers to a strategy for apprehending suspects who murdered police officers in "dangerous" neighborhoods.[37]

Around midnight on January 30, 1970, twenty-five-year-old rookie patrolman Frederick J. Cione Jr. was working the graveyard shift, driving solo around the neighborhood surrounding 17th and Oxford Streets.[38] At 1:08 a.m., Cione exited his red patrol car and approached three black men (at least one of whom was wearing a leather jacket) in a black and white Chevrolet convertible. Not long after, Cione was laying on the street; he was shot three times in the chest and abdomen. The suspects fled south in their car on 17th Street.[39]

Several witnessed the shooting and immediately called the police as Cione lay dying in the street. Within minutes, the Philadelphia Police Department broadcasted an "Operation FIND" alert on all police radios.[40] This plan divided the city into fifty geographical areas and instructed officers from thirty-five to forty-five patrol cars citywide to cordon off the crime scene at key intersections and search streets, homes, and roofs within a six-block radius of 17th and Oxford Streets to

Police search for the "sniper" at the Wilson Park housing project following the shooting of Police Officer John Trettin. February 26–27, 1976, Special Collections Research Center, Temple University Libraries, Philadelphia, PA / Salvatore C. DiMarco / Joseph P. McLaughlin.

question and interrogate anyone who looked like the suspects or might know something about the shooting.[41] Before they started the intensive search, Cione was taken to St. Joseph's Hospital. He died there at 1:30 a.m.[42]

Following the 1970 murder of Patrolman Cione, Operation FIND remained a trusted police tactic.[43] However, Operation FIND would terrorize not only fleeing criminal suspects but also innocent residents who experienced excessive police force when the plan was activated in their neighborhood. Residents of neighborhoods designated as crime hotspots faced the threat of double victimization: social inequity and hard-nosed policing. The executive committee of the Council of Black Clergy even pursued an injunction lawsuit against Police Commissioner Rizzo and three other high-ranking police officials explaining that they observed that following the murder of Patrolman Cione, black residents were deprived of their constitutional rights and privileges to be treated with respect during police investigations and not beaten, repeatedly detained, or insulted with racial epithets: "Operation FIND involved the Philadelphia Police Department in warrantless and illegal arrests of

Mayor Frank L. Rizzo signing autographs for children at the crime scene, located at the Wilson Park housing project. February 25, 1976, *Philadelphia Inquirer* / J. G. Domke.

close to 1,000 non-white residents of the City of Philadelphia."[44] Additionally, Harvey N. Schmidt of the Community Legal Services (CLS) told the press at the *Philadelphia Tribune* that Operation FIND encouraged many citizens who had never been "outspoken" before to express how they were "very disturbed" by the new police tactic and "concerned that there is over-policing in some areas, especially those dealing with young people, and underpolicing in other areas."[45] When certain communities were red-flagged as gang-prevalent or home to the "criminally inclined," police sought to segregate and contain groups and individuals within their "perceived" neighborhood with force. The failure of Operation FIND to locate the "gang" of black youths responsible for the unsolved murder of Patrolman Frederick Cione inspired the Philadelphia Police Department to revamp its use of the apprehension tactic in future cases.[46]

Nevertheless, the police department enhanced Operation FIND by identifying more crime hotspots in several predominantly black and working-class neighborhoods, hyperpolicing housing projects, and stereotyping residents from those locations as potential criminals and gang members. At 8:55 a.m. on December 23, 1974, this scenario became a reality at the Southwark project when twenty-seven-year-old Patrolman Joseph Cavallaro was shot in the stomach by nineteen-year-old Derrick Mays, who was fleeing arrest for an attempted "bar holdup" two days prior.[47] When hundreds of police and Housing Authority guards arrived at the project to find the suspect, they went door-to-door forcibly entering apartments without a search warrant, using "abusive language," ransacking and firing gunshots in homes, and killing a resident's dog, which attempted to protect its owner.[48] Many tenants reported being stopped, searched, strong-armed, questioned, and even falsely arrested by police during the search. Resident and tenants' council representative Mrs. Jennie Haynes told the *Philadelphia Tribune* up to ten police officers (with guns and rifles visible) greeted her at the door when she finally decided to permit them in her apartment for questioning. By January 4, 1975, tenants' council president Jearline Brown organized a petition (signed by 193 tenants) along with five protest letters that were sent through a lawyer to Police Commissioner Joseph O'Neill, condemning the "illegal, terroristic Gestapo tactics" of the police so that an incident like that never occurred again.[49]

Less than two years later, *Philadelphia Tribune* reporter Linn Washington would describe similar police mistreatment at another South Philadelphia project after a patrolman was shot.[50] Washington's March 1976 story even highlighted the discriminatory search procedures police used at the Wilson Park housing project versus those implemented in December 1975 at a high-rise in Rittenhouse Square when a thirty-year-old millionaire was murdered in his home.[51] The article argued that socioeconomic bias motivated police to solve Knight Ridder newspaper heir John S. Knight's murder by being "polite," "professional," and law-abiding when questioning residents at the thirty-two-story luxury Dorchester Apartments because it was a place where "doctors, lawyers, and professional persons" lived.[52] Nevertheless, the use of Operation FIND expanded into a preferred strategy for solving violent crimes at housing projects while excessive and deadly force against alleged nonviolent criminal suspects became normalized behavior in working-class, nonwhite, and "blighted" neighborhoods.

The Culture of Poverty: A Theory in Support of Tough-on-Crime Policing

City officials and police justified the use of Operation FIND and other police tactics involving excessive force because they aligned with the sociological theory of the "culture of poverty." During the late 1950s through the 1960s, social theories about poverty, urban blight, and crime explored how race, culture, and upbringing influenced human criminal behavior. Many anthropologists and sociologists were curious about why certain racial groups experienced generational poverty and marginalization at higher rates than others. Additionally, social scientists wanted to know why urban blight and crime appeared to be much more common with poor and nonwhite people than with the middle-class white majority. In 1959, anthropologist Oscar Lewis released his book *Five Families: Mexican Case Studies in the Culture of Poverty*, in which he discussed how some families living in Mexico City's slums developed a "culture of poverty" marked by a lack of class consciousness and an internationalist mindset that led to not only a bleak outlook on life but also the establishment of a generational "value system" different from that of their white counterparts.[53] Throughout Lewis's career, in

his research on Mexicans and Puerto Ricans along with his brief analytical work on African Americans in poverty, he essentially argued that
there was something pathologically different about how these groups
responded to poverty (compared to white ethnics) because they refused
to acknowledge that class hierarchy was the reason for their socioeconomic struggles, not racism.[54]

In Lewis's research, he explained how some African Americans in
poverty rightly "perceived" the existence of racial discrimination, but
he expressed a conundrum in why many black people remained marginalized and stuck in a generational cycle of poverty.[55] His research
implied the sentiment that if the Irish, Italians, and Eastern European
Jews can overcome obstacles such as employment, housing, and education discrimination, then black people should be able to as well. Although Lewis's goal was to spread awareness about the consequences of
economic inequality, his "culture of poverty" theory suggested that the
nonwhite underclass was either unwilling or unable to pull themselves
out of poverty because they subscribed to a value system in which life
was reduced to being satisfied with disadvantages and indulging in vices
to soothe one's pain.[56] His work did not consider how social institutions
in America like housing, education, and employment discriminately affected the underclass to keep them entrenched in poverty and prone to
criminality. Nevertheless, Lewis's conclusions reaffirmed long-standing
stereotypes identifying the nonwhite poor as lazy, ignorant, and dependent on welfare when uncontrolled and left to their own devices.

Not long after Lewis's theory was disseminated throughout academia,
in 1965, sociologist and the assistant secretary of labor during President
Lyndon B. Johnson's administration Daniel P. Moynihan released a federal report on poverty and the black family entitled *The Negro Family:
The Case for National Action*, later known colloquially as the *Moynihan Report*.[57] In the *Moynihan Report*, which took much inspiration
from black sociologist E. Franklin Frazier's 1939 monograph *The Negro
Family in the United States*, Moynihan nodded toward Lewis's "culture
of poverty" theory in his explanation of why African Americans were
struggling the most socioeconomically in American society. In Moynihan's 1965 report *The Negro Family*, he argued that while slavery and
racial discrimination have hindered the socioeconomic success of African Americans in comparison to white Americans, black culture and

single-parent, matriarchal households are also to blame for the setbacks blacks face in education, employment, wealth, and family life.[58] Although the report led to the creation of social uplift programs under the Great Society, it further stigmatized African Americans, especially the working class and poor, as socially inept and dependent on the federal government to achieve socioeconomic stability. Moynihan's contribution to the "culture of poverty" stereotype was that he suggested black people's criminality was influenced by dysfunctional family lives. Nevertheless, black youth like Andre Martin who grew up in poverty and lived in a "broken home" were labeled by policymakers as doomed to fall into a never-ending cycle of criminality, unless the government intervened in their lives with social welfare programs.

As Lewis's "culture of poverty" theory gained acceptance in federal and local government, several social scientists chose to examine and challenge the controversial conclusions he made through their own research. As anthropologist Carol Stack argued in her 1974 book *All Our Kin: Strategies for Survival in a Black Community*, theories like the "culture of poverty" erroneously portrayed impoverished people as "fatalistic" individuals who lacked value systems similar to those of the middle class that involved dreams and goals of success.[59] Stack further explained that the "culture of poverty" theory was a beneficial tool for policymakers, social workers, and the rich who wanted to cut welfare benefits to the poor and nonwhite and "blame the victim" for not being able to pull themselves "up by their bootstraps like everyone else."[60] Furthermore, Stack's research argued that Lewis failed to realize the intersectionality of stigmatizing identities of race, class, and gender that operated simultaneously in a person's life.[61]

As for city officials and police in Philadelphia, people like Mayor Rizzo believed that poverty was no excuse for crime. Rizzo's unyielding support for tough-on-crime policing as mayor was based on his experience as a Philadelphia police officer from 1943 to 1972. As police commissioner from 1967 to 1972, Rizzo believed "objectionable people" *caused* the crime, unemployment, and white flight that ruined the social, political, and economic reputation of the city.[62] In the 1960s, Rizzo implemented "stop and frisk" and emergency curfews and even purchased armored personnel transports that his critics likened to "military tanks." Additionally, Rizzo did not support the Police Advisory Board (PAB), thought police brutality was rare, and required no departmental investigation of misconduct. If a riot happened, he wanted it to be "treated with a firm hand."[63] During the 1970s, "objectionable people"—nonwhites, the poor, homosexuals, hippies, liberals, or political dissidents—who did not fit the police department's image of a patriotic law-abiding citizen experienced discriminatory policing tactics that included excessive force and civil rights violations.[64] Activists like Spencer Coxe, the executive director of the American Civil Liberties Union's (ACLU) Philadelphia Branch, frequently received complaints regarding Police Captain Rizzo ordering the illegal raids of coffeehouses, public squares, and political offices to disperse "undesirable" people who would offend his "law and order" constituency.[65] As mayor, Rizzo extended these "tough-on-crime policies" to maintain his occupancy of public office and meet the expectations of "law and order" citizens. Rizzo often encouraged police officers, through political rhetoric at press conferences and in interviews, to use excessive force, even against juveniles in marginalized communities.

In Rizzo's opinion, the "culture of poverty" argument was a sociological excuse liberals used to justify social welfare programs and reduced criminal sentences for the poor. Furthermore, Rizzo believed that high crime statistics about nonwhite juveniles were proof that nonwhite children who committed crimes were either inherently criminal and/or the product of bad parental upbringing. In June 1973, Rizzo attended the Pennsylvania Sons of Italy Convention in the Poconos, where he gave a speech outlining his reasoning for supporting tough-on-crime initiatives in Philadelphia:

> One trait that distinguishes Italo-Americans is a firm respect for decency, for properly constituted authority, and for the law. I have learned these things the way most of you learned them—at my mother's knee, and from the back of my father's hand. And we're all better citizens because of it. When I look at the crime statistics today, I realize there are not enough people around like my mother and father, and your parents. Today, whenever a man in politics talks about law and order, the radical liberals call him a dictator. But I do wish to emphasize that in the old days, respect for the law was something that decent people took for granted. It was the left-wingers who made law and order a political issue. Beginning in the early sixties, Americans were fed the malarkey that criminals were not

really responsible for their crimes—that society was to blame. We were told that criminals are the product of their environment, rather than of their own character deficiencies. . . . And, sad to say, some people swallowed that nonsense.[66]

In Rizzo's speech, he denied sociological research from scholars like Frederic Thrasher, William Foote Whyte, Lewis Yablonsky, and Walter Miller who suggested in their studies on gangs and juvenile delinquency that the "underprivileged were more likely to commit crimes."[67] He claimed that the "do-gooders" and "bleeding hearts" who advocated leniency and reduced sentences in the criminal justice system were neither effectively reforming juvenile criminal offenders nor protecting society from violent crime. Rizzo then went on to discuss his concern for law-abiding citizens who reported *terrifying* stories of elderly residents "barricading" themselves in their homes, women walking at night fearful of being robbed and raped, and people on welfare "racing the crooks to the mailbox to get their check." Moreover, Rizzo argued that "law enforcement must be taken out of the sociology classes and put back in the police station" so that penal reforms like the death penalty could be used against juveniles like Andre Martin who committed violent crimes like murder.[68]

"Getting Hassled, Getting Hustled": Containment and Isolation in Housing Projects

While Rizzo argued that bad childhood upbringing and familial culture were no excuse for black juvenile crime, journalists insinuated the idea that poverty induced crime.[69] However, when journalists wrote crime narratives about shootings, gang rapes, and the destruction of property at housing projects, they suggested that some poor black people may be stuck in a culture of poverty where African Americans are victimizing not only outsiders to their community but also one another. In 1957, the *Philadelphia Tribune* began publishing news stories of how tenants of public housing sites like the Raymond Rosen Project in North Philadelphia met with city officials and police officers from seven organizations, including the Gang Unit and Juvenile Aid Bureau, to discuss how police could work with parents to control "wayward children" from the impoverished area.[70] In one news story from 1961, a journalist from the *Philadelphia Tribune* described how a gang of four shot a patrolman with his own gun following a report of a "disturbance" at a wedding reception near the Raymond Rosen Project.[71] In the late 1960s, the *Philadelphia Inquirer* and *Philadelphia Daily News* began to pick up stories on juvenile gang activity near housing projects and recreation centers, and like the *Philadelphia Tribune*, they mentioned how this issue was tied to the poor living conditions residents experienced in these locations.

In the early years of the "public housing project experiment," conditions in low-rise and high-rise units had skip-stop elevators (which stopped at every third floor) along with minimal living arrangements, which included cheap cabinets, doorknobs, and latches that fell apart after limited use.[72] Basic household appliances were installed in apartments to encourage residents to live there temporarily and seek economic upward mobility.[73] Even storage space throughout an apartment in public housing was limited, so families sometimes placed kitchenware and canned food in a bedroom instead of the cupboard, and tricycles and baby strollers were stored in the living room or hallway instead of a closet.[74] Although both black *and* white residents of housing projects were dependent on the government for housing, black residents faced stigmatization for living in these developments because they were the predominant inhabitants of public housing.[75] Philadelphia Housing Authority (PHA) built housing projects that mirrored the racial segregation of the neighborhood when developments were first designed in the 1930s and 1940s. Then PHA gradually integrated all-white public housing with thousands of black families in the 1950s. However, PHA established new public housing in desegregating and all-black neighborhoods from 1956 to 1967 based on some community activists and government officials' demands for de facto segregation, which greatly contributed to the racialized image of who the average public housing resident was in Philadelphia.

From the 1950s to the 1960s, government funding for public housing dwindled, and as a result, housing projects experienced filth, deteriorating infrastructure, and crime (like drugs and gang activity) because PHA could not afford to pay workers to do adequate outdoor cleanup or infrastructural maintenance.[76] Tenants therefore suffered from dangerous and poor housing conditions like the absence of security guards, dimly lit or completely dark hallways and stairwells, no heat, water leaks, and "foul odors" from the incinerators.[77] PHA also was unable to properly regulate entrance requirements for incoming residents, especially when the Department of Housing and Urban Development (HUD) enacted new policies in 1971 that eliminated background checks and evictions for problem tenants who committed crimes, did not pay rent, or kept their apartments unsanitary.[78] To make matters worse, crime in the United States rose in the 1960s due to the surging population of "baby-boom teenagers, increasing availability of handguns, and deteriorating relations between police and minority communities."[79]

At the Wilson Park housing project, residents saw a steady decline in quality of living from the 1960s to the 1970s. Aside from the constant presence of rats and roaches, residents often complained to PHA about trash buildup, malfunctioning elevators, and the lack of security guards patrolling the buildings. In April 1976, residents became so fed up with elevators being out of order that they threatened to hold a rent strike until the infrastructure was fixed.[80] Their anger stemmed from experiencing a six-week elevator outage the previous September and knowing of handicapped and pregnant women being forced to climb the stairs. Although the story made the front page of the *Philadelphia Tribune*, PHA spokesman Bob Alotta responded with an explanation of how vandalism was to blame for the breakdowns and stated that elevator service would return in two weeks.[81]

Furthermore, in the late 1960s, drastically reduced government funding and increased crime rates in major cities exacerbated the horrid conditions housing project residents nationwide experienced. For example, at St. Louis's Pruitt-Igoe in the mid-1960s through the 1970s, residents occupying over seven hundred units at the thirty-three-building project regularly witnessed robbery, rape, drug use, gang activity, and murder. Public spaces like hallways, stairwells, elevators, and courtyards were all potential sites of criminal behavior or assault.[82] Gangs often operated open-air drug markets at projects, engaged in shootouts with rivals, and exerted "control" over multiple buildings at the complex by using fear and intimidation to keep residents silent about the violence and crime that occurred at their doorstep. At Pruitt-Igoe, gangs like Woods engaged in multiple activities at once: they fought to keep rivals from nearby projects like Carr Square off their turf, earned between $100 and

Only Knicknacks Left by Thieves
Mrs. Louise Seale kneels in bare living room after furniture was stolen

Living-Room Suite Stolen
In Project as Family Sleeps

By JOE SHARKEY

Mrs. Louise Seals said on Sunday that she is not surprised occasionally to discover that thieves have stolen something small from the trim townhouse she shares with her five children in the Norman Blumberg housing project, 23d and Jefferson sts. Robberies are epidemic in the area.

But when she walked downstairs Saturday morning, Mrs. Seals, 48, admitted, she was astounded to see her living room as empty as a drum. Mrs. Seals said she remembered quite distinctly having seen a suite of furniture in the room before she went to bed.

"I couldn't believe it," she said.

FAMILY ASLEEP

Working during the dark hours before dawn, industrious thieves had made off with the entire living room set—couch, chairs and tables—as the family slept on the second floor. The intruders apparently pried open a lock on the back door

of the house, then quietly lifted the furniture—valued at $600—outside.

"Can you imagine somebody just walking in and taking out the living room set?" Mrs. Seals sighed. "We all could have been killed in here. Maybe it's a good thing nobody woke up."

Although it was the most spectacular, Saturday's raid was not the most daring robbery at the Seals residence, one of 108 such rowhomes neatly arranged in courts around the Blumberg project's 18-story apartment towers. Last summer, somebody stole into the room where Mrs. Seals' daughter Linda, 17, was sleeping and took a small television set.

Opposed

...minishing the value of having almost 4000 acres of contiguous land. You can't replace it by getting 20 or 30 acres four or five miles away," Coleman continued.

"It's not just the money. No large city in the country can reproduce what we have here in Philadelphia no matter

Norman Blumberg housing project resident Louise Seals in her apartment following a burglary. March 1, 1971, *Philadelphia Inquirer* / Alexander Deans.

$100,000 a day from heroin sales, and maintained their control of the drug market at the project through gun violence.[83] Additionally, criminal activity at housing projects occurred at higher rates than in other residential areas of the city because of the concentrated poverty and lack of surveillance at these derelict-run government facilities. In the 2010 monograph *Blueprint for Disaster: The Unraveling of Chicago Public Housing*, social scientist D. Bradford Hunt described life in Chicago's public housing in the 1970s:

> The earliest project-specific report on crime showed that at Cabrini-Green's four largest high-rises in 1972, residents were five times more likely to be raped, three times more likely to be robbed, four times more likely to

be victims of aggravated assault, and six times more likely to be murdered. With the exception of homicide, these figures likely underreport
actual crimes, as public housing residents feared retaliation and dis-
trusted the largely white police force. Many of the crimes occurred in
public spaces—hallways, elevators, and project grounds—adding to the
fear of residents, many of whom became reluctant to leave the confines of
their apartments after dark.[84]

In fact, violence at other housing projects across America assisted in the
stigmatization of crime and gang activity and the dangers they posed to
police. On July 17, 1970, Chicago's Cabrini-Green made national news
when two police officers were killed by gang members at one of the project's courtyards, nicknamed the "shooting gallery."[85] Eighteen-year-old
Johnny Veal and twenty-three-year-old George Knight targeted Sergeant James Severin and Officer Anthony Rizzato from atop one of the
twenty-three high-rise buildings in celebration of a truce between their
gangs, the Cobra Stones and Blacks, respectively, as the officers crossed a
baseball diamond.[86] The alleged motivation behind the violence against
police was rooted in a police brutality incident in which Chicago police
destroyed their rapport with residents at Cabrini-Green nearly two years
prior. On an autumn day in 1968, officers chased teens into the project
for throwing stones, maced a one-year-old child during the melee, and
made a hollow attempt to rectify the situation by sending in forty-five
black officers to calm residents.[87]

In Philadelphia, citizens had local news stories of crime and gang
violence to color their perception of housing projects. The residents of
housing projects themselves often identified the prime reason for the
proliferation of crime and sometimes mistrust of law enforcement as
the absence of PHA security guards patrolling the buildings and the
faulty protocol system of police as second responders to emergency
calls. In many projects, PHA security guards were severely understaffed,
never available 24/7, and only safely escorted case workers around the
complex.[88] Much of the violence at projects resulted from neighborhood
gang wars among juveniles. On April 2, 1968, forty teens from the newly
merged gang at 22nd and South Streets stormed the recreation center
at Hawthorne Square housing project in South Philadelphia.[89] Around
8:15 p.m., one gang member drew a .32 caliber revolver and fired six

shots into a crowd of thirty people, hitting two teenagers and a gang worker. The incident was retaliation for a confrontation the 22nd and South Street gang had with the 13th and Fitzwater gang at South Philadelphia High School that afternoon.[90]

Additionally, gang rape against women at housing projects was a reoccurring issue. In November 1972, an eighty-four-year-old widow living alone in a sixteenth-floor unit at the Fairhill Apartments was raped and tortured for five days by four boys aged ten to thirteen.[91] In April 1973, news media reported the robbery and rape of a seventy-year-old woman by five boys (aged eleven to fifteen) in the seventh-floor hallway of the Martin Luther King Plaza housing project where she lived.[92] And yet again in December 1975, more rapes were reported, this time from the eleventh floor of the Southwark project, where two women were raped in one week while residents heard their screams as they hid inside their apartments.[93]

In 1974, the *Philadelphia Inquirer* published a front-page article about the story of the October 12th assault on Louise Seals at the Norman Blumberg project, encapsulating the belief that "uncontrollable" violent crimes, especially by *groups* of young men, reigned at housing projects.[94] Around 2:00 a.m. that day, fifty-three-year-old Seals was beaten, raped, and robbed for the sixteenth time when her rowhome at the housing project was burglarized by seven young men. When interviewed, Seals and her neighbors asserted that the suspects most likely lived in the 23rd and Jefferson Street project containing eighteen-story towers surrounded by 108 rowhomes.[95] Additionally, Seals stated that over the course of three years, she lost a kitchen and living room set, Christmas gifts, four televisions, three radios, and two stereos from the home she shared with her children to burglary. Like the previous times when Seals's home was intruded upon, she feared for her life at the project, telling reporters, "It's too dangerous. The Lord only gives you one soul. I don't want to get killed in a place like that."[96] In response to this attack on Seals's home and body, PHA spokesman Robert Alotta explained to the press that these crimes were common at other projects and the police were working hard to investigate. Alotta also added that if Ms. Seals wanted to be transferred to another project, then the request would be granted, but her safety there could not be guaranteed.[97]

In the 1970s (unlike in the 1950s), when newspapers like the *Philadelphia Inquirer* and *Philadelphia Tribune* described these incidents of

A newspaper article about the murder trial of Andre Martin. September 21, 1976, *Philadelphia Daily News*.

"gang" violence, they didn't habitually refer to the suspects as "thugs" and "street thieves" but sometimes sought to humanize them by describing their troubled family lives, impoverished circumstances, and the unaddressed psychological trauma "ghetto life" had on juveniles.[98] Journalists signaled in their articles that poor and volatile conditions at housing projects had psychological effects on residents that sometimes triggered not just gangs but also individuals to prey on others in their community. However, crimes like gang rape incensed journalists. In a 1973 editorial published by the *Philadelphia Tribune*, an author disregarded race and poverty to vent the disgracefulness of "hoodlums" and "wolfpacks" who violated elderly women at housing projects and demand that Mayor Rizzo (despite his history of police brutality) take aggressive action against youth who committed those crimes.[99] Nevertheless, journalists were often unsure how to portray poor African Americans as they received more and more stories from citizens about the structural problems that black people could not control, such as poor conditions in public housing and the police's use of excessive force in their neighborhoods. Journalists relied too heavily on the reports they received from either police or citizens, and as a result, their crime narratives reflected the informants they trusted the most.

Although violence and crime were known realities in housing projects by the 1970s, marginalization and lax government responsibility for uplifting the underclass were not strongly pitted as the root of gang activity and poverty-induced crime. Therefore, stereotypes labeling black people living in housing projects as impoverished, lazy, violent, and criminal were cemented and supported with consequential facts and gang narratives that clearly pointed to a broken system of social equality. Nevertheless, this perception of black gangs and youth at housing projects shaped how police, courts, and the public viewed juvenile crime from teens like Andre Martin, who went on trial in September 1976 for murdering Patrolman John Trettin.

"Save the Children": *Commonwealth of Pennsylvania v. Andre Martin*

During Andre Martin's criminal trial, police, court officials, and journalists faced a conundrum of whether the culture of poverty or poverty-induced crime played a role in black juveniles at housing projects committing violence as gangs and individuals.[100] In *Commonwealth of Pennsylvania v. Andre Martin*, Martin was placed on trial for murdering Philadelphia Patrolman John Trettin while in the company of his two friends. The incident was a major news story from February to December 1976 because it encompassed issues of police brutality, gang violence, the horrors of failed public housing, and the "culture of poverty." When Trettin was shot and killed, his story and subsequently the life of Martin were heavily publicized in news media throughout the Philadelphia metropolitan area. Journalists described Trettin as a twenty-nine-year-old father of three children (six-year-old Tracey, four-year-old Wendy, and ten-month-old John Jr.), a homeowner in Kensington, a law enforcement student at Philadelphia Community College, and devoted banjo player of the Mummers' Quaker City String Band.[101] After five years' service on the police force, Trettin received five commendations, and he (along with his partner Officer Richard Malinowski) was scheduled to receive his sixth commendation at an award ceremony at the Police Administration Building on March 1, 1976, for apprehending Robert Sanchious, a rifle-wielding West Philadelphia man who killed his mother-in-law.[102]

On the other hand, the news media portrayed Martin as a troubled youth from a "broken home," wronged by a "broken system" meant to mollify the social ills that caused juvenile delinquency. In news articles from newspapers like the *Philadelphia Evening Bulletin* and the *Reading Eagle*, journalists summed up his home life by mentioning that when Martin was ten years old, his mother was charged with larceny-shoplifting and assault and battery during Christmastime 1970. Munson was arrested and found guilty of both charges, and municipal court judge Michael Conroy later sentenced her (in her absence from court) to confinement for the crimes.[103] As for Martin's own brushes with the law, he was identified as being arrested for the first time at age eleven, when he was cited for a violation of malicious mischief for throwing stones.[104] In July 1974, Martin was arrested for possession of a hand-gun and later sentenced to nine months' probation by juvenile court. At

Helen Corprew, the creator of the Start Towards Eliminating Past Setbacks (STEPS) program, in 1971. Special Collections Research Center, Temple University Libraries, Philadelphia, PA / *Templar 1971*.

fifteen, Martin entered juvenile court again for possession of marijuana and shoplifting (in the words of his mother) a "cheap necklace" worth thirty-three dollars. He was later referred to STEPS (Start Towards Eliminating Past Setbacks), a part-time, Great Society–era day program that not only offered reading and writing instruction to boys on probation but also paired them with an adult who would teach them a trade like plumbing, carpentry, or photography.[105]

In January 1974, Helen Corprew, a social worker from Philadelphia's family court, established a mentorship program where men could volunteer to "counsel, tutor, and encourage a juvenile in [their] trade" for three hours a week. Black men were strongly preferred as mentors because at least 70 percent of the fifteen thousand juveniles who entered the Philadelphia court system annually were black. Corprew envisioned the project as "a preventive program with hope that he [the troubled youth] never returns" to the court system.[106] However, Martin was later "dropped" from the program "for lack of interest" when he missed two of the mandated biweekly sessions.[107] Amid his personal troubles with the legal system, Martin also had to deal with his mother's mental health issues. Although Munson received individualized psychiatric treatment, Martin and his siblings once had to participate in a psychiatric family conference to ensure progress in their mother's treatment.[108] From the press, readers learned of Trettin's bright and unfulfilled future, while Martin's life appeared to be destined for disaster.

In this criminal case, Martin was also suspected of being a gang member because he committed the crime in the company of two other youths. When Martin gave his confession to police while under interrogation, he claimed that he, Shands, and Chambers used the rifle to fire at a gang of boys from the Tasker Homes housing project prior to the shooting of Trettin.[109] Furthermore, Philadelphians were inclined to believe this gang narrative because from the 1950s through the 1970s, newspapers like the *Philadelphia Tribune* and the *Philadelphia Inquirer* explained how black juvenile gangs began to proliferate housing projects. With these facts about the Martin case laid before the courtroom in tandem with the storied violence news media described as daily life at housing projects since the 1960s, the stigmatizing image of black gang activity latched itself firmly to the residences where some of the most marginalized black families in the city lived.

On the night of March 1, 1976, Martin, Shands, and Chambers "solemnly" faced arraignment in municipal court by Judge Harry Melton and were held without bail on murder charges. In court, Chambers and Shands took public defenders as their legal counsel, and Martin accepted his family-hired lawyer, Daniel Preminger, as counsel.[110] Over the course of six months, charges of murder were dropped for Chambers and Shands, but they remained for Martin.[111] With the help of Assistant District Attorney (ADA) David Strawbridge, Chambers's and Shands's cases were sent to juvenile court (where they could be sentenced to a maximum of five years' jail time) after they agreed to be "state's evidence" during Martin's criminal trial and testify against him.[112]

During the two-week murder trial held in common pleas court in September 1976, Martin never took the stand to tell his version of events.[113] Instead, ADA Strawbridge had Chambers and Shands testify that Martin vowed he was "gonna get a cop" because of the shooting of his friend Croft at the hands of the police one block away from the housing projects where he lived.[114] ADA Strawbridge also brought up Martin's confession to police that his decision to specifically shoot Trettin with a rifle was not a complex one: Trettin was shot because he was the tallest officer at the scene, standing at six feet, seven inches tall.[115]

On the defense side, Attorney Preminger took many approaches to winning the case for his young client. Preminger tried to argue that Martin was not the shooter and was taking the blame for one of his friends, who was the real sniper. Preminger brought in medical experts like toxicologist Dr. Richard Phillips of Upton Pharmaceutical Company and Dr. Sidney Schnoll of Eagleville Hospital to testify that Martin was impaired after he consumed Valium and marijuana on the night of the shooting.[116] Preminger even attempted to claim Martin was of too low intelligence to commit the crime when he asked clinical psychologist Dr. Gerald Cooke to testify that Martin was "bordering on the mentally retarded" because he had a verbal IQ of sixty-seven, appeared "fearful," and saw "the world as a hostile place where he [Martin] doesn't know what to do." Moreover, the defense's strategy was to play on the racial stereotype of black inferiority and argue that Martin was too mentally incompetent to commit first-degree murder against Trettin.

On September 21, 1976, a jury found Martin guilty of murder. Before the sentencing hearing took place, Munson pled before the jury and Judge Robert A. Latrone to spare her son's life from the death penalty. She said, "Take my boy off the streets and place him in a juvenile home. . . . I was begging him [juvenile court judge] to take my child off the streets. . . . I told him something bad would happen . . . gangs . . . drugs."[117] Although Munson was unaware of her son's daily activities, she knew that gangs, drugs, and other negative external elements that were prevalent at housing projects were potential influences on Martin. Therefore, she shared that information with Judge Latrone hoping that he would empathetically sentence her son to prison instead of death.

At the sentencing hearing on September 22, 1976, the jury remained deadlocked on whether to sentence Martin to the death penalty, and Judge Latrone sentenced him to life in prison.[118] On December 8, 1976, Shands and Chambers pled guilty to charges of possession of a gun and conspiracy in juvenile court and were, respectively, sent to Cornwell Heights and Glen Mills institutions for juvenile delinquents.[119] The immediate legacy of Martin's case was that it not only caused citizens to question the validity of racist theories like the culture of poverty but also triggered public outcry about the potential for violence and crime to happen in blighted neighborhoods. The case also inspired public interest and concern from investigative journalists about the social conditions of public housing that drove young men like Andre Martin to engage in delinquency, join gangs, and commit violence in their neighborhoods. Criminal cases like Martin's would inspire the Philadelphia Police Department to heavily police not only gangs but also any black male body in the city, particularly in hypersegregated, impoverished black communities that represented the "jungle." Moreover, as historian Lisa Levenstein has explained, since working-class and poor black people were often confined to "segregated or transitional low-income neighborhoods," whatever structural inequalities operated at black housing projects would inevitably determine the "fate of Philadelphia's working-class black communities" as a whole.[120]

From 1970 to 1978, tough-on-crime policing would lead to hyperpolicing and police brutality in black and poor neighborhoods. This technique would support a system of racial capitalism that expropriated value from black communities and bestowed financial wealth to the police department and City Council. The arrest and incarceration of black men and boys for real and manufactured crime provided police officers with extra income through paid overtime for hours served during criminal interrogations and court appearances. City Council also benefited from tough-on-crime policing because the crime-prevention program could be used as a tool to convince the white middle class to stay in the inner city, pay taxes, and protect the tax base as Philadelphia struggled with financial debt.

Conclusion

On September 27, 2017, forty-one years after he was first sentenced to life imprisonment for killing Patrolman John Trettin, a teary-eyed and handcuffed Andre Martin stood before Trettin's family in room 506 of the Juanita Kidd Stout Criminal Justice Center and publicly apologized for his crime at his resentencing hearing:

> I am deeply sorry for the tremendous pain and loss I have caused each of you. By killing your father, I have hurt you every day and in so many ways. I think of the times you needed advice or a hug, or just the comfort of a loving father. I know I took that from you, and I'm sorry. I'm getting this chance, and I'm so sorry it means you have to relive that awful night that gave you a lifetime of pain. I pray every day for your peace and comfort.[121]

For two days, the Trettin and Martin families sat together (for a second time) in a courtroom as prosecutors and defense attorney Louis Natali recounted the series of events that led up to Trettin's murder. Members of both families (Martin's siblings and Trettin's three children) gave witness testimonies of the night when Trettin was killed. Martin's family talked about the troubled childhood he had, filled with poverty, abandonment from his father, and domestic abuse from his mother. Trettin's family testified about how Martin should remain imprisoned, expressing how every day they painfully mourned Trettin's death, Trettin's children had been cheated out of sharing special milestones with their father (like birthdays, graduations, marriages, the births of grandchildren), and Trettin's wife lived the rest of her life for her kids—still brokenhearted over the death of her husband.[122] After all witness testimonies were made by family members, prison staff, a psychologist, and one of

Martin's fellow inmates, Judge Barbara McDermott resentenced Martin to forty-four years to life, stating that he was rehabilitated but "needed a few more years."[123]

With opposing feelings of happiness and sorrow engulfing Martin and Trettin's families, respectively, both sides were able to make some peace over the judgment when one of Martin's relatives embraced one of Trettin's daughters. In 2020, fifty-nine-year-old Martin was released from Phoenix Maximum Security Prison in Skippack Township, PA, after serving forty-four years in prison.[124]

Martin's second chance at freedom was granted to him because the Pennsylvania Supreme Court ruled unanimously in June 2017 that life sentences for juvenile offenders without parole were unconstitutional. The Pennsylvania Supreme Court argued that the sentence was "not appropriate" because a juvenile's "transient immaturity" makes it difficult for prosecutors to successfully argue that a murder committed in adolescence is "deliberate," "premeditated," or the result of a "permanent" character trait of violence.[125] Furthermore, aside from the controversy surrounding Martin's resentencing and release from prison, his case highlighted how acts of violence often stem from anger and frustration over some perceived inequality in life. Societal inequalities like racism, nativism, discrimination, poverty, and abuse affect people in unique ways. Martin's choice to react to social inequality and police brutality by rebelling against society with random violence was not the only option he had, but it was the one he chose to take given the uncontrollable circumstances he was offered in life.

6

A Trip to 8th and Race

I submit that until the people of Philadelphia admit to themselves, in the face of incontrovertible evidence, that the police
are human and can commit crimes like any other human, we
shall have no real justice in our city.
—Victoria A. Brownworth, Witness to the 1977 police beating
of William Cradle

On April 29, 1977, twenty-three-year-old William Cradle was driving
in his 1971 Mercury after midnight in Queen Village, on his way to pick
up his wife, Carol, from work at 5th and Walnut.[1] When Cradle reached
3rd and Fitzwater Streets, he was stopped by police for speeding after he
ran a stop sign. Patrolman Lyle Sprague questioned Cradle, who, over
the course of approximately seven minutes, expressed that he was eager
to pick up his wife. There was a brief but tense verbal exchange between
Cradle and Sprague, and eventually, Cradle slowly drove off after the
officer insulted him by saying, "Take your black ass back into the car."[2]

Cradle soon reached 5th and Spruce Streets in Society Hill, where he was
stopped again, this time by multiple officers. According to nine witnesses
at the scene, including twenty-one-year-old Victoria A. Brownworth, who
stood just twenty feet away, Cradle was dragged out of his car by three officers. They punched, kicked, and severely beat Cradle with nightsticks, hitting him on the head, shoulders, chest, back, and legs. Two nightsticks broke
from the impact. Five other patrolmen looked on and said nothing. Cradle
was taken to Metropolitan Hospital and treated for cuts, bruises, a broken
rib, and multiple injuries to his head and limbs.[3]

On July 8, Judge Lynne Abraham issued a warrant for the arrest of Officer Sprague on seven charges, which included aggravated assault and
falsifying police reports.[4] If he was found guilty at the trial, he faced a
maximum of thirty years in prison.[5] In November 1977, Sprague along
with two other officers, Patrolmen Roy Land and Raymond Casper, were

placed on trial for charges of police brutality and the violation of Cradle's civil rights. At the trial, the prosecution presented nine citizens who witnessed the beating and argued that the incident was a case of brutality.[6] The defense responded with testimony from eight policemen who claimed there was an altercation between Cradle and the officers that provoked the use of force. During the trial, the defense asked Patrolman Land to testify that he punched Cradle in the face after Cradle slapped him to demonstrate to the court that the accusations of a police beating were exaggerated by witnesses who were telling untrue stories for the "money" or because of "psychedelic imagination."[7] On November 21, 1977, the three officers were acquitted by an all-white federal jury of eight men and four women, with *only* one juror being an actual Philadelphia resident.[8] Two days later, Philadelphia's first assistant district attorney John Morris announced that the DA's office had rescinded its decision to prosecute Sprague, Land, and Casper because "it would be unfair to attempt to proceed against the three defendants in light of their acquittal after a full, fair trial."[9] DA Morris also explained to news media outlets that he did not want to risk committing "double jeopardy" by prosecuting the men under charges similar to those made in the federal trial.[10]

Victoria A. Brownworth, a court witness and aspiring journalist, was so shocked by the outcome of the case that she wrote an editorial for the *Philadelphia Inquirer*.[11] In her November 1977 opinion piece, she argued that justice was not served in a case of blatant use of excessive police force. She expressed not only disgust for the failure of the justice system to find the officers guilty of a crime she witnessed with her own eyes but also fear of corrupt patrolmen who unknowingly walk the streets and have access to such unlimited police power: "I have lived in Philadelphia all my life and I shall continue to live here. I want to feel safe here and I want to know that the police are the good and just people they should be. I don't want to live in fear of the police, nor do I want anyone else to share in that fear."[12] Additionally, Brownworth's editorial "took issue" with the Fraternal Order of Police, Mayor Frank Rizzo, and "anyone else" who believed she was exaggerating in her accusation of police brutality. In the second-to-last column of her half-page news editorial, Brownworth concluded with the argument that for society to be fair and equal, there must be blind criminal justice, even for police: "The people of Philadelphia must take the blinders from their eyes and see the realities that exist. Crime is a reality and it has many sources. . . . I do not call for a wholesale indictment of the police department. However, Philadelphians, and the police themselves, must have the courage to punish crimes where they exist, irrespective of their source."[13]

The 1977 police beating of William Cradle was one of many examples of injustice surrounding tough-on-crime policing in Philadelphia. In the 1970s, many Philadelphians harbored criticism and animosity toward the police because anyone, from a doctor to a juvenile delinquent, could experience excessive and authoritarian police power and violence during this tough-on-crime era. The Philadelphia Police Department often made the newspapers (locally and nationally) for its many cases of alleged police brutality. Residents throughout the city regularly petitioned the police department to investigate officers and detectives for manhandling, verbal abuse, false arrests, torture-filled interrogations, and deadly force. These cases publicized the evolution of how commonplace excessive force was against not just African American males but also nonwhite and working-class citizens near low-income neighborhoods and housing projects in the city.

In June 1972, the Pennsylvania State Committee published an investigative report on corruption within and the use of excessive force against other socioeconomic groups by the Philadelphia Police Department.[14]

Cradle beating witness says justice was not served

Victoria A. Brownworth's six-column editorial condemning the acquittal of police officers who beat William Cradle. November 29, 1977, *Philadelphia Inquirer*.

This was the beginning of a series of investigations on police brutality conducted by government and nonprofit organizations in Philadelphia. By April 1977, local journalists were publishing groundbreaking articles on how Philadelphia beat officers and detectives were profiting from the existence of "crime" by arresting marginalized citizens: the nonwhite, poor, or anyone appearing to be outside of their residential neighborhood.[15] Nevertheless, state investigations into police brutality revealed police and city officials' biases, insecurities, and improprieties, while serial exposés written by investigative journalists in Philadelphia revealed a system of racial capitalism where many police officers falsely arrested, interrogated, and brought people to lengthy court trials to gain financial rewards like paid overtime as salaried government officials.

"As If I Were Some Criminal": The Pennsylvania State Committee Investigates Police Brutality in Philadelphia

From March 3 to March 23, 1971, the Pennsylvania State Committee investigated the prevalence of excessive force used by police. The Pennsylvania Committee was established under Section 105 (c) of the Civil Rights Act of 1957.[16] The committee consisted of eleven appointed state residents (serving without compensation) to investigate citizens' reports of police brutality in Philadelphia. The United States Commission on Civil Rights, an agency of the federal government's executive branch, requested the investigation because, since 1969, the commission had collected news reports, police reports, and citizens' complaints about the Philadelphia Police Department's tense relationship with African Americans, which one journalist described as a "war of the cops."[17] The commission decided to take action in 1970 following the shooting of three police officers, the police raid of the Black Panther Party's headquarters, and black residents reporting to Secretary William Wilcox of the Commonwealth of Pennsylvania Department of Community Affairs that at one moment in their lifetime, they experienced some kind of "excessive police harassment," "psychological brutality," or "physical brutality."[18] The committee's investigation consisted of ten hours of closed executive sessions and nineteen hours of open town hall meetings to discuss, document (in over six hundred pages of transcript), and evaluate incidents of police brutality.[19] After the investigation, the Pennsylvania

State Committee sent its report to the United States Commission on Civil Rights, detailing how police not only engaged in excessive force against alleged criminals but also attempted to cover up their illegal behaviors through evidence tampering. The Pennsylvania State Committee's major achievement in its investigation was discovering that officers' use of excessive force against suspects was not limited to impoverished black males but also included poor whites, working-class Latino men, and middle-class black men.[20]

From March 4 to March 5, 1971, forty-one Philadelphians testified before the Committee about their experiences with police brutality. The common goal among these witnesses was not to argue for the abolition of the police force but to insist that their civil rights be protected and abusive police be held accountable for their actions.[21] From these testimonies, the Committee discovered that the "role of the police in the minority community appears to be one of containment and control rather than protection and service."[22] This observation was made once the Committee learned from the testimonies of black teenagers that police often committed false arrests, physical and verbal abuse (like slapping, manhandling, beating, and using slurs), unlawful detention at the "Roundhouse" (the Police Administration Building and the city's main jail, located at 8th and Race), and "turf dropping" (abandoning a released individual in a racially hostile neighborhood or gang territory) against them.[23] When the Committee heard similar testimonies of police violence from poor white teenagers and other nonwhite witnesses, it concluded that the "powerlessness that comes from poverty and minority group membership substantially increases an individual's chance of being a victim of police abuse."[24] Nevertheless, the Committee determined that police brutality in Philadelphia was contingent on police officers' racial and class biases.

Among the forty-one witnesses at the town hall meeting was a working-class Puerto Rican man who described how, in August 1970, he was falsely arrested by police in North Philadelphia after a bar fight between a white teen and a Puerto Rican youth erupted in his neighborhood.[25] The witness stated (through an interpreter) that as he was leaving his mother-in-law's house with his two children, a policeman "attacked" him from behind, separated him from his children, and arrested him. The witness was taken to the Twenty-Sixth Police District (serving the majority-Latino neighborhoods of Fairhill, Juniata Park /

Feltonville, and Hunting Park) and then transferred to the Twenty-Fifth District (serving the predominantly white neighborhoods of Norris Square, Kensington, and Fishtown), where, in addition to police forcibly tightening his handcuffs, he was detained for seventeen hours without water or a phone call to his family.[26] Even though this witness was later released, he was upset about not only the police brutality he faced but also acquiring an arrest record: "I had to pay $12.50 as a fine, and this spoiled my record because I never been involved in police problems at all in the past, so [now] I have a record. . . . Now whenever I have something else happening, I have that record to condemn me in the future."[27]

Another witness at the town hall meeting was a middle-class black man, pharmacologist Raymond Ragland Jr. In Ragland's testimony, he stated that on May 19, 1970, he was walking four blocks away from his Mount Airy home (where 10 to 15 percent of neighborhood residents were black) to buy cigarettes at a nearby store when an unmarked police car riding down the opposite side of the street made a U-turn and stopped him at 10:30 p.m.[28] Dr. Ragland was then questioned, pinned against the police car, searched, and arrested. During his testimony, Dr. Ragland shared his thoughts as police falsely arrested him: "For one thing, the school that my oldest son goes to was right across the street. I had lived in this neighborhood. I just didn't think it was right for me to be leaning against a police car as if I were some criminal."[29] When Dr. Ragland resisted officers who roughly handcuffed him and threatened to "twist his black arm over," one officer "jabbed" his spine with a nightstick, "spun" him around, and "punched him in the stomach." The pharmacologist then feared that his confrontation with the officers would result in him being shot. Once the police wagon arrived to take Dr. Ragland to jail, the arresting officer lied to the approaching officer, stating that he found the doctor "hiding in the bushes."

At the police station, Dr. Ragland was detained for over three hours, questioned, and charged with assault and battery, threatening a police officer, and resisting arrest.[30] After a detective recognized that Dr. Ragland was his wife's employer, the charges were dismissed, and the doctor was released following an argument between the detective and the arresting officer. Within two months after the incident, Dr. Ragland filed a complaint with the police department, hired a lawyer, and filed a lawsuit when police refused to investigate the incident. Dr. Ragland concluded his testimony with this statement: "You hear some slogans about people being innocent until proven guilty. When I was there [police headquarters] . . . I was less than a human being. I was an animal that could not drink out of the fountain. . . . Unfortunately, that's the way it works."[31]

A third testimony came from the executive director of the Lawyers' Committee for Civil Rights Under Law, Edwin Wolf, who insinuated that local investigations into cases of police brutality were hindered, delayed, or dismissed to protect corrupt police officers.[32] In Wolf's testimony, he described how six men—black, white, teenage, young adult, and middle-age—were shot and/or killed by police in six separate incidents in two days for allegedly committing a crime and attempting to attack an officer with a gun or knife. In one incident of blatant excessive force, police shot and wounded a "20-year-old boy" who allegedly did not pay his subway fare because he "drew a knife" forty feet from an officer.[33]

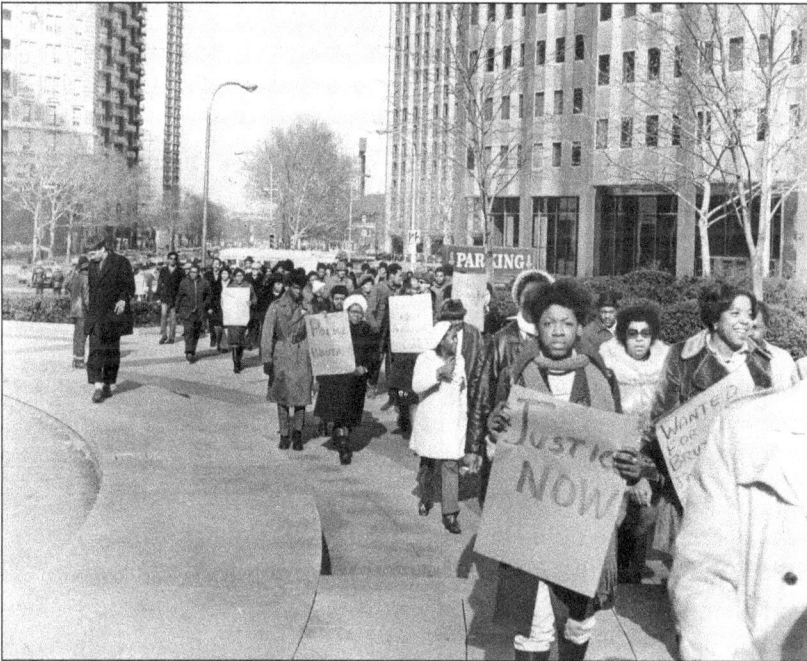

Philadelphians march to City Hall protesting the shooting death of Roger Allison by police. February 16, 1971, Special Collections Research Center, Temple University Libraries, Philadelphia, PA / Wasko.

Wolf's testimony also provided another example of flagrant police brutality when he described an incident of evidence tampering and cover-up by the police department after a "white youth" who "allegedly failed to stop at the scene of a burglary" was shot. In this case, Wolf suggested that police intentionally withheld the bullet-pierced clothing of the alleged suspect from the chemical experts at the Philadelphia Textile Institute for two months and then cut out the bullet hole because two eyewitnesses were prepared to testify in court that officers shot the suspect in the back as he laid on the sidewalk face down.[34] Overall, Wolf gave his statement before the State Committee to persuade them to investigate incidents in which police officers frequently and unjustifiably wounded and killed suspects but never faced prosecution for blatant police brutality.

Throughout the 1970s, the Philadelphia Police Department condoned officers' use of martial law and excessive force on suspects regardless of the race and/or class of the suspect. In 1970, police violence against citizens spiked after three police officers (black officer Charles R. Reynolds in October 1969, white officer Frederick Cione Jr. in January 1970, and black officer Harry Lee Davis in April 1970) were shot and killed during confrontations with criminals.[35] One day that Wolf describes as particularly violent was August 29, 1970, when white Fairmount Park Police sergeant Frank Von Colln was ambushed, shot five times, and killed by five members of the revolutionary group the Black Unity Council as he worked alone at his desk inside a Cobbs Creek guardhouse.[36] Certainly, these police murders made officers paranoid, prompting Wolf to suggest that police officers used excessive force against suspects because they feared for their safety, were angry about recent police murders, and were influenced by the police department itself to thwart crime with force.

As the Pennsylvania State Committee gathered testimonial evidence on police brutality cases, it discovered that several high-ranking city officials refused to hold abusive officers accountable for their actions. In the first place, the Committee's investigation found that countless complaints of police abuse filed by the city's Commission on Human Relations, Lawyers' Committee for Civil Rights Under Law, Philadelphians for Equal Justice, American Civil Liberties Union (ACLU), and Community Legal Services were unresolved by the city and police department.[37] Secondly, numerous participants in the town hall meetings expressed that former police commissioner Mayor Rizzo contributed to the "deterioration of police-community relations for minorities and white dissidents" because his politically charged, antiprotest responses to events in the city "escalated tensions" that led to violence between the two groups.[38] And third, several city officials and aspiring politicians ignored the issue of police-community conflict to maintain or attain their seats in public office.

During the investigation, several incumbent city officials, including Mayor Rizzo, dismissed citizens' complaints of police brutality and refused to attend the town hall meetings hosted by the Committee.[39] From January 7, 1971, to April 13, 1972, representatives from the United States Commission on Civil Rights and the Pennsylvania State Advisory Committee exchanged letters with Police Commissioner O'Neill, District Attorney Arlen Specter, Mayor James H. J. Tate, and Mayor Rizzo requesting that they attend the town hall meeting and respond to citizens' complaints of police violence or provide support in the investigation.[40] Only DA Specter responded positively to Director of the US Commission on Civil Rights Isaiah T. Creswell Jr.'s request by attending the town hall meetings, testifying before the Committee, reviewing the meetings' transcripts, and proposing the creation of a municipal advisory board to further investigate problems in police-community relations.[41]

When Police Commissioner O'Neill responded to Chairman Richard K. Bennett of the Pennsylvania State Advisory Committee in March 1971, he declined the invitation by arguing that he had to prioritize reevaluating police policies after the murders of two policemen over listening to community complaints about police abuse, an issue that may have originally triggered antipolice violence.[42] In Mayor Tate's January 1971 response letter to Assistant Director of the US Commission on Civil Rights Theodore W. Robinson, he declined to participate in the Committee's investigation, claiming he did not want to aggravate police-community tensions.[43] In Mayor Rizzo's April 1972 response letter to Director Creswell Jr., he vehemently chastised Creswell for hosting town hall meetings that were (in Rizzo's opinion) antipolice: "The record, of course, does not include the testimony of police . . . who have paid the supreme sacrifice. Call upon the families of Officers Fred Cione, Frank Von Colln and other officers who were assassinated without provocation while performing their duties."[44]

Community meeting at Canaan Baptist Church in Germantown about police violence following the murder of Michael Sherard. February 1976, *Philadelphia Inquirer* / J. G. Domke.

In March 1974, the Pennsylvania Crime Commission published its eighteen-month investigative report on corruption in the Philadelphia Police Department. While the Pennsylvania Crime Commission did not investigate police brutality, it focused on collecting citizens' testimonies to uncover all the reasons many citizens mistrusted the police. Like in the 1940s, Philadelphians complained there were a slew of officers who engaged in, permitted, or financially benefited from the operation of illegal drug dealing, prostitution, speakeasies, and numbers racketeering in black and white communities.[45] Furthermore, the Pennsylvania Crime Commission's investigation opened the door for another organization to delve into the issue of police brutality in Philadelphia.

By 1977, police violence had not waned. The Public Interest Law Center of Philadelphia (PILCOP) had received dozens of citizens' complaints about abusive patrolmen and detectives who violated their rights. The abuse complainants made against officers ranged from being denied an attorney to having a chair thrown at them during an interrogation.[46] PILCOP's attorneys then addressed letters to Police Commissioner Joseph O'Neill on behalf of their clients detailing how some juveniles, men, and women were persecuted and brutalized while in police custody. In 1976 alone, PILCOP received 201 complaints of police abuse that took place on streets, in district police stations, in clients' homes, in the police van, and at the Roundhouse.[47] Some complaints entailed harassment and false arrest, like a December 1976 case where a fourteen-year-old boy was arrested at his job at Levi's Hotdog Stand in South Philadelphia for possessing a toy gun.[48] Other cases described visceral brutality, like the April 1976 beating of a Cedarbrook man by multiple officers that led to him being hospitalized for lacerations of the skull and face, a broken jaw, and subconjunctival hemorrhages.[49] Moreover, despite the presence of state investigations, lawsuits, and press coverage on police brutality, the issue remained unresolved on an institutional level. If there were no accountability or serious consequences for police who violated citizens' civil and human rights, then people of color, the working class, and the poor would never be truly safe or protected in their own city.

"An Eye for an Eye": Fighting Back against Racial Violence

In the 1970s, police violence was sometimes met with retaliation—for example, when African American suspects killed white policemen as a response to past black-police confrontations they believed to be police brutality. Some of these incidents involved *groups* of two or more young black men targeting white patrolmen in black neighborhoods red-flagged by the police department as crime hotspots. Consequently, when African American men retaliated against white policemen for police brutality happening in the city, some police officers not only stereotyped black men as violent but also felt justified in using excessive force in black-police confrontations.

According to criminologist Sean Patrick Griffin, when the Black Unity Council murdered Police Sergeant Frank Von Colln in 1970, their motivation for the killing was to fulfill their philosophy of "killing the pigs and declaring war on police officers for what they thought was brutality in their community."[50] The five suspects were later charged with murder and sentenced to life in prison.[51] On February 21, 1971, two white officers were found shot dead in their patrol cars within five hours of each other, in two different city neighborhoods.[52] Around 10:00 p.m. on February 20, twenty-five-year-old Officer John McEntee was found slumped over his steering wheel with two gunshots to the back of the head in Stanton, a predominantly black neighborhood in North Philadelphia. Police Commissioner Joseph O'Neill would later report to the news media that before McEntee was "executed," he "stopped two youths for questioning." Early the very next day, forty-five-year-old Officer Joseph Kelly was found slumped over in his patrol car with two gunshots to the chest in Roxborough. When police arrived at the scene, they discovered Kelly with his police radio microphone in his right hand and his revolver on the car floor. Kelly fired five shots before his death.[53]

The killings were news across the country. A journalist from the *St. Petersburg Times* wrote that Philadelphia Police "refused to speculate" whether the killings of McEntee and Kelly were done in retaliation for the shooting and wounding of a twenty-two-year-old African American man, Roger Allison, who threatened police with a whiskey bottle on February 15, 1971. Furthermore, the journalist suggested that since Allison was shot six blocks away from where McEntee was killed, it was possible that the murderers may have killed the white officers to avenge the shooting of an allegedly mentally disabled black man.[54] Since Von Colln, McEntee, and Kelly were killed by African American suspects who wanted to retaliate against police, it is possible that fear and anger drove some white police officers to mistrust certain members of the black community who appeared to hate white patrolmen. Since all the suspects involved in killing these four officers were black males, this pattern developed a stereotype that all black men were violent, especially against police. This stereotype had great importance in the second half of the decade when police killed several black males for alleged crimes.

Newspaper headline about the acquittal of Officer Thomas Bowe Jr. for the murder of Cornell Warren. August 17, 1979, *Philadelphia Inquirer* / William F. Steinmetz.

As Rizzo grew to be an influential police commissioner and mayor throughout the 1970s, some officers adopted his stance on using excessive force in black communities to keep crime rates down. As a result, there were many incidents where police wounded and killed unarmed black men and teens suspected of crime. Three cases that impacted the city at large morally and financially were the shooting deaths of Michael Sherard, Michael Carpenter, and Cornell Warren.[55] Additionally, Rizzo and the Fraternal Order of Police (FOP) consistently petitioned the city to provide higher wages and overtime to patrolmen and detectives who wanted to work beyond their eight-hour shifts while also blindly defending officers who violated the civil rights of citizens.[56]

At noon on February 15, 1976, as he sat in his patrol car near the Queen Lane Apartments housing project, twenty-five-year-old Officer Donald Woodruff saw sixteen-year-old Michael Sherard walking down a street in Germantown carrying a portable television set.[57] Woodruff suspected the television was stolen and ordered Sherard to stop. Sherard continued walking until Woodruff got out of the car and followed him. Sherard then ran and threw the television toward Woodruff, who chased the teenager into an alley and a playground before fatally shooting him in the back of the head.[58] Days after Sherard was killed, Germantown residents called for Officer Woodruff's suspension from the police force.[59] Woodruff was later charged with manslaughter.[60] Months later, Woodruff faced a two-week trial in common pleas court in which he testified that he "didn't want to do it [kill Sherard]" and he now believed it was "better for him [Sherard] to escape than to take his life." By November 4, 1976, the jury acquitted Woodruff of manslaughter, and he was released.[61] Despite the court ruling, Sherard's family pursued a $3 million damage suit against Officer Woodruff, the city, Mayor Frank Rizzo, and Police Commissioner O'Neill.[62]

On February 27, 1978, nineteen-year-old Michael Carpenter was riding in a Thunderbird (with broken headlights) with four friends in their Kensington neighborhood when a Twenty-Fifth District patrol wagon spotted them.[63] The police signaled for Carpenter to pull over at the red light near Tioga Street and Aramingo Avenue (located eight minutes away from the Whitehall Apartments housing project), but Carpenter sped off, and a police chase ensued. Soon the police broadcasted the incident, and Officer Marcus Giardino and his partner William Atkinson joined the chase. Officers Giardino and Atkinson soon caught up with Carpenter and stopped the car for a traffic violation.[64] During the traffic stop, Carpenter fled from the vehicle, and Giardino pursued him into an alley and then fatally shot him in the back. The officers later discovered Carpenter's friends hiding nearby, found beer and five dollars' worth of marijuana in the car, and arrested the men for drunk driving.[65] In April, District Attorney Ed Rendell obtained a murder warrant for Giardino. When detectives interrogated Giardino, he lied to them, stating that when Carpenter threatened him, he shot the teen in the chest.[66] By September, an autopsy of Carpenter's body reported that Giardino shot Carpenter not in the chest but in the back. Giardino later confessed the truth, pled guilty to manslaughter, and resigned from the police force.

In October, Judge Robert Latrone sentenced Giardino to five years' probation, ordered him to pay $5,000 in funeral expenses to Carpenter's family, and instructed him to join the Big Brothers Association as part of his rehabilitation program.[67] After the sentencing, members of the Big Brothers Association stated that Giardino was unfit to mentor children because of his involvement in Carpenter's death. Judge Latrone responded with surprise, stating that Giardino was "not a criminal type" but a "good father" and he did not understand why an organization in need of volunteers would refuse Giardino. Judge Latrone later stated that he would not force the organization to accept Giardino and placed him in another community-based organization, the Police Athletic League (PAL).[68]

On September 23, 1978, twenty-year-old Cornell Warren, a North Philadelphia resident, was stopped by white officer Thomas Bowe Jr. and black officer Daryl Bronzeill. They suspected Warren of speeding in a stolen car in the Tasker Homes housing project, located in Grays Ferry.[69] Warren was later arrested, handcuffed by officers, and placed in a police van. The police officers took Warren to the Police Administration Building to further investigate his case, but Warren escaped and ran down the street, still handcuffed.[70] The officers pursued Warren and shot him in the head two blocks from the police van. Warren died in the hospital thirteen days later.[71] Philadelphia district attorney Ed Rendell responded to the incident with great conviction against the officers:

> I took great pains to tell the Philadelphia police department and the police officers of this city of what constitutes deadly force. . . . The police do not know the law. You can't shoot a fleeing suspect for something other than a forcible felony, like murder or rape. It does not cover a suspected stolen car. . . . The whole concept is distasteful for a prosecuting officer to bring charges against police, but it's the law. This has got to stop. This man could have been your nephew or my nephew or your son or daughter. Any nineteen-year-old is susceptible to panicking and running away from police.[72]

After Warren died, Officer Bowe Jr. claimed his gun accidentally fired and hit Warren. Assistant District Attorney Robert Campolongo later pursued a charge of third-degree murder, believing the shooting was not premeditated but done in a "moment of rage."[73] In Bowe's August 1979 trial, a jury of eight women (two were African American) and four men acquitted him of murder.[74] After the verdict was read, Cornell Warren's mother, Margaret Warren, left the courtroom exclaiming that

Officer Bowe Jr. was a "murderer," and another relative shouted in the courtroom that the verdict was similar to the "Ku Klux Klan days in Alabama." Bowe's acquittal occurred at a crucial time when the Pennsylvania Justice Department charged the city, Mayor Rizzo, and nineteen top officials in Philadelphia with "systematically condoning police brutality," particularly against African Americans and Latinos.[75] Furthermore, Bowe's acquittal was shocking but not surprising, since police brutality was an endemic issue in the police department.

In all three cases of deadly officer-involved shootings, the police spotted and pursued these young men near housing projects in predominantly working-class African American neighborhoods that appeared "blighted" because of the many abandoned homes and factories that lined city streets. Since "blighted" areas were often associated with black crime, any potential black suspect who fled police, resisted arrest, or questioned his treatment from officers faced excessive (and sometimes deadly) force, especially when their presence in a neighborhood seemed out of place—for example, if they were riding around in a luxury car or participating in recreational activities outside of the confines of a housing project development.

In addition to this form of police bias, another consequence of Rizzo's unspoken approval of excessive force was the police department's unwillingness to properly screen potential police recruits for possible violent outbursts toward suspected citizens.[76] Giardino, who joined the force in 1974, was a Vietnam veteran who was medically discharged from the air force because he suffered a nervous breakdown. Toward the end of Giardino's military career, he was afraid of loud noises and could not handle stress. Military officials became aware of Giardino's psychological illness when he *repeatedly* dived under his cot, covered his ears, and cried every time he heard a plane fly overhead.[77] While it is unknown whether police officials knew of Giardino's post-traumatic stress disorder (PTSD) when they hired him, it is known that Giardino had a tendency to lie about his behavior because, in addition to lying about shooting Carpenter in the chest, he tried to conceal his medical history from court officials during his trial, stating that he was released from the military for a perforated eardrum.[78] Like Giardino, there were numerous officers who were military veterans—possibly suffering in secret from undiagnosed PTSD that, in turn, made them prone to using excessive force when they became stressed, afraid, or angry with suspects.

While many police-involved shootings led to murder trials for accused officers, few were convicted. Nevertheless, much social activism from civil rights attorneys took place to expose and demand an end to police brutality. From 1970–79, black, white, and Latino citizens circulated petitions demanding the suspension of accused police officers, held demonstrations in courtrooms, and participated in mass marches to police stations and City Hall in protest of police shootings.[79] Some Philadelphians conducted extensive research on the trend of police brutality. On April 19, 1979, Attorney Anthony E. Jackson, director of the Police Project for PILCOP, released an eighty-four-page statement that gave a full report on the findings of the Police Project's study on police brutality in Philadelphia from 1970–78.[80] Jackson's opening argument was as follows: "The Police Project's study on the use of deadly force by Philadelphia police reveals a pattern and practice of alleged shootings that are condoned by the police and city administration by the lack of disciplinary action against offending officers. Nearly 50% of the shootings by Philadelphia police are in violation of Pennsylvania law in that those victims were not engaged in any forcible felony or threatening serious bodily harm to officers or others."[81]

Jackson's research also provided a plethora of statistics on police-involved shootings. In his study, Jackson analyzed 469 shootings by police from 1970–78. Out of 469 shootings, 60 victims were juveniles, 162 individuals died, and 297 people were wounded. Seventy-five people who were shot by police did not commit a violent felony (like rape or murder) but fled officers. In Jackson's 1978 case study, he discovered that of twenty-three people killed by police, eight were unarmed, seven had guns, five had other types of weapons, and for three individuals, police could not determine whether the suspect was unarmed. Also, five out of eight unarmed suspects murdered were fleeing police when they were shot.[82] Among these five individuals were Michael Carpenter and Cornell Warren. Furthermore, Jackson claimed the police shootings of the eight suspects were even more unjustifiable because the individuals were not committing violent crimes when the police shot them.[83] Jackson's research also documented every police-involved shooting from 1970 to 1978, the names of officers and shooting victims, officers involved in multiple suspect shootings, statistics on police use of deadly force, police districts with the highest percentages of police shootings per year, and the criminal charges and lawsuits filed against officers. Overall, Jackson's report determined that although African Americans composed 33 percent of Philadelphia's population, the trend in police shootings was racially motivated, since 66 percent of the identifiable police-involved shooting victims were black.[84] Nevertheless, the data revealed that police officers patrolling low-income black neighborhoods identified as "crime hotspots" expected suspects in these areas to be "armed and dangerous" and therefore felt justified in using deadly force against black men even when their lives were *not* threatened.[85]

Maintaining "Law and Order" Means Fighting Black Crime

In 1978, director Robert Mugge released his controversial documentary *Amateur Night at City Hall: The Story of Frank L. Rizzo*, which explored the meaning of "law and order" in Philadelphia's Rizzo era. From start to finish, the film explored how Rizzo's tough-on-crime movement sparked police brutality when politicians feared white flight from a "blighted" and "crime-ridden" city.[86] With interviews from citizens, politicians, civil rights activists, and journalists, Mugge's film painted Rizzo as a "demagogue" who was (for the most part) admired and supported by the Italian American community for breaking down white ethnic and socioeconomic barriers for Italians seeking public office. Most importantly, Rizzo was portrayed as a local spokesman for a "law and order" political base that desired "hard-nosed" policing to combat street crime—the supposed cause of job flight, white flight, and blight.

As mayor, Rizzo maintained his tough-on-crime agenda because he wanted to meet the expectations of the "law and order" citizens who supported him and retain his seat in public office. Supporters of this political base feared the proliferation of particularly black street crime in the city while also contemplating an escape to the suburbs. To please these citizens, Rizzo often encouraged police officers to use excessive force against the "animals" who committed street crime through his political rhetoric in press conferences and news interviews.[87] Rizzo's public statements such as "The guy that kills police should be strung up . . . after he receives that fair trial" were covert signals to policemen that he condoned excessive force. His words sent the message to officers that no matter what they did to curb crime (like injure, maim, or kill a suspect), he would support them. Nevertheless, police officers ranking from the president of the Fraternal Order of Police to the beat cop were indirectly granted permission from Rizzo to use excessive force against a suspect if they believed it was necessary, felt threatened, or were insulted:

> We have a uniform . . . a badge . . . a blackjack . . . a gun, and a club. If somebody takes a punch at you and tries to put you down, it's just like being in a fight. You're going to put them down best you can until they stop swinging. And if you want to call it violence, it's violence, but we're not out there to be punching bags, we're out there to protect the public and that's what we intend to do.—Thomas McCarey, President of the Fraternal Order of Police Lodge #5[88]

Additionally, Mayor Rizzo was focused on black crime because Philadelphia's economic issues were exacerbated by industrial decline, job flight, and continual white flight. Rizzo maintained his stance on law and order against black crime because it was a familiar narrative to the white middle class. In fact, during Rizzo's two terms as mayor of Philadelphia, deadly police-involved shootings increased by approximately 20 percent per year.[89] He promoted tough-on-crime policing and increased spending on the police department to convince white residents that inner-city Philadelphia was safe and there was no need to move to the suburbs. Political fears about black crime triggering white flight existed long before Rizzo arrived in public office. Since the Great Migration, negative racial stereotypes about black migration, black residency, and black crime in Philadelphia triggered white fear and white flight from the city. However, it wasn't until the 1960s, when City Council had to determine how to effectively control its budget spending, that white flight decreased the city's tax base at the same time the police department began requesting more funds to "protect and serve" Philadelphia.

In the late 1960s, city officials were concerned about budgetary spending during periods of economic downturn. As police commissioner, Rizzo was aware of this when he promoted his 1968 police plan, Operation FIND, as one requiring no additional municipal funds. However, in the 1970s, the police department gradually received more and more funding from the city budget through paid overtime. In 1961, the FOP first achieved paid hourly overtime for police officers ranking from lieutenant to beat cop.[90] Officers earned overtime when they remained on duty beyond their eight-hour shifts to continue investigations, conduct interrogations, appear in court, or increase manpower during public safety emergencies. By July 1970, the FOP (with support from the police department and Rizzo) signed a contract with the city achieving overtime pay for officers at one and a half times the usual hourly rate.[91]

Despite the increased costs of overtime, the police department's director of administration, Philip H. Carroll, explained in a 1971 interview how elevated levels of crime from June 15 to September 15 made extra manpower a necessity: "During warm weather, we have most of our problems in the city. Last summer, there was a riot in Holmesburg prison and the trouble at Tasker Homes and in Fairmount."[92] In these three examples, to justify increased spending on the police, Carroll described incidents from summer 1970 where groups of black men and boys committed crimes of violence and murder. The riot at Holmesburg Prison involved about four hundred predominantly black inmates who attacked over one hundred mostly white guards and inmates in retaliation for physical abuse, poor living conditions, and racism.[93] The "trouble" at the Tasker Homes housing project involved three hundred "helmeted" and "club-carrying" police officers breaking up a race riot between black juveniles from the project and white residents from the surrounding area who were throwing bottles and bricks at one another.[94] And the "trouble" at Fairmount Park was the shooting of two police officers by the Black Unity Council in which Sergeant Von Colln was murdered.[95] As a result of incidents like these, the police department had continuously run overbudget for emergencies, and with narratives of recent black crime palpable, City Council relied on reserves to cover the costs.[96]

By March 1971, *Philadelphia Inquirer* reporters began to note the city's uncontrollable budgetary spending on the police department when it received twice as much funding as any other city office: $82 million.[97] In that month, Philadelphia reportedly offered members of its 7,904-man police force approximately two thousand hours of overtime each day, costing the city $15,000 a day and $5.5 million a year. As the fourth largest city in the country, Philadelphia was spending more money on overtime with a smaller police force than the top three: New York, Chicago, and Los Angeles, respectively.[98] Since 90 percent of overtime went to "street patrolmen who spend a lot of time in court" and 10 percent went to the Warrant Squad, crime scene staff (in the radio room and crime laboratory), and community relations staff like PAL officers, police were earning extra money from the existence of crime.[99] While actual crime was present in a society filled with economic uncertainty, instances of officer-citizen confrontation, false arrests, and police brutality may have also been induced to give police a greater opportunity to earn overtime.

Furthermore, in a city where government officials were obsessed with curbing job flight, white flight, depopulation, and budget deficits, fighting black crime was a simple strategy that would yield a multitude of supposedly positive economic results. During the 1920s and beyond, African American migrants of the Great Migration were scapegoated as the cause of economic downturns, racial tension between black and white people, and the changing demography of a diversifying city. City officials and residents who refused to watch Philadelphia evolve into a more racially and culturally diverse city fought back with not only overt and covert forms of social discrimination but also police power. By the 1970s, city officials positioned the highest-contributing taxpayers as their ideal constituency at the expense of people of color, the working class, and the poor, who also uplifted Philadelphia and desired an equitable place in their city. City officials who believed there were more benefits in appeasing the middle and upper classes, which were majority white, allowed the police department to seize larger and larger pieces of Philadelphia's budgetary spending, even if it resulted in race and class-based stigmatization, discriminatory policing, police violence, and the violation of citizens' civil rights. Nevertheless, the police abuses of power and citizens' resistance to that issue in the 1970s demonstrated how Philadelphia's city government operated from the perspective that profit-yielding residents are ideal citizens and everyone else is less important. Moreover, black citizens and their allies' struggle for social justice and police accountability were part of a larger movement seeking to curb the widening of the racial wealth gap, hypersegregation, and the defunding of social welfare programs that largely benefited the working class and people of color. Philadelphians' hopeful struggle to have African Americans seen as ideal citizens regardless of their economic status is an ongoing affair, and peaceful protest and testimony highlighting government-sanctioned police injustices make up one of many steps toward the realization of that goal.

Conclusion

In an era of tough-on-crime policing, street crime (real and imagined) was commonplace, and police were encouraged by the mayor, the police department, and the city to control it. Since social welfare programs appeared to be incapable of curbing crime, the city engaged in a form of racial capitalism by investing in the police department to curb black crime. While funds to other city offices and programs decreased, the police department and its labor force were financially strengthened.[1] From the 1950s through the 1970s, Philadelphia's city officials believed tough-on-crime policing was the best crisis-prevention plan for achieving financial stability. Many politicians and police believed and even witnessed how community-centric social welfare programs were capable of solving black gang violence and the roots of "black crime" like poverty, racism, and marginalization. Over time, those ideas were largely ignored because they would challenge the socioeconomic hierarchy that privileged some while disadvantaging others. Instead, Philadelphia city officials chose a strategy that exists to this day. As Larry Krasner—former defense attorney, civil rights activist, and current district attorney (2017–25)—explained in his observation of Philadelphia as a policed city for more than thirty years, they "continued to fund cops at the expense of desperately needed resources for public education, treatment for mental illness, addiction, and trauma, and economic development—all the things we know actually prevent crime."[2] City officials chose to maintain the social caste system by investing in the police to assist with everything: curbing crime, stopping white flight, halting the dwindling tax base, and hopefully reinvesting as loyal taxpayers to uplift the city out of its never-ending budget deficit.

For Philadelphia City Council, interest in maintaining a stable tax base went from a common postwar big-city concern about its decreased revenue in the 1950s to panic about its steady decline in the 1970s and onward. For three decades, city officials entrusted the police department to assist in halting the city's financial deficit in unique ways. For Philadelphia, the 1950s began as a decade where city government could have a fresh start after City Council spent four years investigating and eliminating citywide corruption with the help of the press and the Committee of Fifteen, composed of five councilmen and ten civic group representatives. Following the investigation, approximately 128 city officials—including ward leaders, magistrates, a tax official, a fire marshal, and the head of the police vice squad—faced criminal charges of public stealing, forgery, and embezzlement, and approximately $40 million in city spending was deemed missing. After Philadelphia faced local and national embarrassment over the "exposure of municipal corruption," City Council sought to reform the government by granting the mayor more political power under a new city charter approved by voters and taking a firmer responsibility over municipal budget spending.[3]

Furthermore, one way city officials saw fit to maintain an "austere" budget and replenish the city's coffers was to tackle parking meter theft committed by youth and adults from ages eight to eighty-two, which cost the city approximately $250,000 in revenue each year. In 1957 alone, the police department made 588 arrests for "larceny from parking meters" with 223 cases involving youth. Adults were sent to jail, dismissed, or held for grand jury, while youth like ten-year-old Marshall Chandler and his eight-year-old brother William, who were repeat offenders of the crime, were sent to the Youth Study Center as punishment. In search of a finite solution to the issue, city officials took advice from the police department instead of the courts to curb widespread parking meter theft. Police Commissioner Thomas J. Gibbons responded to city officials' concern about the loss in revenue from theft or damage of any one of the fourteen thousand parking meters across Philadelphia's twenty-three police districts by stating that the police department needed "complete cooperation from the court" by issuing fines for people arrested for the crime. "We're using precious manpower trying to end this loss of hundreds of thousands of dollars a year," Gibbons added. "If we can't discourage it by confinement, or fines to pay the average of $22 it costs to repair a meter, there's no sense wasting our men on the job. They [the police] could be out fighting crime." By December 1957, City Council set the penalty for parking meter vandalism as a fifty-dollar fine or thirty days in jail. Then revenue commissioner Mortin E. Rotman added more collectors to the payroll to shorten the time frame between collections, which reduced how much money could be stolen from the meters, but increased city expenses in funding workers to complete the job.[4]

By 1959, City Council president James H. J. Tate argued before City Council that the city's real estate tax base be widened by spending $10 million on land, industries, and programs that would lead to the creation of new jobs and real estate along with the collection of tax revenue from newly constructed houses, apartments, hotels, commercial properties, and industrial plants for the 1960–61 fiscal year to meet the growing costs of government services, including the funding of public schools.[5] For Tate, this strategy was a preemptive maneuver to halt tax revenue losses incurred during an era of job flight and white flight and spark consumer interest in new homes, highway-accessible businesses, and even a sports stadium. Additionally, the chairman of City Council's finance committee, Victor E. Moore, supported Tate, stating that there was no need for additional city taxes that would burden residents because Philadelphia had a "carefully budgeted" fiscal program that was designed to keep the city stable until January 1961. However, Moore suggested that there was hope in getting the city out of financial debt and possibly a budget surplus if the state and federal governments granted the city at least $2 million in funding for Philadelphia General Hospital (which largely treated poor African Americans), public housing, and urban redevelopment. He predicted that with rising costs and inflation, city budgeting would be difficult in years to come: "The going will be grim for all big cities. The demand for municipal services will increase, wages will be higher, pension obligations will go up and debt costs will rise." Moore also emphasized that City Council "must strive desperately to halt emigration from the city to the suburbs" and said he would implement austerity in how he granted or denied funding to city departments and programs: "I shall continue to strive for a thorough appraisal of the economic and social consequences of each city program put forth and to give proper priority to those judged worthy. When prices rise, more money must be found to pay our bills or we are compelled to deny ourselves some of the things we deem essential."[6] Nevertheless, this era in which city officials sought to tighten Philadelphia's budget was also a time when the police department fought to keep the city's neighborhoods safe and moral by pursuing violent crimes like rape, murder, robbery, and burglary as their first priority, while policing social disorder and vice that allegedly occurred in bars, cafés, parks, and city streets came second.[7]

During the 1960s, city officials were focused on not only expanding local real estate to boost the tax base but also using police power to protect it on behalf of the tax-paying business owners who feared the destruction of their commercial property when protests, marches, rallies, uprisings, and riots around the issue of civil rights "threatened" their existence in residential, commercial, and tourist districts. At the start of this decade, Mayor Richardson Dilworth agreed with City Council president Tate on broadening the realty tax base to "renew and rehabilitate" the city and proposed that the municipal government and residents continue to support the effort. In his August 1960 editorial in the *Philadelphia Inquirer*, Dilworth explained to the public that upon recommendation of the city administration to increase city revenue by $93 million in four years, he planned to maintain investments in real estate and industry expansion rather than increase the wage tax, real estate tax, and gross receipt tax on businesses. Dilworth's editorial acknowledged that the decline of industry and construction of new real estate along with the loss of taxpayers to the point where "it could no longer support the needs of the city" had left Philadelphia with a shrinking tax base, the looming threat of a defunded Board of Education, and the "decay into which our city had been permitted to sink." However, he also expressed hope that Philadelphia's current redevelopment projects involving what would become new housing and industries (of tourism, commercialism, and industrialism) in the neighborhoods of Washington Square East and Society Hill in Center City and Eastwick in Southwest Philadelphia would achieve City Council's four-year revenue goal. Dilworth claimed that the city already attracted private capital that would add over $200 million to real estate tax values and his next goal was to attract $200 million worth of industrial plants and forty thousand industrial jobs in the next five years to increase the real estate tax and wage tax revenue without increasing taxes on current taxpayers. Overall, Mayor Dilworth was highly aware that Philadelphia was in a serious competition with the counties of Delaware, Montgomery, Chester, and Bucks in Pennsylvania and Camden, Burlington, and Gloucester in New Jersey for taxpayers and revenue, so he set out to reverse the "flight of business, industry, and building construction" to those counties and "re-attract" them to Philadelphia by 1964.[8]

In addition to City Council's fears of job flight and depopulation, city officials were also concerned about meeting the increase in municipal pension payments to over eight thousand retired policemen, firemen, and other former city employees when the price tag reached over $14 million per year. The overworked staff at the Board of Pensions and Retirement were worried about retirees receiving their checks on time, especially individuals who left Philadelphia to live on the Jersey Shore or in Florida. However, City Council was concerned about having enough funds over time to pay retirees and survivors with money from approximately 27,000 city workers who were currently paying into retirement, the 13,500 former city employees who had their contributions on deposit, and the over $38 million in assets held in the municipal retirement system. Philadelphia needed more taxpayers, employed and retired, to boost the city's revenue and help it survive during times of a budget deficit.[9] Nevertheless, while the mayor and City Council spent years trying to avoid raising taxes, from 1961 onward, the real estate tax and wage tax increased almost annually, and special taxes were implemented from time to time to meet certain municipal needs.[10]

From 1963 to 1968, local iterations of the Civil Rights Movement involving protests, marches, rallies, and even uprisings occurred often in Philadelphia. These events presented a financial issue for city officials who wanted to maintain social order on city streets with assistance from multiple city departments, particularly the police. City officials labeled events like the 1963 Municipal Construction Project protests against employment discrimination, the 1964 Columbia Avenue Riots against police brutality, and the 1965 Girard College protests for school desegregation as "civil emergencies" even if some events were peaceful or organized by highly esteemed institutions like the National Association for the Advancement of Colored People (NAACP), the Congress of Racial Equality (CORE), and the Black People's Unity Movement (BPUM).[11] Since these social protests challenged Philadelphia's race- and class-based hierarchies and had the potential to cause tension among tax-paying residents who could leave the city at any time, the Tate administration sought to contain them with police power.

From January 1, 1968, to June 30, 1969, the city's planned budget was $693.5 million, with $85 million slated to fund the police. In December 1968, Mayor Tate, who once referred to the Girard College demonstration as an "extremist action" causing an "unsavory condition" in the community, took issue with the fact that $24.5 million of the city's surplus fund was nearly gone due to protests and uprisings that required extra services from the police, fire, and streets departments.[12] According to Philadelphia's finance director, Edward J. Martin, twelve city departments overspent approximately $23.5 million of the surplus fund, with $14.2 million going to the police department for overtime, equipment, and other services. The 1968 protests and civil unrest situations that were singled out by Tate's administration for causing the depletion of the surplus fund included a Rittenhouse Square antiwar rally in February, the aftermath of the assassination and funeral of Dr. Martin Luther King Jr. in April, a Temple University student sit-in and the Poor People's March in May, and the National Black Power Conference in August. According to Martin, "extraordinary additional expense" for the police was necessary because city officials believed these social activist events would yield "unanticipated and potentially riotous conditions" in which, by their estimation, the police were best suited to "maintain calm in the troubled neighborhoods and to prepare for dangerous situations." Nevertheless, Police Commissioner Frank Rizzo, aware that city officials heavily relied on the police department to curb social disturbances that would disrupt everyday life and business in the city, requested that City Council grant the police department an additional $2 million in six months to handle future emergencies with firearms training, fifty-four new police cars, gas masks, three buses, and foot patrol radio equipment.[13] Thus began a tradition in which the police department could make a believable yet expensive plea for funding outside of the city's budget, and City Council felt bound to approve it rather than pursue other options to maintain peace on city streets.

By January 1969, Director of Finance Edward J. Martin advised Mayor Tate's Tax Study Advisory Committee to cut $12.4 million in spending from thirty-nine municipal agencies to preserve the city's emergency fund and increase taxes for the 1969–70 fiscal year. In light of the potential budget cuts, Police Commissioner Rizzo requested a twelve-month budget of $93 million for the police department. Despite Rizzo's demands,

City Council planned to cut $2,997,246 from the police department's budget, which included eliminating all police overtime worth $1.8 million. The city would garner an additional savings of $729,500 by leaving current officer vacancies unfilled. The Tax Study Advisory Committee also proposed cutting $4.5 million in spending from other vital agencies, which included approximately $1.7 million for Philadelphia General Hospital, $1.6 million for the streets department, and $1.2 million for the public welfare department mainly by eliminating payments for outpatient and emergency care, overtime, and childcare in foster homes and private institutions, respectively. Additionally, the committee advised cutbacks that affected education, social life, and recreation—like $198,341 for the Free Library, $407,000 for Fairmount Park, $430,935 for the public health department, and $677,400 in contributions to the Academy of Natural Sciences, the Franklin Institute, and the Pennsylvania Academy of the Fine Arts.[14] Moreover, although the police department was allotted a budget of $80 million in 1970, city spending on the police budget and overtime ballooned to over $150 million per year during the 1970s despite City Council's desire to be frugal across all city departments.

By the 1970s, Frank Rizzo's transition from police commissioner to mayor of Philadelphia shaped the city into becoming a big tough-on-crime spender while simultaneously expanding the realty tax base by redeveloping malls, shopping districts, and tourist attractions—particularly in Center City—that would draw in consumers and revitalize the city. From 1970 to 1980, Philadelphia lost 10 percent of its population when over two hundred thousand people left the city, and the surrounding suburbs grew in population by 23 percent. In North, West, and South Philadelphia, where historic immigrant and black communities had lived for the past one hundred years, the population decreased by 15 to 30 percent. However, the Northeast, a nearly all-white area located adjacent to the suburbs, saw a 6 percent population increase, while Center City's population remained unchanged. Additionally, from about 1951 to 1977, the city's factory-based work force decreased from 46 percent to 24 percent, demonstrating that the manufacturing industry was no longer the "backbone of Philadelphia's economy."[15] Therefore, when Rizzo became mayor of Philadelphia in 1972, he continued the asset-building strategies of investing in real estate that James H. J. Tate and Richardson Dilworth promoted as city councilman and mayor of the city.

Rizzo gave his approval for a series of public and private construction projects totaling $635.5 million to improve Center City and beyond. Among the projects Rizzo greenlighted were the creation of three private office buildings, four major hospital projects that included the Children's Hospital of Philadelphia (CHOP), the downtown commuter tunnel linking the subway, elevated train, trolley, and regional rail systems together, the restoration of several historic buildings and homes surrounding Independence Hall, the Gallery Mall, and the renovation of the historic Bellevue-Stratford Hotel. Overall, city government prioritized the services industry in these revitalization projects meant to spark a return of residents to the city and steer consumers away from suburban "department stores, supermarkets, family restaurants, movie theaters, and specialty shops," since approximately 60 percent of the projects focused on improving medical, educational, and governmental institutions, 18 percent were geared toward "residential and commercial activity," and 3 percent were for industrial building.[16]

However, after the recession of 1974–75 occurred, the Rizzo administration was prepared to implement major cutbacks when Philadelphia faced a budget deficit of $100 million by May 1976.[17] During that time, Finance Director Lennox Moak proposed that City Council raise the city wage tax and real estate tax while also laying off 1,013 city employees, including 264 from the streets department. This decision presented many disadvantages for Philadelphians. Aside from general cutbacks in city services, the most immediate consequences residents would face were inadequate trash collection and street cleaning along with major delays in sanitation workers handling the roughly three hundred complaints per day they received concerning potholes, streetlight outages, and other maintenance and repair issues throughout the city. The two long-term consequences of those cutbacks were that city officials would have to fund overtime for streets department employees in times of emergency and there was the looming threat of a strike organized by overworked yet unionized city workers across all municipal departments who wanted to support their fellow employees who were laid off. Additionally, the city could risk having "dirty streets" when 10 to 15 million tourists were expecting to visit a beautified city for the 1976 bicentennial celebration of the thirteen colonies' declaration of independence from Great Britain and the subsequent founding of America.

Since City Council facilitated the investment of hundreds of millions of dollars into new real estate and industries throughout the city, the local government needed police to protect their financial investments, investors, consumers, and "ideal" residents from crime to ensure that economic growth continued to rise in Philadelphia. As historian Stephanie G. Wolf explained, Mayor Rizzo and his supporters saw the local government as an "institution for providing citizens with protection and only secondarily as an instrument for the delivery of social services."[18] Despite over one thousand municipal workers being laid off, countless city employees in fear of a pay freeze, and the closing of Philadelphia General Hospital due to budget cuts, Rizzo won the 1976 Democratic primary election that would lead to his mayoral reelection later that year. Although Rizzo made campaign promises of "holding the line" on taxes, protecting city jobs, and granting twenty thousand municipal workers a pay raise, he had no definite plan for how to get the funds to pay for it. Eventually, Rizzo had to ask the state legislature and City Council for a 30 percent increase in income and property taxes, while Finance Director Moak had to balance the budget like he did in the prior year when he turned a $19 million budget deficit into a surplus by recording expected state and federal financial commitments to Philadelphia as revenue.[19] However, Rizzo was committed to granting police (and firemen) a 4 percent wage increase despite the budget crisis, and so during the 1976 fiscal year, city budget spending for the police and prisons increased by 90 to 110 percent of their 1970 figures, with each department receiving $152.5 million and $18.8 million, respectively.

Rizzo's continued advocacy for the police department from the time he was appointed police commissioner in 1967 to the end of his mayoral term in 1980 involved making sure that the police were fully funded and received as much overtime as the department requested at the expense of taxpayers and other city departments. For example, in February 1971, two homicide detectives were known as the "kings of overtime" because they nearly doubled their two-week salary by working between sixteen and nineteen hours beyond their usual shift.[20] For overtime to continue, hyperpolicing—particularly in stigmatized, poor, and nonwhite neighborhoods—had to exist.

In the April 1977 *Philadelphia Inquirer* article "The Homicide Files, Part I," journalists Jonathan Neumann and William K. Marimow theorized that "money" was the motive behind overtime being a popular task within the eighty-four-member homicide division.[21] Based on three years of research, Neumann and Marimow investigated how, among 433 homicide cases handled by the police department, eighty of them were ruled by common pleas court judges to have involved illegal police investigations. In many of these cases, suspects and witnesses were handcuffed, tortured with beatings and threats, and forced by detectives to make false confessions during interrogations that could last up to twenty-four hours.[22] The article also mentioned that while people were brutalized and actual criminal offenders were never pursued once a case was "closed," homicide detectives in 1976 earned an average of $7,575 in overtime according to the city's payroll records. In that same year, one detective, Michael Chitwood, received a salary higher than Police Commissioner O'Neill's due to overtime: $36,293.[23] Crime narratives, including ones about uncontrollable black gangs, provided justification for hyperpolicing and intense police interrogations. Citizens were, in part, conditioned to solely rely on police instead of community interventionists to effectively combat social unrest and crime, giving the Philadelphia Police Department's director of administration, Philip H. Carroll, the ease of making statements like this in 1971: "You can call for a police officer here and you get one fast or someone's not doing their job. In other cities, New York for instance, you can wait an hour. By that time it's usually too late."[24] Overall, the article highlighted how power and greed played a role in a capitalist system where disadvantaged communities were exploited to garner wealth for others. Today, the issue, though widely known, largely remains unresolved.

According to urban anthropologists Judith Goode and Jo Anne Schneider, at least 75 percent of Philadelphia's current labor force operates in nonmanufacturing fields, which include services in business, education, law, and health care, FIRE (finance, insurance, and real estate), retail and wholesale trade, TCPU (transportation/communication/public utilities), and construction.[25] From these industries, Philadelphia gets the bulk of its taxpayers; however, tax revenue from these citizens still isn't sufficient to produce a healthy tax base for the city. And as a result of continued deindustrialization, job flight, and white flight since the 1970s, we have a city dependent on a system of racial capitalism in which not only police but also many other middle- and upper-class professionals profit from the existence of crime and gun violence that largely affects African Americans and other people of color. Surgeons, nurses, forensic investigators, medical examiners, morticians, bail bondsmen, lawyers, judges, bailiffs, correctional officers, wardens, journalists, and politicians all profit financially in a carceral state. The unresolved issues of poverty-induced crime and racially biased policing mean that unfortunately, there will always be a dysfunctional cycle in which society thrives on a constant oversupply of working-class, poor, and people of color to arrest, hospitalize, bury, prosecute, incarcerate, and report crime narratives about for the general public's consumption. History has shown us that as long as poverty, institutional racism, and social inequality rooted in antiblackness persist, our society will always be wrought with racial tension, violence, crime, police abuse, and greed.[26] Ultimately, the question that remains is what are we, as everyday citizens, voters, and activists for our community, going to do to change the future ahead of us?

Afterword

They are, in effect, still trapped in a history which they do not
understand; and until they can understand it, they cannot be
released from it.
—James Baldwin, *The Fire Next Time*, 1963

Around 5:00 p.m. on May 24, 2019, I visited Old Pine Presbyterian Cemetery after a long week of researching to find the grave of slain graduate student In-Ho Oh. It was the Friday before Memorial Day weekend, and in the historic cemetery, adjacent to Old Pine Street Church in Society Hill, were miniature American flags and emblems lining the graves of military veterans from the colonial era to the twentieth century. At the southbound end of the cemetery was Oh's grave, not far from a red-brick walkway that led to a square, brown-stoned veterans' memorial. Oh's grave was shaded by a pine tree and surrounded by magenta-colored geraniums lying in direct sunlight. And like in the 1958 newspaper articles I read about Oh's death, his headstone read, "To Turn Sorrow into Christian Purpose."[1] After having perused several newspapers, letters, and photographs about the short life of twenty-six-year-old Oh in the archives, my experience of sitting on a bench beside his grave in such a patriotic environment made this book go full circle.

Next to Oh's headstone was a stone marker describing in trite detail how Oh lost his life to "hoodlums" who only wanted "35 cents." Predictably, the obituary silenced the "hoodlums" who murdered Oh and suggested that the crime the eleven black youth committed was senseless because Oh was "bludgeoned" for pocket change.[2] The murder of Oh was an unprovoked tragedy, but the obituary ignored the larger picture of this crime. Beyond the teenagers' motive to acquire money for admission to a party in the integrating middle-class neighborhood of Powelton Village was a bigger story of social rejection and exclusion. It was a story of rage and rebellion birthed from socioeconomic ostracism and

Author's photos of the George Floyd Protests against police brutality in Philadelphia, June 3, 2020.

stigma based on race, class, and residency.[3] Philadelphia's history of segregation, poverty, slum housing, job discrimination, and racially biased policing partially created the social conditions for the murder to occur. Nevertheless, the life experiences of the black teenage boys from Mantua who killed Oh were largely ignored and forgotten.

Throughout Philadelphia's history, the murders of innocent victims like Oh and citizens' fear of crime triggered social and political action from community activists, police, and politicians to prevent crime. Although it has been more than sixty years since Oh's death, American society still has not fully realized the correlation between inequality and poverty-induced crime. Today, no one seems to care about issues of poverty, crime, and violence unless someone of high esteem or youthful innocence is murdered. So many human tragedies in our communities could be prevented if our society was truly equal and fair for all.

As sociologist Alex S. Vitale argues in his 2017 book *The End of Policing*, poverty, racial segregation, and the lack of socioeconomic opportunities for youth and adults are the roots of crime, including gang violence.[4] In 1958, Oh's parents offered the city of Philadelphia five hundred dollars to create a rehabilitation fund for the eleven boys who robbed and murdered their son. As Oh's father, Ko-Phung Oh, explained, "I understand that American laws are very strict, but we will make every effort to achieve our objectives and help these errant youth."[5] Moreover, Oh's family donated the funds because they suspected that the dysfunctional nature of racial ostracism and poverty influenced the teenagers to commit the crimes without considering the moral and legal consequences of their actions.

Today, the United States holds more than 20 percent of the global prison population despite composing only 5 percent of the world's population. As a result, American metropolises like Philadelphia are among the top carceral cities in the world.[6] Philadelphia's history of socioeconomic criminalization and tough-on-crime policing has definitely shaped its carceral identity, but state laws and politics have facilitated the mass incarceration of marginalized groups. And consequently, to this day, there is inconsistent government support for citywide programs offering poverty alleviation, nonviolent crime prevention, and rehabilitation to citizens.

Since the 1970s, Pennsylvania legislators have increased the number of criminal offenses from 282 to nearly 1,500 while also heavily utilizing

Response Time vs. Resident Demographics by Police District for All 911 Calls

Majority-minority districts with the longest response times are shown in blue

Average Call to Dispatch Time

More white residents →

Faster response times ↓

40 min. — **35**th

25th

30 min. — **19**th

12th

20 min.

10 min.

0%   20%   40%   60%   80%

Percent of White Residents in District

Source: PPD report entitled MIS police response times by event type for calls in calendar year 2021

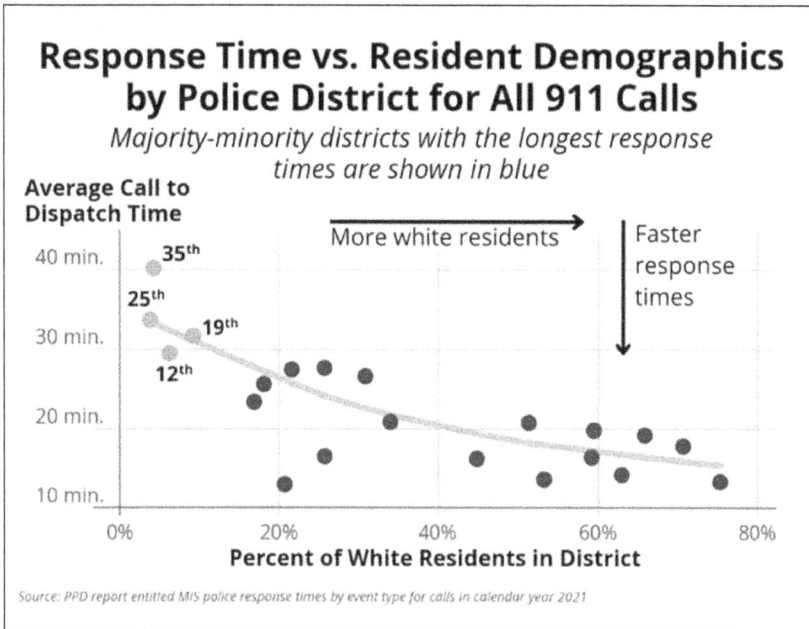

Chart featured in City Controller Rebecca Rhynhart's "Review and Analysis of the Philadelphia Police Department and Other Related Police Spending" detailing the racial disparity in how fast police respond to 911 emergency calls by police district in Philadelphia.

mandatory minimum sentencing laws and high sentencing guidelines for individuals convicted of crime.[7] Although Pennsylvania Supreme Court cases like *Commonwealth v. Bradley* (1972) temporarily succeeded in making capital punishment unconstitutional, by 1978, the legislature edited the death penalty bill and received approval from the Pennsylvania and US Supreme Courts to reinstate the controversial sentencing. With this significant increase in carceral legislation, Philadelphia had been the only big city in the Northeast region of the United States to legally sentence countless juveniles to life imprisonment and even death until Governor Tom Wolf declared a death penalty moratorium in the state in 2015.[8]

From the 1980s to 2017, the mass incarceration of people in jails and prisons increased by 500 percent nationally, but in Pennsylvania, the rate was over 700 percent.[9] The drastic increase in incarcerated persons was largely a consequence of the nationally recognized "law-and-order" approach to fighting (black) crime that Rizzo utilized to make Philadelphians feel safe enough to continue their lives, jobs, and businesses in the city. To some residents, white *and* black, Philadelphia appeared to be safer under Rizzo's term in office. Unfortunately, crime persisted, and police-community violence continued in the 1980s as society became less economically collectivist and racially integrated. President Ronald Reagan's "trickle-down" economics policy, which lowered corporate and estate taxes while providing tax benefits that included retirement savings, lower mortgage rates, and charitable giving incentives for the wealthy, disadvantaged the lower and middle classes, who paid higher taxes but received few tax breaks and inefficient government services.[10]

Additionally, the national Cocaine Epidemic not only sparked a rise in theft, drug dealing, drug possession, gun violence, and murder but also triggered Reagan's War on Drugs, which involved overpolicing lower-income urban (black) neighborhoods for drug-related crimes instead of treating them the same way as white suburban communities, which were often humanized for their drug offenses with the offering of rehabilitation instead of incarceration.[11] As a result of the War on Drugs's race and class bias in policing, arresting, and incarcerating, black people are ten times more likely than white people to be incarcerated for drug offenses even though both groups use drugs at approximately the same rates. Aside from incarceration due to drug-related crimes, the American Civil Liberties Union (ACLU) estimates that general rates of imprisonment remain racially biased, since one out of three black boys, one out of six Latino boys, and one out of seventeen white boys today are likely to go to jail or prison in their lifetime.[12]

By 2017, among Pennsylvania's sixty-seven counties, 27 percent of state prisoners received their sentence in Philadelphia. While the national rate for adults on probation or parole was 1.8 percent, Philadelphia's rate was the highest among big cities in America at 4.3 percent for the general population and 7.1 percent for African Americans.[13] On September 28, 2022, the Public Interest Law Center of Philadelphia (PILCOP) and the Prison Policy Initiative released the report *Where People in Prison Come from: The Geography of Mass Incarceration in Pennsylvania*, in which they detailed how Philadelphia sends the most people to prison in Pennsylvania at a rate of 463 per 100,000 residents. The report also suggested that historic racial segregation and inequality in

TABLE 3: 911 RESPONSE TIMES VS. DEMOGRAPHICS BY DISTRICT, CY 2021
Sorted by response time for all calls (Priority 1-6), from fastest to slowest

Police District	Average Call To Dispatch Response Time by Priority in Minutes							Resident Demographics, as a Percent of Total			
	1	2	3	4	5	6	1 - 6	White	Black	Hispanic	Asian
22	01:52	19:45	21:59	19:27	11:03	22:35	12:59	21%	64%	6%	5%
5	01:39	16:05	15:29	22:52	15:19	24:58	13:18	75%	10%	5%	4%
1	01:39	19:01	19:05	21:44	19:45	36:47	13:36	53%	22%	6%	15%
7	01:43	16:14	14:53	20:19	18:12	23:46	14:10	63%	8%	7%	17%
17	01:39	21:59	20:52	26:07	15:19	32:02	16:11	45%	34%	7%	9%
6	01:57	20:39	21:07	25:32	21:01	33:45	16:22	59%	14%	7%	15%
18	01:34	24:58	25:12	27:49	22:56	31:53	16:28	26%	51%	5%	12%
9	01:54	21:31	22:08	27:17	23:24	28:41	17:47	71%	8%	6%	11%
8	02:11	25:57	21:24	29:17	23:42	30:55	19:08	66%	14%	11%	6%
3	02:03	26:18	26:35	31:08	27:40	42:46	19:44	59%	7%	13%	17%
26	02:14	31:32	32:50	36:06	22:57	42:16	20:42	51%	15%	23%	6%
15	02:54	32:03	25:19	23:08	20:39	27:36	20:48	34%	26%	28%	7%
39	02:35	40:17	38:04	31:00	51:52	23:18	17%	71%	5%	2%	
14	02:14	39:48	33:38	37:17	33:49	49:39	25:32	18%	72%	4%	1%
24	03:05	37:59	46:36	53:26	38:27	71:20	26:32	31%	15%	47%	4%
16	02:14	38:09	46:14	44:13	30:44	54:08	27:22	22%	60%	5%	9%
2	04:01	39:57	34:21	33:22	27:43	34:04	27:34	26%	29%	24%	15%
12	02:17	45:35	45:09	46:15	32:51	65:40	29:26	6%	81%	4%	5%
19	02:45	47:08	48:33	55:03	37:32	71:25	31:38	9%	81%	3%	2%
25	03:30	48:32	55:45	55:04	43:30	79:42	33:37	4%	27%	65%	2%
35	02:46	62:15	58:39	58:11	59:51	76:12	40:07	4%	71%	14%	8%

Table featured in City Controller Rebecca Rhynhart's "Review and Analysis of the Philadelphia Police Department and Other Related Police Spending" detailing the racial disparity in how fast police respond to emergency calls (ranging from life-threatening Priority 1 Calls to nonviolent and nuisance Priority 6 Calls) in Philadelphia.

Philadelphia have played a role in the neighborhoods most affected by mass incarceration when it identified the majority-black, low-income North Philadelphia neighborhood of Nicetown-Tioga as a place where residents are "more than fifty times as likely to be imprisoned" than residents of the majority-white and upper-middle-class "Center City–West neighborhood."[14]

The issues of double victimization and racial capitalism disproportionately affect poor communities of color in regard to crime and policing. Poor black communities often face double victimization through government neglect and economic exploitation but are also blamed for crime, real and imagined. City governments like Philadelphia's have had the ability to reduce crime through poverty alleviation initiatives like decent housing, education, and jobs for generations, but they refuse to wholeheartedly do so and instead invest in the police department and corrections to curb crime. This system of racial capitalism involving the overfunding of police and the underfunding of social welfare programs that could lift people out of poverty creates social conditions that lead to higher rates of poverty-induced crime, black incarceration, black unemployment, and black recidivism.[15]

Today, Philadelphia's poverty rate is approximately 23 percent, with many of the same neighborhoods suffering from concentrated poverty also experiencing high crime and overpolicing (or, in some cases, underpolicing). In the 1970s, the Philadelphia Police Department argued that a large, fully equipped and funded police force was necessary to reduce crime, but today, many Philadelphians experience long wait times in response to their 911 emergency calls, especially in neighborhoods with large percentages of people of color.[16] Although the Philadelphia Police Department's goal is to answer 911 calls within ten seconds, from 2017 to 2021, the percentage of calls that met that goal dropped from 95 percent to 68 percent. From July to September 2022, the rate increased to 85 percent, which was still below the Pennsylvania Emergency Management Agency's mandated benchmark of 90 percent. Additionally, in 2021, the average call-to-dispatch response time differed based on the racial composition of the neighborhood. For example, in the Fifth Police District (serving the Northwest neighborhoods of Roxborough and Manayunk), where 75 percent of residents are white, police took an average of one minute and thirty-nine seconds to respond to a Priority 1 call (involving a violent, life-threatening crime in-progress, like a shooting or burglary) and under twenty-five minutes to respond to a Priority 6 call (involving a nonviolent and/or nonlife-threatening crime, like vandalism or theft). However, in comparison to the majority-white Fifth Police District, the Twenty-Fifth and Thirty-Fifth Police Districts (serving the North Philadelphia neighborhoods of Hunting Park, Fairhill, Juniata Park, Feltonville, Olney, Oak Lane, and East Oak Lane), where the population of African Americans, Latinos, and Asians combined made up 93 to 94 percent of residents, saw police respond to Priority 1 calls at an average of two and a half to three and a half minutes and Priority 6 calls at an average of seventy-six to nearly eighty minutes.[17]

Since 2017, Philadelphia's twenty-one police districts have approximately 70 to 190 officers in each, with 10 to 22 officers available for patrol depending on whether the area served is a low-crime or high-crime district. Although there are often more police officers stationed in districts with higher percentages of people of color and working-class status, unpredictable staff shortages due to officers on vacation or sick leave, unequal spending on officers' salaries and overtime compensation (regardless of crime levels) across the districts, and low officer morale greatly contribute to the delayed response police have to emergency calls.[18] For more than half a decade, the police department has tried to reduce crime, gun violence, and excessive police force by implementing a series of strategies to break the cycle of poverty, crime, and incarceration. In 2017, Philadelphia launched the Police Assisted Diversion (PAD) program, which trains officers to divert low-level and nonviolent criminal offenders who engage in retail theft, prostitution, and drug possession to social services instead of funneling individuals through the carceral system and increasing the economic and social costs of "incarceration, court-time, and employment / family disruption resulting from arrest."[19] In 2019, the police department piloted Operation Pinpoint, a program that uses intelligence-based research from "historical gang information"; data from stops, arrests, and crimes; reports of blight (like graffiti, abandoned cars, illegal dumping, and inadequate lighting); and "social network analysis" along with "community-oriented" yet racially stigmatizing maneuvers involving police patrols (by foot, bike, and car) and "mere encounters" of officers randomly questioning residents to curb crime in forty-five "hotspot areas" or "grids" across the city.[20] And most recently, in 2020, the Philadelphia Police Department began the Crisis Intervention Team (CIT), in which the department trained over 50 percent of its officers in how to handle mental health crises during emergency calls, while its 911 Triage and CoResponders Strategy program (started in 2022) has behavioral health navigators from the Department of Behavioral Health and Intellectual Disability Services act as coresponders with police on mental health crisis events in the Philadelphia Police Department's radio room and on city streets.[21] However, many of our issues with crime, gangs, and gun violence can be solved with stricter gun control laws and regulations (or just gun abolition altogether), defunding (and possibly, in the future, abolishing) the police, and reappropriating the city government's budget spending to finance widespread poverty alleviation programs. These changes could yield major benefits for Philadelphians.

Like in New York and Chicago, Philadelphia's city budget allocates tremendous amounts of money to police. For Philadelphia's 2021 fiscal year, the city's budget was approximately $4.9 billion, with $760 million slated to fund the police department.[22] According to an October 2022 review of the Philadelphia Police Department and its spending released by City Controller Rebecca Rhynhart, the Philadelphia Police Department neither conducts a "strategic" analysis of how many officers and hours are needed to meet "public safety goals" nor asks communities what they need from police before proposing its budget request but refers to "historical spending levels" to determine how much money it wants City Council to grant them each year. In fact, the Philadelphia Police Department's request of $760 million for an ideal department of 6,500 personnel was misleading because, in actuality, the Philadelphia Police Department has experienced serious staff shortages since the 2019 fiscal year due to attrition, low recruitment rates, and hundreds of officers being unavailable for patrol duty because of Injured on Duty (IOD) claims (though still receiving partial or full salaries).[23] As of June 30, 2022, the police department had 5,983 uniformed officers but approximately 2,500 assigned to patrols, 572 officers out on medical leave, and more than 400 vacancies.[24] Moreover, with nearly 1,000 officers unavailable to protect and serve the city, the costs for maintaining the police department are inflated and suggest internal issues of disorganization, a lack of oversight and accountability in maintaining sufficient records, and potential fraud.[25]

Since 1976, Philadelphia's city budget has decreased its funding of the police from 19 percent to 15.2 percent, but the Fraternal Order of Police (FOP) has often expropriated more money from the city through the settlement of criminal cases involving officers who engaged in corruption, sexual assault, and police brutality.[26] Additionally, numerous cases of police corruption and police brutality against nonwhite people continue to be a major cause of citizens' animosity toward and mistrust of the police, especially those from the black community.[27] For example, on May 13, 1985, a police helicopter bombed the 6221 Osage Avenue rowhome of John Africa, the founder of the back-to-nature black liberation group MOVE, after he and his followers refused to vacate the city-condemned home when five hundred police officers attempted to issue arrest warrants. The incident resulted in eleven deaths, the destruction of sixty-five homes, and 253 residents left homeless.[28] In an effort to take responsibility for the tragedy, Mayor W. Wilson Goode appointed the Philadelphia Special Investigation Commission (PSIC) to investigate the incident, and Police Commissioner Gregore Sambor resigned from his position that November. The city would also promise to restore homes to the 253 residents who were displaced in a twenty-three-year-long ordeal that would inevitably be marked with shoddy construction, extensive litigation, and an eventual payout of $5.4 million to thirty-six families who had to find new homes elsewhere.[29] Moreover, Goode and Sambor's original statement that MOVE was a "terrorist organization" that was not only a nuisance to Cobbs Creek homeowners but also a threat to police was a memorable narrative of police violence that still haunts the city today.[30] A year after the MOVE bombing, the Philadelphia Police Study Task Force conducted a survey on citizens' perceptions of the police and found that only 53 percent of African Americans gave a favorable rating of the department.[31] The survey also revealed that many Philadelphians, black *and* white, held animosity toward the police because they witnessed officers using excessive force, using illegal drugs, and receiving free meals, gifts, and sexual favors from criminals.[32]

More recently, police corruption specifically has been a serious and expensive issue in Philadelphia. From 2011 to 2019, there were approximately 170 cases of police misconduct in which the FOP sought to have cases dismissed, criminal charges reduced, and officers reinstated for crimes they allegedly committed on and off duty.[33] As a result of this extensive litigation, the City of Philadelphia spent $5 million for arbitration to review the criminal cases of accused officers, $4 million to settle federal lawsuits involving fifteen policemen, and $1.2 million in retroactive pay and other payments to officers who were fired and later reinstated.[34] Additionally, since 2015, Philadelphia has spent an average of $10 million each year to settle police misconduct claims. From 2017 to 2022 alone, the city spent $108,474,000 on settlement and litigation costs accrued by the police department, which composed 37 percent of the $297 million paid by the law department for Philadelphia's citywide litigation expenses.[35] Nevertheless, as *Philadelphia Inquirer* journalist Larissa Mogano summed up in her October 2019 article on the financial and social costs of an uncontrolled police department, "Philly's police misconduct cases drain taxpayer money. . . . These hefty bills take city money that could help renovate our schools or staff our libraries. Even worse, these payouts do not lead to a safer community for Philly residents, and they fracture communities' faith in the more trustworthy and law-abiding officers."[36]

By the end of 2019, the Institute for Survey Research at Temple University (ISR) conducted a survey of Philadelphians' opinions of the police that suggested a significant number of residents mistrusted the police based on their personal experiences with officers. The survey revealed that 43 percent of residents rated police officer conduct as "excellent or good" and only 26 percent of residents rated the police's ability to prevent crime as "excellent or good."[37] Among people of color, 22 percent of black residents and 21 percent of Hispanic residents rated police officer conduct as "poor," in comparison to 10 percent of white residents who expressed a similar sentiment in the survey.[38] Nevertheless, as in previous decades, the historically troubled reputation of the police department along with recent accounts of police misconduct have led many residents to feel uncomfortable and, at times, unsafe around police.

Racial capitalism driven by poverty-induced crime is also secretly embedded in the tax system. Police officers are guaranteed a well-paying job as long as crime exists. Between the 2017 to 2021 fiscal years, approximately 95 percent of the Philadelphia Police Department's budget went to personnel costs at a rate higher than Los Angeles, New York, and Chicago.[39] Within the costs for employee compensation, 8 percent of that budget (approximately $13.5 million) goes to overtime spending, but oftentimes the police department exceeds that allotment each year. In Philadelphia, police officers have the opportunity to participate in two types of overtime under the discretion of their district captain: nonreimbursable and reimbursable. Nonreimbursable overtime is the traditional type in which officers receive compensation for work outside of their usual schedule, while reimbursable overtime involves the police department essentially "hiring out" officers to "private sector" businesses like supermarkets and department stores to guard and patrol facilities as if they were armed security guards. Although the police department claims that police officers working reimbursable overtime can be called away to handle 911 calls at any time, this form of for-profit labor is detrimental to the city because it reduces the number of officers patrolling city streets, particularly in neighborhoods dealing with the issue of gun violence.[40] Additionally, the City of Philadelphia has also granted members of the FOP tax privileges that economically disadvantage the city, which relies heavily on the tax base fed by middle-class residents. For example, in 2010, the FOP petitioned and won the right for police officers to live outside of the city limits if they had served on the force for at least five years. In 2012, the revised residency requirement went into effect, and as a result, approximately 15 percent of the city's roughly 6,500-officer police force moved to the suburbs, taking their tax dollars with them.[41]

In 2017, Mayor Jim Kenney rejected the FOP's desire to completely eliminate the residency requirement on the grounds that the loss of property taxes from middle-class municipal workers like police officers would harm government funds to schools: "They should hang in the neighborhoods and help make the schools better. All of our residents need to pitch in and help with our schools."[42] At that time, the average police officer earned a salary of $75,000 a year. Although Philadelphia had approximately thirty thousand municipal workers, many of whom were confined to the residency requirement, the loss of even one thousand middle-class taxpayers would plunge the city further into debt.[43] In fact, since 1976, the city has often frozen the salaries of municipal workers and increased wage, property, and business taxes as short-term debt solutions that inevitably burden taxpayers in Philadelphia.[44] The other financial privileges uniquely granted to the FOP are an abundance of paid overtime and a 2.5 percent salary raise at the time of an officer's contract renewal. Benefits such as these for police—particularly the salary increase, which is 0.5 percent higher than that of other city workers—have historic precedence, as the former president of the AFSCME District Council 47 union supporting municipal workers in nonprofits and higher education, Thomas Paine Cronin, stated in a June 2020 interview: "They [police] were always given favored status. It's just part of the tradition in Philadelphia."[45]

Since June 2020, the municipal power of the police and the FOP has been called into question following mass protests against police brutality nationwide. The catalyst for these protests was the police killings of several unarmed black people over the span of four months: Breonna Taylor, Ahmaud Arbery, and George Floyd. The murder of George Floyd was particularly shocking because it was caught on camera and witnessed by several onlookers.[46] On May 25, 2020, Floyd, a forty-six-year-old black Minneapolis man, was arrested for counterfeiting, handcuffed, and later fatally restrained by Officer Derek Chauvin, who pinned his knee to Floyd's neck for approximately nine minutes and twenty-nine seconds as he laid in the street. The other three officers at the scene, J. Alexander Kueng, Thomas Lane, and Tou Thao, assisted Chauvin in the deadly incident by helping restrain Floyd, delaying the call for medical assistance, and preventing witnesses from intervening in the situation.[47]

Nationwide outrage over Floyd's death led to weeks of multiracial and multigenerational protests organized by groups like the Black Lives Matter movement in countless cities, including Los Angeles, Portland, Atlanta, and Washington, DC. In Philadelphia, thousands of protestors marched and chanted for justice down city streets while also holding rallies and calling for police reform, using slogans promoting "defunding" and "abolishing" the police.[48] In the midst of these peaceful protests were individuals who physically and verbally assaulted police, looted local businesses, and destroyed public and private property, including defacing structures with graffiti and burning buildings and police cars throughout the city.[49] Similar to the 1960s protests and riots against police brutality, some police conflated rioters and looters with peaceful protestors and chose to use unnecessary and brute force against the individuals they encountered during these demonstrations. Before the National Guard arrived to "restore order" and protect property and city landmarks, some police manhandled and beat protestors on city streets, while others dispersed crowds marching on the Vine Street Expressway and in the residential neighborhoods of West Philadelphia with teargas, rubber bullets, and allegedly long-range acoustic devices (LRADs).[50]

Additionally, there were even incidents of white vigilantism against black protest of police brutality in Philadelphia. In one event, a "group" of nearly one hundred white male residents from Fishtown sought to "protect" their neighborhood *and* police by walking the streets armed with baseball bats to deter "looters" and "rioters" from "destroying" their community.[51] In some instances, white police officers permitted the vigilantes to roam the neighborhood with "household weapons," while a few other officers took photos, did high-fives, and made friendly conversation with the armed men. Not only did these Fishtown vigilantes conflate protestors with rioters, but their use of dog whistle terms like *looters* enabled them to justify their desire to protect their majority-white neighborhood from the "spillage" of black rioting and vandalism happening in majority-black communities that they saw televised on the news.[52] However, the only "imminent threat" to their neighborhood was a multiracial and multigenerational group of Black Lives Matter protestors who wanted to march through Fishtown to protest the white supremacy that has often been undergirded by police power. Interestingly, the George Floyd–inspired mass protests against police brutality in part convinced Philadelphia City Council to reassess the city's relationship with police. On June 18, 2020, City Council announced that it was reducing the police department's 2021 budget by $33 million to finance a police oversight commission, provide body cameras and implicit-bias training for police, and install therapists to assist police in mental health crisis emergency calls. The budget revision also appropriated approximately $26.35 million toward health care, affordable housing, antipoverty initiatives, job training, and the arts.[53]

Despite the gradual acts of reconciliation city government has made in recent months, the relationship between police and black citizens in Philadelphia continues to be tumultuous. On October 26, 2020, the police shooting of twenty-seven-year-old Walter Wallace Jr. in Cobbs Creek caused outrage that sparked new peaceful protests but also violent uprisings over the issue of police brutality.[54] On that day, Wallace, a sufferer of bipolar disorder, had threatened his family with a knife and later went out into the street carrying the weapon. A relative called 911 for medical assistance to calm Wallace down, as he was experiencing a mental health episode, but police were sent to 61st and Locust Streets to deescalate the situation instead.

When police arrived at the scene, Officers Sean Matarazzo and Thomas Munz ordered Wallace to put down the knife eleven times before they shot him ten times in the shoulder and chest.[55] The shooting caused much uproar because Wallace was killed by police in front of his mother and neighbors, who repeatedly begged officers not to shoot him because he was mentally ill. Over the course of a week following the shooting, many Philadelphians peacefully protested in the streets about the death of Wallace. However, there were also uprisings and rioting that resulted in 225 residents arrested, sixty officers injured, 617 incidents of looting, eighteen vehicles damaged, and twenty-four ATM explosions throughout the city.[56] Both the peaceful protests and the uprisings had an impact on the city, but the antipolice uprisings that caused property damage and financial loss sent a clear message to city leaders that citizens would relentlessly demand police accountability in officer-involved shootings.

Immediately following the police shooting of Walter Wallace Jr., city officials and the police department attempted to regain citizens' trust by first apologizing to the Wallace family. Then the police department released police body cam footage of the shooting to the public to demonstrate that the police department was committed to transparency about the details of the case. The other actions city officials and the police took to gain Philadelphians' trust in handling the incident were discussing police-community relations with residents on the street and in town hall meetings along with pledging to equip more police officers with tasers so that they had a nondeadly weapon they could use to subdue a suspect. However, the death of Wallace called more attention to the idea of defunding the police.

The fact that police were the first responders to Wallace instead of medical officials is a prime example of how the institution of policing is ill-equipped to handle certain emergency calls that are assigned to them and a 411 crisis hotline should be established to handle mental health issues.[57] In fact, the entire situation involving Wallace was reminiscent of the February 1971 police shooting of Roger Allison, a mentally ill black man who was killed by police for threatening them with a whiskey bottle.[58] But Allison's death in 1971 was not the only precedent in which police were ill-equipped for an emergency call and mishandled the situation. On November 7, 1980, an incident of excessive force against a mentally ill man occurred when police attempted to arrest thirty-eight-year-old James Willis for murdering a construction worker in Brewerytown.[59] Willis, a former patient at the Fairview State Hospital for the Criminally Insane, died in police custody after more than one hundred firefighters and police used high-pressure water hoses and nightsticks, respectively, to subdue him.[60] Although police spent two hours trying to convince Willis to put down the knife he used to stab forty-four-year-old Walter Starks to death, the fire department's use of water hoses to force Willis to surrender was a racialized police control tactic similar to that used by Southern police departments during peaceful protests for integration during the Civil Rights Movement. Moreover, the recent police shooting of Wallace not only increased antipolice sentiment throughout the city but also bolstered the movement to defund police and reappropriate funds to social welfare programs and resources supporting social work and rehabilitation. However, city officials and law enforcement are gradually learning how powerful and influential citizens' relentless protests against racial injustice and police brutality can be. On April 20, 2021, national news syndicates announced that former Minneapolis police officer Derek Chauvin was found guilty of murdering George Floyd in May 2020. Countless Philadelphians, like many others throughout the country, expressed relief that an officer was held accountable for police brutality. This event came at a time when mass protest finally forced law enforcement and the justice system to reckon with America's roots in white supremacy and antiblackness and take action to prevent police abuse, brutality, and misconduct in the future.

Five years since I sat beside Oh's gravesite pondering this book, I have come to the realization that despite Oh's "unachieved future," his life had purpose and meaning. Oh may not have been able to control when and how he died in 1958, but his life as a loving, hardworking student with a passion for politics and international relations inspired societal change that benefited many others. Throughout the 1960s and 1970s, most city officials were hesitant to fully invest in social welfare and poverty alleviation programs, while numerous community activists like Herman Wrice, Falaka Fattah, and Harvey Wearing would risk their lives to stop police, gang, and gun violence in Philadelphia. Many antigang organizations like Herman Wrice's Young Greats Society and Arlen Specter's Safe Streets, Inc., involved community activists, city officials, and police working together to keep youth away from crime with education, recreation, and job training.[61] However, most of these organizations were short-lived, and only a few from the era remain—namely, Queen Mother Falaka and David Fattah's House of Umoja.[62] Today, organizations like Urban Youth Kings & Queens, Inc.; EMIR (Every Murder Is Real) Healing Center; and Philadelphia CeaseFire are combining education, rehabilitation, and community service to combat community violence.[63] Moreover, if we are ever to solve police brutality, gang activity, gun violence, and crime in Philadelphia and cities across the nation, it must start with people who acknowledge the negative effects of institutional racism and poverty and are willing to make the ultimate sacrifice to fight for change.

ACKNOWLEDGMENTS

This book was the product of nine years of research on race and policing in Philadelphia. I am indebted to Temple University's Special Collections Research Center, the Public Interest Law Center of Philadelphia, the Arlen Specter Center at Jefferson University, the Charles L. Blockson Afro-American Collection, the National Archives Records and Administration, the Philadelphia Municipal Archives, and the Free Library of Philadelphia for the countless archival documents I gained access to through their collections. The Free Library of Philadelphia, in particular, was not only where I volunteered and gained firsthand experience about community activism in Philly but also where I pondered and wrote this book, usually at the branches in Germantown, Mount Airy, Chestnut Hill, Chinatown, Nicetown, and Center City.

I am thankful for my family, friends, Temple University colleagues from grad school, and mentors who supported me as I completed this book. Additionally, I give thanks to the editors of the Urban History Association's the *Metropole*, the *Washington Post*, the *Journal of Urban History*, and the African American Intellectual History Society's *Black Perspectives* who read, reviewed, and published my research at various stages of the writing process. To Bryant Simon, Lila Corwin Berman, and Harvey Neptune, thank you for your never-ending support, patience, and guidance as professors and mentors. Additionally, to Matthew F. Delmont, Elizabeth K. Hinton, Max Felker-Kantor, Timothy J. Lombardo, and Walter C. Stern, thank you for your support, encouragement, and feedback during the late stages of this project. To my editor, Clara Platter, thank you for your enthusiasm and faith in this project from the start. Last but not least, this book is for all the friends, neighbors, and strangers who shared their own Philadelphia stories with me about race relations, gangs, and police at libraries, bus stops, coffee shops, and offices and even in their own homes. I am overwhelmingly grateful for their time, respect, and interest in my research about our city.

APPENDIX

TABLE 1: Police spending in America's largest cities. Source: *USA Today*, "Here's How Much Money Goes to Police Departments in Largest Cities across the U.S.," June 26, 2020.

City	Population (2018)	Police Department as Percentage of City Budget (2020)	Total Police Budget for Fiscal Year	Total City Budget for Fiscal Year
New York	8,398,748	5.9%	$6 billion (2021)	$95.30 billion (2021)
Los Angeles	3,990,469	17.6%	$2 billion (2021)	$10.53 billion (2021)
Chicago	2,705,988	15.3%	$2 billion (2020)	$11.65 billion (2020)
Houston	2,326,090	17.3%	$965 million (2021)	$5.56 billion (2021)
Phoenix	1,660,272	22.0%	$721 million (2021)	$3.27 billion (2021)
Philadelphia	1,584,138	15.2%	$760 million (2021)	$5.00 billion (2021)
Detroit	672,681	15.1%	$317 million (2021)	$2.10 billion (2021)
Washington, DC	702,455	3.3%	$544 million (2021)	$16.70 billion (2021)
Baltimore	602,495	18.3%	$536 million (2020)	$2.93 billion (2020)
Atlanta	498,073	9.3%	$205 million (2020)	$2.20 billion (2020)
Miami	470,911	23.4%	$266 million (2020)	$1.14 billion (2020)
New Orleans	391,006	17.1%	$194 million (2020)	$1.13 billion (2020)
Memphis	650,632	38.3%	$273 million (2020)	$711.56 million (2020)
Las Vegas	644,664	44.9%	$656 million (2021)	$1.46 billion (2021)

TABLE 2: Philadelphia's population by race, 1900–1980. Demographics table of white and black populations in Philadelphia.

Census Year	Total Population	White Population (Number and Percent)	African American / Black Population (Number and Percent)
1900	1,293,697	1,229,673 (95.1%)	62,613 (4.8%)
1910	1,549,008	1,463,371 (94.5%)	84,459 (5.5%)
1920	1,823,779	1,688,180 (92.6%)	134,229 (7.4%)
1930	1,950,961	1,728,806 (88.6%)	219,599 (11.3%)
1940	1,931,334	1,678,577 (86.9%)	250,880 (13.0%)
1950	2,071,605	1,692,637 (81.7%)	376,041 (18.2%)
1960	2,002,512	1,467,479 (73.3%)	529,240 (26.4%)
1970	1,948,609	1,278,717 (65.6%)	653,791 (33.6%)
1980	1,688,210	983,084 (58.2%)	638,878 (37.8%)

TABLE 3: Chart of active, sporadic, and dormant gangs in Philadelphia as of May 13, 1968 (printed in Phineas M. Anderson's *The Gang Unit*). Source: Gang Control Unit, Philadelphia Police Department.

Gang	Area (Defined by Streets)	Foes	Members	Status
2-4 Counts	25th to 27th; Passyunk to Snyder	Hill; PJ's	25	Sporadic
PJ's	25th to 27th; Passyunk to Snyder (claims same territory as 2-4 Counts)	2-4 Counts; 22nd & Greenwich	30	Active
5th Street	3rd to 7th; Federal to South	13th Street	45	Active
13th Street	9th to Broad; Christian to South	All gangs in South Philadelphia	60	Active
5th and Porter	4th to 6th; Moore to Porter	7th Street	25	Sporadic
7th Street	Mifflin to Wolf; 5th to 8th	5th and Porter	30	Active
15th and Clymer Street	Broad to 17th; Washington to South	13th Street	30	Active
19th and Dorrance Street	19th to 20th; Reed to Dickinson	None at this time	40	Sporadic
21st and Titan Street	19th to 22nd; Reed to Washington	13th Street	20	Active
22nd and Greenwich Street	22nd to 24th; Wharton to Watkins	Roads; PJ's	25	Active

(continued)

TABLE 3: Chart of active, sporadic, and dormant gangs in Philadelphia as of May 13, 1968 (printed in Phineas M. Anderson's *The Gang Unit*). Source: Gang Control Unit, Philadelphia Police Department. (*cont.*)

Gang	Area (Defined by Streets)	Foes	Members	Status
22nd and South Street	17th to 23rd; Washington to South	13th Street	45	Active
20th and Carpenter Street	22nd to 25th; Washington to Carpenter	None at this time	20	Sporadic
2-T-6	26th to 30th; Wharton to Moore	Taylor Street; PJ's	25	Sporadic
30th and Tasker Street	26th to 33rd; Morris to Reed	Any gang from outside their area	30	Sporadic
Roads	25th to 30th; Wharton to Grays Ferry	13th Street; Taylor Street	25	Active
Taylor Street	23rd to 25th; Tasker to Federal	Roads; 2-T-6	25	Sporadic
Wine	20th to 21st; Christian to Washington	22nd and South Street	20	Sporadic
20th Street	20th to 22nd; Gerritt to Watkins	Have several corners but will band together	70	Active
10th and Carpenter Street	10th to 9th; Washington to Christian	Any gang in South Philadelphia	10	Sporadic
12th and Poplar	8th to 12th; Green to Girard	Moroccans; 12th and Oxford	50	Active
T.G.O.'s	Broad to 13th; Fairmount to Parrish	12th and Poplar	20	Sporadic
16th and Wallace Street	Broad to 20th; Fairmount to Spring Garden	Moroccans	20	Active
Moroccans	Broad to 20th; Fairmount to Girard	12th and Poplar; 16th and Seybert	75	Active
16th and Dauphin	Broad to 18th; Lehigh to Susquehanna	21st and Norris	30	Active
21st and Norris	19th to 22nd; Susquehanna to Berks	16th and Dauphin; Valley	40	Active
28th and Montgomery	24th to 27th; Columbia to Montgomery	Valley; DeMarco's; 28th and Oxford; 30th and Norris	50	Active
2-9-D's	28th to 32nd; Norris to York	30th and Norris	30	Active
30th and Norris	30th to 33rd; Susquehanna to Montgomery	Valley; 32nd and Turner; 28th and Montgomery	30	Active

(continued)

TABLE 3: Chart of active, sporadic, and dormant gangs in Philadelphia as of May 13, 1968 (printed in Phineas M. Anderson's *The Gang Unit*). Source: Gang Control Unit, Philadelphia Police Department. (*cont.*)

Gang	Area (Defined by Streets)	Foes	Members	Status
32nd and Turner	31st to 33rd; Columbia to Oxford	30th and Norris	25	Active
LT's	29th to 33rd; Huntingdon to Lehigh	Village	45	Dormant
Village	24th to 27th; Dauphin to Cumberland	LT's	60	Sporadic
Valley	Broad to 26th; Columbia to Diamond	15th and Oxford; 30th and Norris	250	Active
15th and Oxford	Broad to 18th; Columbia to Jefferson	16th and Montgomery; 21st and Montgomery; 19th and Montgomery	20	Active
DeMarco's	20th to 25th; Thompson to Columbia	21st and Montgomery; 28th and Oxford	45	Active
19th and Harlan	18th to 20th; Jefferson to Columbia	Valley; 21st and Montgomery	30	Active
16th and Seybert	Broad to 18th; Girard to Jefferson	Moroccans; 12th and Poplar	40	Active
2-4-R'S	24th to 25th; Oxford to Jefferson	28th and Oxford	25	Sporadic
28th and Oxford	22nd to 32nd; Girard to Oxford	DeMarco's; 24th and Redner	20	Active
MMF	8th to Broad; Lehigh to Clearfield	Zulu Nation	30	Active
Camac and Butler	10th to Broad; Erie to Hunting Park	None at this time	20	Sporadic
Uptown Norris	6th to 10th; Somerset to Allegheny	None at this time	50	Sporadic
8th and Diamond	6th to Broad; Berks to York	8th and Oxford; Zulu Nation	100	Active
8th and Oxford	5th to Broad; Jefferson to Berks	8th and Diamond; 12th and Poplar	60	Active
Zulu Nation	Front to 7th; Columbia to Lehigh	MMF; 8th and Diamond	200	Active
Stars	2nd to 5th; Diamond to Huntingdon	None at this time	50	Dormant
Soul Diplomats	2nd to 5th; Diamond to Huntingdon	None at this time	25	Sporadic
Sommerville	Chew to 21st; Chelten to Ogontz	Dogtown; Haines Street	200	Active

(continued)

TABLE 3: Chart of active, sporadic, and dormant gangs in Philadelphia as of May 13, 1968 (printed in Phineas M. Anderson's *The Gang Unit*). Source: Gang Control Unit, Philadelphia Police Department. (*cont.*)

Gang	Area (Defined by Streets)	Foes	Members	Status
Dogtown	Gorgas Lane to Walnut Lane; Chew to Germantown	Sommerville; Haines Street	75	Active
Pulaski Town	Queen Lane to Chelten; Pulaski to Wissahickon	Sommerville; Haines Street	30	Dormant
Haines Street	Germantown to Belfield; Walnut Lane to Chelten	Dogtown; Sommerville; Brickyard	60	Active
Brickyard	Penn to Logan; Germantown to Rubicam	Haines Street	40	Sporadic
Clang	68th to 65th; Ogontz to Broad	Sommerville	75	Active
15th and Venango	Broad to 17th; Erie to Tioga	MMF; 21st and Westmoreland	35	Active
23rd and Atlantic	Hunting Park to Ontario; 21st to 23rd	21st and Westmoreland	30	Active
21st and Westmoreland	Broad to 22nd; Lehigh to Westmoreland	23rd and Atlantic; 15th and Venango	50	Active
39th and Aspen	39th to Union; Aspen to Brown	36th and Market; Empires; 41st and Brown; 43rd and Pennsgrove	35	Active
Theta Phi Omicrons	33rd to 34th; Haverford to Mantua	36th and Market	20	Active
36th and Market (this gang moved but still carries the old corner's name)	51st and Sansom	39th and Aspen 34th and Haverford	40	Active
Empires	35th to 36th; Haverford to Wallace	39th and Aspen	20	Active
41st and Brown	41st—Fairmount to Brown	39th and Aspen	20	Active
43rd and Pennsgrove	40th to 43rd; Westminster to Mantua	39th and Aspen; June and Parrish	15	Active
Coast	57th to 60th; Spruce to Market	Moons; Cedar Avenue	30	Active

(*continued*)

TABLE 3: Chart of active, sporadic, and dormant gangs in Philadelphia as of May 13, 1968 (printed in Phineas M. Anderson's *The Gang Unit*). Source: Gang Control Unit, Philadelphia Police Department. (*cont.*)

Gang	Area (Defined by Streets)	Foes	Members	Status
Cedar Avenue	55th to 57th; Baltimore to Cedar	Coast; Creeks; 49th and Woodland	25	Active
49th and Woodland	48th to 50th; Upland to Chester	Cedar Avenue	30	Sporadic
60th and Webster	59th to 60th; Christian to Pine	Creeks; 49th and Woodland	20	Active
Moons	58th to 63rd; Market to Jefferson	Coast	50	Active
June and Parrish	June to 48th; Parrish to Brown	43rd and Pennsgrove	20	Dormant
Lansdowners	54th to 58th; Lancaster to Lansdowne	Moons	20	Sporadic
Creeks	61st to 63rd; Cobbs Creek Parkway to Christian	Cedar Avenue; Coast	20	Dormant

TABLE 4: Chart of additional gangs in Philadelphia as of April 1970 (printed in Phineas M. Anderson's *The Gang Unit*). Source: Youth Conservation Services, Philadelphia Welfare Department.

Gang	Area	Foes	Members	Status
31st and Reed	—	Unknown	Unknown	Unknown
20th and Dickinson Streets	—	Unknown	Unknown	Unknown
2-S-6	26th and South Streets	Unknown	Unknown	Unknown
2-E-6	26th and Earp Streets	Unknown	Unknown	Unknown
2-M-1	21st and Morris Streets	Unknown	Unknown	Unknown
Hill Gang	31st and Mifflin Streets	Unknown	Unknown	Unknown
Toppers	—	Unknown	Unknown	Unknown
Main Streeters	—	Unknown	Unknown	Unknown
Black Bridge	—	Unknown	Unknown	Unknown
Centaurs	—	Unknown	Unknown	Unknown
Counties	—	Unknown	Unknown	Unknown
CC Counts	—	Unknown	Unknown	Unknown
31st and Montgomery Avenue	—	Unknown	Unknown	Unknown

(continued)

TABLE 4: Chart of additional gangs in Philadelphia as of April 1970 (printed in Phineas M. Anderson's *The Gang Unit*). Source: Youth Conservation Services, Philadelphia Welfare Department. (*cont.*)

Gang	Area	Foes	Members	Status
28th and Oxford Streets	—	Unknown	Unknown	Unknown
31st and Cumberland Streets	—	Unknown	Unknown	Unknown
Cambria Streeters	20th and Cambria Streets	Unknown	Unknown	Unknown
Cool World Valley	—	Unknown	Unknown	Unknown
58-W's	58th Street and Willows Avenue	Unknown	Unknown	Unknown
Wallace Streeters	12th and Wallace Streets	Unknown	Unknown	Unknown
Twine Debs of Soul	Chelten and Ardleigh Streets	Unknown	Unknown	Unknown
Da Nang Delta	Chelten and Ardleigh Streets	Unknown	Unknown	Unknown
Black Volunteer Society	13th and Fitzwater Streets	Unknown	Unknown	Unknown
Last Siders	Roxborough	Unknown	Unknown	Unknown
32nd and Haverford Avenue	—	Unknown	Unknown	Unknown
58th and Whitby Avenue	—	Unknown	Unknown	Unknown
58th and Chester Avenue	—	Unknown	Unknown	Unknown
Mill Creek Area	—	Unknown	Unknown	Unknown
42nd and Mantua Avenue (Girls)	—	Unknown	Unknown	Unknown
23rd and Diamond Streets	—	Unknown	Unknown	Unknown
25th and Diamond Streets	—	Unknown	Unknown	Unknown
Upsetters—24th and Master (Girls)	—	Unknown	Unknown	Unknown
Fishtown—Lutheran Center Minis (Girls)	—	Unknown	Unknown	Unknown
Fishtown—Lutheran Center Minis (Boys)	—	Unknown	Unknown	Unknown
Venice Islanders	Northwest Philadelphia	Unknown	Unknown	Unknown
Mayfair Area (Boys)	Northwest Philadelphia	Unknown	Unknown	Unknown
Mayfair Area (Girls)	Northwest Philadelphia	Unknown	Unknown	Unknown
3-T-0	South Philadelphia	Unknown	Unknown	Unknown
7th and Morris Streets	—	Unknown	Unknown	Unknown

(*continued*)

TABLE 4: Chart of additional gangs in Philadelphia as of April 1970 (printed in Phineas M. Anderson's *The Gang Unit*). Source: Youth Conservation Services, Philadelphia Welfare Department. (*cont.*)

Gang	Area	Foes	Members	Status
2nd and Harps Streets	—	Unknown	Unknown	Unknown
Hawthorne Area (Girls)	—	Unknown	Unknown	Unknown
Wilson Park (Girls)	—	Unknown	Unknown	Unknown

TABLE 5: Philadelphia spending to fight crime. Source: *Philadelphia Evening Bulletin*, "Billions for Safe Streets Yield Failure, Fear, Fury," September 11, 1977.

Purpose	Fiscal 1970	Fiscal 1976
Police	$80 million	$152.5 million
Prisons	$8.6 million	$18.1 million
Defender Association	$1.2 million	$3.2 million
Sheriff	$1.9 million	$3.6 million
District Attorney	$2.2 million	$6.0 million
Clerk of Courts	$1.4 million	$2.5 million
Courts	$15.5 million	$39.8 million
Youth Study Center	$1.6 million	$3.0 million
Juvenile Commitment	$3.0 million	$5.7 million
Citizens Crime Prevention	—	$1.6 million
Total	$115.4 million	$236 million

TABLE 6: Pennsylvania spending to fight crime. Source: *Philadelphia Evening Bulletin*, "Millions for Safe Streets, and Crime Still Climbs," March 10, 1974.

Year	Law Enforcement	Corrections	Courts	Total
1969	$968,000	$349,000	$85,000	$1,427,000
1970	$4,598,000	$2,778,000	$1,383,000	$10,590,000
1971	$6,757,000	$9,176,000	$2,286,000	$22,276,000
1972	$6,908,000	$12,112,000	$2,811,000	$26,469,000
1973	$9,512,000	$13,052,000	$3,724,000	$30,715,000

TABLE 7: Gang-related homicides in Philadelphia, 1965–76. Source: *Philadelphia Evening Bulletin*, May 23, 1976.

Year	Number of Homicides
1962	1
1965	13
1966	14
1967	12
1968	30
1969	45
1970	30
1971	43
1972	39
1973	43
1974	32
1975	15
1976	3

TABLE 8: Police apprehensions made under Operation FIND (as of November 1971). Source: Federal Bureau of Investigation, *FBI Law Enforcement Bulletin*, November 1971.

Crime	Number Apprehended
Bank Robbery	12
Other Armed Robberies	59
Rape and Kidnap	1
Homicide	3
Assault with Intent to Kill	9
Burglary	11
Auto Theft	2
Vehicles Recovered without Occupants	42

TABLE 9: Top three national police department salaries by city (1971). Source: *Philadelphia Inquirer*, "Police Department Overtime Runs $6.3 Million in 7 Months," March 21, 1971.

City	Starting Annual Police Salary
Los Angeles	$10,105
Chicago	$9,600
Philadelphia	$9,578

TABLE 10: National Police Department Strength and Overtime Expenditures by City (1971) Source: Gerald McKelvey and Howard Shapiro, "Police Department Overtime Runs $6.3 Million in 7 Months," *Philadelphia Inquirer*, March 21, 1971.

City	Police Force Strength	Estimated Annual Overtime Budget
New York City	29,000	$7 million
Los Angeles	8,991	$6 million
Chicago	12,500	N/A; Compensatory time off
Philadelphia	7,409	$5.5 million
Pittsburgh	1,600	$500,000
Baltimore	4,283	$460,000

NOTES

PROLOGUE

1 Weisenbach, "Boy, 9, Is Slain."
2 Weisenbach.
3 "Innocent Bystander Again."
4 "Innocent Bystander Again."
5 *Gang Killing.*
6 *Gang Killing.*
7 "Stray-Bullet Death of Boy."
8 Dougherty and Griffenberg, "5 Held in 'Get Anybody' Killing of Temple Graduate Student."
9 Murphy and Lintz, "Bullet Kills Girl, 7."
10 Caparella, "Gang Leader Who Pledged Peace Held in Killing."
11 Du Bois and Eaton, *Philadelphia Negro*, 385.
12 Muhammad, *Condemnation of Blackness*, 33.
13 Muhammad, 68–69.
14 Franklin, "Operation Street Corner."
15 Thrasher, *Gang*, 38.
16 United States Congress Senate Committee on the Judiciary Subcommittee to Investigate Juvenile Delinquency, *Hearings*, 48–58.
17 Anderson, *Gang Unit*, 12.
18 Dirkson, "Hyper-segregation, Inequality, and Murder Rates."
19 Nutter, "Philadelphia Homicides 1960–2020."
20 Janson, "Gangs Face Drive in Philadelphia."
21 Miller, *Violence by Youth Gangs and Youth Groups*, 1–10.
22 Miller, 27.
23 *Black Panther Party.*
24 Romero, "How Philly's Poverty Rate Has Changed."
25 "City of Philadelphia Five Year Financial and Strategic Plan."
26 "Mapping Philadelphia's Gun Violence Crisis."
27 Sullivan and Baranauckas, "Here's How Much Money Goes to Police Departments."
28 Thompson, "Why Mass Incarceration Matters."

INTRODUCTION
Epigraph: LoBianco and Killough, "Trump Pitches Black Voters." The selection of this quote from Donald Trump was inspired by the sound bite that opens Philadelphia-born

rapper Meek Mill's 2020 song "Otherside of America." The song was released in summer 2020 following the global outbreak of the COVID-19 virus and the national George Floyd protests against police brutality. Meek Mill's lyrics describe what life is like in America's neglected urban black neighborhoods, where there are issues of poverty, inequality, crime, police brutality, and gun violence. Furthermore, my usage of Trump's quote is to introduce my reaction to his statement with a thorough explanation of how these urban issues don't come out of a vacuum but have origins in racial segregation and discrimination in housing, employment, and education. Today, past racial oppression and socioeconomic exclusion have, in part, contributed to many urban problems like racially distinct gun violence that are more pronounced in our society than general poverty.

1 Perales, "Letters to the Editor." Southeastern Pennsylvania Transportation Authority, or SEPTA, is the public transportation system that operates in the Philadelphia metropolitan area. The opening story of this introduction is a tribute to sociologist Elijah Anderson, who opened his 1999 book *Code of the Street: Decency, Violence, and the Moral Life of the Inner City* with an introduction describing black street life along Philadelphia's 23 bus route.

2 Levenstein, *Movement without Marches*, 8. Like the route 33 bus, SEPTA passengers have also associated the route 23, 16, and 54 buses with crime, possibly because they travel through many low-income black neighborhoods in North Philadelphia.

3 In this book, a moral panic is defined as a widespread fear based on a contemporary narrative of an exaggerated public safety issue that is disseminated to the public through mass media, political rhetoric, and everyday word of mouth.

4 Robinson, *Black Marxism*, 27.

5 "SEPTA Riders Speak Out."

6 *TED*, "Danger of a Single Story."

7 Hinton, *From the War on Poverty to the War on Crime*, 1–2.

8 Harriot, "Maybe America Is Racist."

9 Taub, "Behind 2016's Turmoil."

10 KODX Seattle, "Robin D. G. Kelley."

11 Robinson, *Black Marxism*, 177.

12 Jordan, *White over Black*, 7. Jordan's *White over Black* is a controversial text on slavery, race, and racism. His book is often referenced to explain how social constructions about race came into existence in early American society and the European and American Enlightenments (1685–1815). However, his personal beliefs about whether people of African and European descent are truly equal human beings regardless of their phenotype, language, and culture are unclear at best. In regard to scholar Ibram X. Kendi, who explained in his 2016 book *Stamped from the Beginning: The Definitive History of Racist Ideas in America* how assimilationists are racists in that they argue the causes of racial disparities are the racial inferiority of black people and racial discrimination from white people, Jordan's book

can be read as an apology for white supremacy, intellectually cloaked in political correctness during the era of the African American Civil Rights Movement. See H. Reuben Neptune's 2023 article on the hypocritical nature of Jordan's writing and his belief in race science and racial difference as a biological determinant of who is inferior or superior: H. Reuben Neptune, "'The Baby of Biological Race': The Issue of Racial Science in Winthrop Jordan's White over Black," *Journal of the Early Republic* 43, no. 2 (Summer 2023): 199–243.

13 Morgan, "'Some Could Suckle over Their Shoulder.'"

14 Muhammad, *Condemnation of Blackness*, 8.

15 Muhammad, 22–23.

16 Muhammad, 22–23.

17 Shaler, "Negro Problem."

18 Muhammad, *Condemnation of Blackness*, 17–18.

19 Muhammad, 19.

20 Muhammad, 35–36.

21 Hoffman, "Vital Statistics of the Negro."

22 Muhammad, *Condemnation of Blackness*, 35–36.

23 Cunningham, "Morbidity and Mortality of Negro Convicts."

24 Blackmon, *Slavery by Another Name*, 118.

25 Muhammad, *Condemnation of Blackness*, 43.

26 Ball, "Correspondence."

27 Muhammad, *Condemnation of Blackness*, 48.

28 Hoffman, *Race Traits and Tendencies*, 217–34.

29 Muhammad, *Condemnation of Blackness*, 42.

30 Muhammad, 10.

31 Muhammad, 247.

32 Muhammad, 9.

33 Muhammad, 165–66.

34 Agyepong, *Criminalization of Black Children*, 9.

35 Agyepong, 13–14.

36 Agyepong, 90.

37 Suddler, *Presumed Criminal*, 7.

38 Suddler, 26–27.

39 Suddler, 81.

40 Suddler, 123.

41 Hinton, *From the War on Poverty to the War on Crime*, 1–4.

42 Hinton, 29–30.

43 In this book, a *riot* refers to unjustified violence, murder, and reckless destruction of public and private property to further an immoral cause such as segregation, hate crimes, and other forms of racial intimidation to oust "undesired" people from a community. An *uprising* refers to justified violence as a form of active protest to bring awareness to social issues and spark immediate and positive change in a community. An uprising can occur in response to a moral issue

like police brutality and involve the destruction of property to make the voices of the marginalized minority heard by the majority.

44 Hinton, *From the War on Poverty to the War on Crime*, 29.

45 Hinton, 38.

46 United States Department of Labor, *Negro Family*, 16–37.

47 United States Department of Labor, 17.

48 Hinton, *From the War on Poverty to the War on Crime*, 269–70.

49 AP, "Youth Gangs Seen Growing Threat."

50 Hinton, *From the War on Poverty to the War on Crime*, 2.

51 Schneider, *Ecology of Homicide*, ix.

52 Schneider, 1–2.

53 Schneider, xvi. In this book, *desegregation* refers to neighborhoods naturally becoming racially heterogeneous when new migrants arrive to all-white communities under their own volition and free of political, legal, or social motives to make change. *Integration* refers to a premeditated, strategic plan to diversify an all-white neighborhood to further political, legal, or social motives, like pursuing a civil rights lawsuit to challenge restrictive covenants for homes and ending legalized segregation.

54 Schneider, 6.

55 Schneider, 6–10.

56 Schneider, 28.

57 *A1: NPR*, "To Be in a Rage."

1. "THE GREAT 'BLACK INVASION'"

1 The introduction of this chapter was inspired by Isabel Wilkerson's *The Warmth of Other Suns: The Epic Story of America's Great Migration* and Dan Berger's *Stayed on Freedom: The Long History of Black Power through One Family's Journey*, which heavily focus their narratives on bottom-up, first-person accounts while also highlighting and uplifting the words and memories of everyday people.

2 "Interview: Crosby Brittenum."

3 Equal Justice Initiative, "Reconstruction in America: Racial."

4 Litwack, "Hellhounds," 14.

5 Adero, preface to *Up South*, vii–xiv. According to the Equal Justice Initiative, approximately 30 percent of lynchings that occurred in Southern states between 1877 and 1950 were based on accusations of murder, while 25 percent of these incidents of violence were the result of sexual assault accusations.

6 "Interview: Kathryn F. (Kitty) Woodard."

7 Countryman, *Up South*, 14.

8 Henri, *Black Migration*, 54–55.

9 "Interview: Beulah Collins."

10 United States Bureau of the Census, "Migrations."

11 Yax, "Population of the 100 Largest Cities."

12 "Interview: Crosby Brittenum."

13 "Interview: Crosby Brittenum."

14 "Interview: Ralph Jones."

15 "Interview: Crosby Brittenum."

16 "Interview: Crosby Brittenum." Broad Street Station was a major train station located at 15th and Market Streets. It was designed by Philadelphia architect Frank Furness and operated by the Pennsylvania Railroad from 1881 to 1952. From 1952 to 1953, the station was demolished, and an urban renewal project featuring new Center City skyscrapers adjacent to City Hall was developed in its place.

17 "Interview: Ralph Jones."

18 J. J. Johnson, "ReMemory," 102–3.

19 Mossell, "Standard of Living," 177. After Sadie Tanner Mossell outlined her critiques of rural black migrants of the Great Migration, she ironically later married attorney and activist Raymond Pace Alexander, the son of former slaves from rural Virginia.

20 Hornblum, *Sentenced to Science*, 14.

21 Dixon, *Clansman*, 182. The Dunning school of historiography was based on the historical interpretation of Columbia University professor of history William Archibald Dunning (1857–1922).

22 Cook, *Thomas Dixon*, 68.

23 D'Ooge, "'Birth of a Nation.'"

24 A. Clark, "How 'The Birth of a Nation' Revived the Ku Klux Klan."

25 Mossell, "Standard of Living," 175.

26 Wilkerson, *Warmth of Other Suns*, 528.

27 Mossell, "Standard of Living," 173–77.

28 Simon, *Philadelphia*, 74–75.

29 Simon, 74–75.

30 Spencer, *In the Crossfire*, 23.

31 Wilkerson, *Warmth of Other Suns*, 528–31. In Isabel Wilkerson's *Warmth of Other Suns*, she cites census analysts Larry H. Long and Lynne R. Heltman, whose research data revealed that Southern-born blacks in the North not only had higher incomes than African Americans who stayed in the South but also were more likely to be economically successful than Northern-born blacks.

32 Wilkerson, 528–31.

33 Henri, *Black Migration*, 48–80.

34 Callard and Germantown Historical Society, *Images of America*, 7.

35 Hingston, "What Two Centuries of Census Records Taught Us."

36 Wolfinger, *Philadelphia Divided*, 17.

37 Burt and Davies, "Iron Age, 1876–1905," 471–523. In 1900, Philadelphia's Irish population was the third largest in the country after Boston and Providence.

38 Avery, "As Neighborhoods Change, So Do the Names."

39 Whalen, *From Puerto Rico to Philadelphia*, 1–22. Following World War II (1941–45), hundreds of thousands of Puerto Ricans moved to the urban areas of the island and the mainland United States. By 1970, approximately 700,000 left

Puerto Rico's rural communities and 388,000 traveled to the mainland. Philadelphia's Puerto Rican population increased from under 2,000 in the 1940s to 27,000 in 1970. For decades, Philadelphia had the third largest Puerto Rican population on the mainland after New York and Chicago. Since 2010, Philadelphia's Puerto Rican population of over 122,000 is the second largest in the country.

40 Farr, "Spanish Merchants Association of Philadelphia."

41 Gross, *Colored Amazons*, 81. From the 1860s through the 1910s, Philadelphia's downtown region was known as the "center of the city." By the 1920s, the downtown area was referred to as "Center City" in newspapers by advertising companies and journalists to identify the central area of the city for suburbanites looking for work in Philadelphia.

42 Wilson, "From Bachelor Enclave to Urban Village." One staple institution established in Chinatown was the Chinese Cultural and Community Center at 125 North 10th Street by T. T. Chang in 1966. From 1966 to 2004, the center offered calligraphy, tours, meals, and Tai Chi classes, helping Chinatown become known as more than "restaurants & gift shops." The institution closed in 2007.

43 Lee, *Dynamics of Ethnic Identity*, 55–59.

44 "As Neighborhoods Change, So Do the Names."

45 Wolfinger, *Philadelphia Divided*, 16.

46 "As Neighborhoods Change, So Do the Names."

47 Franklin, "Operation Street Corner."

48 Bauman, "Black Slums / Black Projects."

49 Spencer, *In the Crossfire*, 22–23. Marcus Foster (1923–73) was a well-known and respected educator who served as principal at Simon Gratz High School in North Philadelphia and later became the associate superintendent of schools in Philadelphia during the 1960s. Despite his renowned record for improving student achievement and morale along with his success as an administrator, he was never promoted to the position of school superintendent of the district. Foster later left Philadelphia to accept the school superintendent position in Oakland, California, in 1970. In 1973, Foster was assassinated by members of the militant group the Symbionese Liberation Army, who murdered Foster because they disagreed with his proposed public safety policy of requiring student identification cards in schools to curb vagrancy and off-campus drug-dealing.

50 Wolfinger, *Philadelphia Divided*, 127.

51 Burt and Davies, "Iron Age, 1876–1905," 488.

52 Muhammad, *Condemnation of Blackness*, 128.

53 Franklin, "Operation Street Corner," 197.

54 Franklin, 197. Historians like Khalil Muhammad and Saidiya Hartman have also discussed in their research the charity work settlement houses like the Wharton Centre did for black migrants in North Philadelphia. However, V. P. Franklin's 1998 article was a precedent for their scholarship. Franklin's article is based on boxes of archival documents on the Wharton Centre and its impact on the black community from 1930 through the 1960s. His scholarship on the Wharton

Centre's founding and antigang program Operation Street Corner is a foundational text on the role settlement houses played in attempting to improve slum communities.

55 Franklin, 197. Aside from organizing a neighborhood library and a housing program for black residents in Philadelphia, in 1895, Susan Parrish Wharton initiated arrangements for W. E. B. Du Bois to investigate black life in the city's Seventh Ward with sponsorship from the University of Pennsylvania.

56 Franklin, 198–200.

57 Countryman, *Up South*, 19.

58 Du Bois and Eaton, *Philadelphia Negro*, 311–14.

59 McGrail, "Philadelphia Negro (The)."

60 Du Bois and Eaton, *Philadelphia Negro*, 385.

61 Muhammad, *Condemnation of Blackness*, 33.

62 Muhammad, 68–69.

63 Hingston, "What Two Centuries of Census Records Taught Us."

64 Hingston.

65 Hardy, "Historical Overview."

66 Bauman, "Black Slums / Black Projects," 312–16.

67 Webber, "Slum Profits in Philadelphia."

68 Webber.

69 Sugrue, *Sweet Land of Liberty*, 202.

70 Meyer, *As Long as They Don't Move Next Door*, 219.

71 Meyer, 202–11.

72 Meyer, 229.

73 Meyer, 229.

74 L. T. Brown, *Black Butterfly*, 66.

75 "Black Invasion of Harlem Stirs Up Bitter Feud." Adena C. E. Minott (1879–1955) was a Jamaican-born scholar, author, and activist who studied phrenology, physiology, and psychology. In 1906, she founded the Clio School of Mental Sciences, and in 1910, she operated as the institution's principal. In 1921, she earned her doctorate in metaphysics from the College of Metaphysics in St. Louis. She was a member of a Colored Women's Club, which participated in social activism, including antilynching campaigns and care for aging African Americans. Additionally, she was often featured in the black newspaper *New York Age*, where editors highlighted her business and activist endeavors.

76 "Black Invasion of Harlem Stirs Up Bitter Feud."

77 "Teagle's White Wife." A trinity house, also known as a bandbox house, was an attached, two- or three-story town house under one thousand square feet with a winding staircase and one room per floor. Today, Philadelphia's "rowhomes" are the closest likeness to bandbox homes of the nineteenth and early twentieth centuries.

78 "West Phila. House Stoned."

79 "Police Stop Raid on Colored Household."

80 "To Reimburse Negro."

81 "Teagle's White Wife."

82 "Baltimore Resents Negro in White Block."

83 Yanker, "Moving."

84 Yanker.

85 An Evader, "Race Irritation."

86 An Evader.

87 "Different Black Invasion."

88 "Different Black Invasion."

89 Finkel, "Roots of Hypersegregation in Philadelphia."

90 Wolfinger, *Philadelphia Divided*, 2.

91 Webber, "Slums No Accident."

92 Shertzer and Walsh, "Why US Cities Are Segregated by Race."

93 United States of America, Bureau of the Census, *Fifteenth Census of the United States, 1930*, Philadelphia, PA.

94 United States of America, Bureau of the Census. Both John M. Boiling and Randolph Thompson are interesting figures who lived in Philadelphia as accomplished, middle-class African Americans but are largely unknown. According to US Federal Census records, Boiling was a South Philadelphia music teacher who gradually worked toward owning his own music store. Thompson was born in Warsaw, Virginia, and at the age of twenty-four, he joined the army during World War I, did two years of service, and fought in major battles at Saint-Dié-des-Vosges and Meuse-Argonne in 1918. Both Boiling and Thompson are subjects worthy of deeper historical investigation.

95 United States of America, Bureau of the Census.

96 United States of America, Bureau of the Census, *Fourteenth Census of the United States, 1920*, Philadelphia Ward 32, Philadelphia, PA, roll T625_1633, page 2A, enumeration district 1066.

97 Pennsylvania Historic and Museum Commission, *Pennsylvania, U.S., Death Certificates, 1906–1967*, "Frank C. Brooker," certificate number range 117001–120000.

98 United States of America, Bureau of the Census, *Fifteenth Census of the United States, 1930*, Philadelphia, PA, page 14A, enumeration district 0727.

99 United States of America, Bureau of the Census, *Sixteenth Census of the United States, 1940*, Abington, Montgomery, PA, roll m-to627-03576, page 8B, enumeration district 46–6.

100 United States of America, Bureau of the Census, *Twelfth Census of the United States, 1900*, Philadelphia Ward 32, Philadelphia, PA, page 6, enumeration district 0814.

101 United States of America, Bureau of the Census, *Thirteenth Census of the United States, 1910*, Philadelphia Ward 32, Philadelphia, PA, roll T624_1403, page 4B, enumeration district 0757.

102 United States of America, Bureau of the Census, *Fourteenth Census of the United States, 1920*, Philadelphia Ward 38, Philadelphia, PA, roll T625_1636, page 1B, enumeration district 1345.

103 Pennsylvania Historic and Museum Commission, *Pennsylvania, U.S., Death Certificates, 1906–1967*, "Thomas Washington Hitchcock," certificate number range 102001–105000.

104 United States of America, Bureau of the Census, *Fifteenth Census of the United States, 1930*, Philadelphia, PA, page 19B, enumeration district 0785.

105 Webber, "Slums No Accident."

106 Webber.

107 Webber.

108 Webber.

109 Storey, *Study of Municipal Recreation in Philadelphia*, 22.

110 "Interview: Edgar Campbell."

111 "Act 132."

112 Royal, *Not Paved for Us*, 1.

2. "THUGS," "BANDITS," AND GANG ATTACKS

1 Webber, "In Philadelphia."

2 Webber.

3 J. J. Johnson, "ReMemory," 102.

4 Webber, "In Philadelphia."

5 Webber.

6 Simon, *Philadelphia*, 74–75.

7 Carlisle, "In Logan Square."

8 K. Glover, *Leisure for Living*, 60–61. Based on archival records at Temple University's Special Collections Research Center, Philadelphia's Crime Prevention Association (CPA) existed well into the mid-1970s.

9 K. Glover, 60–61.

10 K. Glover, 60–61.

11 United States Congress Senate Committee on the Judiciary Subcommittee to Investigate Juvenile Delinquency, *Hearings*, 33–34.

12 Webber, "In Philadelphia."

13 Webber.

14 Webber.

15 Webber.

16 Webber.

17 Webber.

18 Avery, "As Neighborhoods Change." The Pearl Theatre was a popular jazz venue known for its upper-class clientele, its dances, and the celebrities who performed there, like Count Basie, Duke Ellington, and Pearl Bailey. It was in operation from 1927 to 1963 and demolished in 1970. In 1987, Columbia Avenue in North Philadelphia (from 33rd Street to Frankford Avenue) was renamed Cecil B. Moore Avenue. Cecil Bassett Moore (1915–79) was a lawyer, civil rights activist, and Philadelphia City Council member whose career was defined by his strong advocacy for working-class and poor African Americans in North Philadelphia.

19 Webber, "Slum Profits in Philadelphia."

20 Rothstein, *Color of Law*, 1.

21 Webber, "In Philadelphia."

22 Corson, *Article Soliciting Funds*.

23 Barbour, "Gangs and Their Locations."

24 Barbour.

25 Franklin, "Operation Street Corner," 197.

26 Franklin, 209–11.

27 Franklin, 204.

28 Franklin, 204.

29 *Children Play Ping Pong.*

30 *Youth Cleaning Streets and Lots.*

31 Simon, *Philadelphia*, 81.

32 Simon, 79–80.

33 Altschuler and Blumin, *GI Bill*, 118.

34 Desmond and Emirbayer, *Racial Domination, Racial Progress.*

35 Cohen, *Consumer's Republic*, 170–71.

36 Sugrue, *Sweet Land of Liberty*, 229.

37 Sugrue, 225.

38 Spencer, *In the Crossfire*, 23–26.

39 Spencer, 23–26.

40 Spencer, 23–26.

41 See Matthew F. Delmont's 2012 book *The Nicest Kids in Town: American Bandstand, Rock 'n' Roll, and the Struggle for Civil Rights in 1950s Philadelphia* for a thorough discussion of de facto school segregation in the city, particularly involving Northeast High School.

42 Asquith, *Emergency Teacher*, 1.

43 Asquith, 1–4.

44 Asquith, 4.

45 Kitzmiller, *Roots of Educational Inequality*, 109. Today, black student enrollment in the School District of Philadelphia is approximately 60 percent.

46 Asquith, *Emergency Teacher*, 5.

47 Whalen, *From Puerto Rico to Philadelphia*, 55–82.

48 Asquith, *Emergency Teacher*, 5.

49 Smart, "Old Northeast Was Built for Learning."

50 Asquith, *Emergency Teacher*, 5–6.

51 Asquith, 6–8.

52 Asquith, 7–8.

53 Asquith, 7–8.

54 Levenstein, *Movement without Marches*, 127.

55 Levenstein, 127.

56 K. E. Johnson, "Police-Black Community Relations in Postwar Philadelphia."

57 Wolfinger, *Philadelphia Divided*, 2.

58 K. E. Johnson, "Police-Black Community Relations in Postwar Philadelphia," 120.

59 K. E. Johnson, 120–22.

60 K. E. Johnson, 120–22.

61 K. E. Johnson, 120–22.

62 K. E. Johnson, 120–22.

63 Schneider, Agee, and Chronopoulos, "Dirty Work." The term *dirty worker* origi-
    nates from sociologist Lee Rainwater, who described it as someone who does
    undesirable tasks that mainstream society wants completed but the society itself
    refuses to publicly recognize. Rainwater's original use of the term *dirty worker* can
    be found in this article: Rainwater, "Revolt of the Dirty Workers."

64 Schneider, "Crime."

65 Ward, "Police Athletic League."

66 "Philadelphia Strike in 1903 Gave Rise to 'Children's Army.'"

67 Antosh, "Gus Rangnow."

68 PAL centers also offered children arts and crafts, homework clubs, and literacy
    programs.

69 "Tribune Sports."

70 "Sniper Shoots Down Police."

71 Ward, "Police Athletic League."

72 Franklin, "Operation Street Corner," 198–200. Wilbur Miller Barbour (1907–57)
    was a celebrated social scientist and housing activist who later served as regional
    director of the Urban League in Los Angeles.

73 Thrasher, *Gang*, 38.

74 Dimitriadis, "Situation Complex."

75 Park and Burgess, *City*, 62.

76 Coughlin and Venkatesh, "Urban Street Gang after 1970," 41–64.

77 Thrasher, *Gang*, 286–92.

78 Ngai, *Impossible Subjects*, 42.

79 Pasto, "'Street Corner Society' Revisited."

80 Whyte, *Street Corner Society*, 1–25.

81 *Hearings before the United States Senate Committee to Investigate Juvenile Delin-
    quency*, 48–58. A gang worker is a social worker who directly interacts with gang
    members on street corners and in recreation centers. From the 1940s through the
    1970s, gang workers from settlement houses and antigang programs spent hours talk-
    ing with gang members to gain the youths' trust, direct them to a recreation center
    for positive mentorship, and educate them about the pitfalls of gang life so that they
    would abandon gang activity in the future. During the 1970s, some gang workers in
    programs like Safe Streets, Inc. (from 1969 to 1976), were college-educated in the field
    of social work, while others were former gang members who relied on their personal
    experiences to educate and guide youth away from gang activity.

82 Barbour, "Gangs and Their Locations."

83 *Hearings before the United States Senate Committee to Investigate Juvenile Delin-
    quency*, 48–58.

84 Barbour, "Gangs and Their Locations."

85 *Hearings before the United States Senate Committee to Investigate Juvenile Delinquency*, 48–58.

86 Barbour, "Gangs and Their Locations."

87 Franklin, "Operation Street Corner," 195–218.

88 *Hearings before the United States Senate Committee to Investigate Juvenile Delinquency*, 48–58.

89 Sugrue, *Sweet Land of Liberty*, 224–29.

90 Wolfinger, *Philadelphia Divided*, 2.

91 Wolfinger, 203.

92 Police Study Task Force, *Philadelphia and Its Police*, 122–23.

93 According to Pennsylvania law, a forcible felony crime is rape, murder, armed robbery, or kidnapping.

94 Police Study Task Force, *Philadelphia and Its Police*, 122.

95 Police Study Task Force, 132.

96 Police Study Task Force, 122–23.

97 Schneider, *Ecology of Homicide*, 52.

98 Singer, "Dawn Patrol."

99 Lisowski, "Police Officers Waking Teen Sleeping in Bus Station."

100 Karafin, "Problem of Teen-Age Street Gangs."

101 Karafin.

102 "Five Typical Cases Handled by the Juvenile Aid Bureau."

103 Monahan, "Police Dispositions of Juvenile Offenders," 133. In December 2012, the YSC closed, and a new twenty-four-hour facility opened in West Philadelphia at 91 North 48th Street as the Juvenile Justice Services Center.

104 Karafin, "Problem of Teen-Age Street Gangs." The Juvenile Aid Bureau regularly collected, managed, and possessed files of statistics along with arrest and court records of juveniles aged six to seventeen. In 1955, Philadelphia's Central Statistical Unit became responsible for compiling data from juvenile record forms when the city was admitted into the Federal Bureau of Investigation's (FBI) reporting system.

105 Hornblum, *Sentenced to Science*, 19.

106 Karafin, "Problem of Teen-Age Street Gangs."

107 Karafin.

108 Karafin.

109 Karafin.

110 "Thug Kills Businessman on Broad St." In 1956, the Silver Dollar Check Cashing agency was located at 711 South Broad Street in South Philadelphia.

111 "Thug Kills Businessman on Broad St."

112 Hornblum, *Sentenced to Science*, 9–20.

113 United States of America, Bureau of the Census, *Seventeenth Census of the United States, 1950*. Based on US Federal Census records, military registration cards, and vital records (particularly birth and death certificates) from 1910 to 1950,

Thomas J. Gibbons (1904–88), a Philadelphia native, grew up in a blue-collar family in which his father spent much of his life working as an engineer for the Baltimore and Ohio Railroad. In 1910, Gibbons and his family lived at 2043 South Cecil Street, and from 1918 to 1930, they lived at 2035 South 58th Street in Southwest Philadelphia. From 1940 to 1950, Gibbons, along with his wife and four children, lived at 3031 Knorr Street, while his parents lived a four-minute walk away from his home, at 2927 Longshore Avenue in the Northeast, where many white families often moved to escape desegregation throughout inner-city Philadelphia before migrating to the suburbs. Prior to Gibbons's death in 1988, he lived in Hollywood, Florida, where the population was over 78 percent white. For more discussion on covert racism and the usage of euphemisms to hide racist attitudes during this era, see Stephanie G. Wolf's article "The Bicentennial City, 1968–1982" in the 1982 book *Philadelphia: A 300-Year History*.

114 AP News, "Thomas Gibbons."
115 "Thug Kills Businessman on Broad St."
116 "Thug Kills Businessman on Broad St."
117 "Thug Kills Businessman on Broad St."
118 Karafin, "Problem of Teen-Age Street Gangs."
119 "Street-Corner Slaying of Youth."
120 "4 in Teen Gang Jailed in Killing."
121 "Kid Gloves Won't End Gang Wars."
122 "Kid Gloves Won't End Gang Wars."
123 Cassidy, "Most Explosive Race Problem Is in the North," 1–4.
124 Cassidy, 2.
125 Cassidy, 3–4.
126 Cassidy, 4.
127 Binzen, *Nearly Everybody Read It*.
128 Cassidy, "Most Explosive Race Problem in North."
129 Lombardo, *Blue-Collar Conservatism*, 28–30.
130 Lombardo, 28–30.
131 Lombardo, 28–30.
132 Lombardo, 30–33.
133 Lombardo, 28–30.
134 Hirsch, *Making the Second Ghetto*, xii.

3. TOUGH ON CRIME

1 Shubin, "Memorial to a Murder"; "Fatal Beating Hearing for 11 on Wednesday."
2 "DA to Ask Adult Trials for 8 Teeners in Killing."
3 Shubin, "Memorial to a Murder."
4 Shubin.
5 "DA to Ask Adult Trials for 8 Teeners in Killing."
6 "Police Capture 11 in Korean's Fatal Beating." The eleven teenage boys involved in the murder of In-Ho Oh were Alfonso Borum, Douglas Clark, Harry McCloud,

Sonny (Edward) McCloud, Lonnie Collins, Harold Johnson, Leonard Johnson, Percy Johnson, Franklin Marshall, James Wright, and Robert Williams. See Eric C. Schneider's 2020 book *The Ecology of Homicide: Race, Place, and Space in Postwar Philadelphia* for a detailed account of the murder case.

7 "125 Police Ordered into Murder Area to Curb Teen Gangs."

8 "In-Ho Oh's Parents to Give $500 to 'Help' His Slayers."

9 Shubin, "Memorial to a Murder."

10 Peters, "Race Mortician Directed Rites for In-Ho Oh."

11 "Mayor Starts Drive for Fund to Honor Slain Student."

12 "CITIES."

13 Lewis, "Gang Murders Korean Student in West Phila."

14 "CITIES."

15 Schneider, *Ecology of Homicide*, 34–35.

16 Schneider, 32–50.

17 J. Clark, "Shotgun Blast Triggers Young Great Society."

18 Schneider, *Ecology of Homicide*, 41–42.

19 Geffen, "Industrial Development and Social Crisis."

20 Clark and Clark, "Rally and Relapse," 664–68.

21 Clark and Clark, 676.

22 Finkel, "Roots of Hypersegregation in Philadelphia." In Finkel's article, he argues that hypersegregation was not in Philadelphia's "original DNA" because Philadelphia was "designed" and "destined" for "social, economic, and racial integration." Finkel suggests that eighteenth-century Quaker William Penn's idea of Philadelphia as a society of religious and racial harmony was the original design. However, when the Great Migration sparked an influx of thousands of African Americans who were "overwhelmingly rural and predominantly Southern" to Philadelphia, many white people embraced white flight and segregation in "accommodations, services, education, and religion."

23 Kim, "Death in Philadelphia, 1958."

24 Eric Schneider's *Ecology of Homicide* offers a detailed discussion of how universities in Philadelphia gentrified black neighborhoods located near their campuses for profit and to provide public safety for their students. Davarian L. Baldwin's recently published book *In the Shadow of the Ivory Tower: How Universities Are Plundering Our Cities* offers an additional look at this issue.

25 Forman, *Locking Up Our Own*, 44–45. The idea of black activists providing "guardianship" over criminal black youth comes from Forman's book. In the book, Forman describes how black court officials, community organizers, and elected officials promoted a range of policies to deter criminality and protect black people's reputation in mainstream society: incarceration, rehabilitation, and strict drug and gun laws. These policies had positive and negative effects on black youth. Strict crime laws and incarceration were particularly detrimental to African Americans in the long run because many individuals experienced recidivism and social stigma for the rest of their lives.

26 Perkiss, *Making Good Neighbors*, 36–51.
27 Lee, *Dynamics of Ethnic Identity*, 38–40. For a closer look at the topic of Asian Americans cast as the "model minority," see Madeline Hsu's book *The Good Immigrants: How the Yellow Peril Became the Model Minority.*
28 Perkiss, *Making Good Neighbors*, 36–51.
29 Perkiss, 50–54.
30 "Capt. Rizzo Refuses to Stop Arrests." See Timothy J. Lombardo's 2018 book *Blue-Collar Conservatism: Frank Rizzo's Philadelphia and Populist Politics* for the most recent history on Frank Rizzo and his effect on the city of Philadelphia.
31 Hamilton, *Rizzo*, 47–57.
32 Paolantonio, *Rizzo*, 35–41. See Fred Hamilton's 1973 book *Rizzo: From Cop to Mayor of Philadelphia* (particularly page 58) for a detailed description of the organizations, locally and internationally, that commended Rizzo's efforts to curb crime in Philadelphia.
33 Perkiss, *Making Good Neighbors*, 50–54. On the "racial theory of property value," see Carl Nightingale, *Segregation: A Global History of Divided Cities* (Chicago: University of Chicago Press, 2012), 305.
34 Schneider, *Ecology of Homicide*, 32–39.
35 Schneider, 36.
36 "Other Editors' Views."
37 "11 Lashed as 'Vermin' and Held without Bail in Killing of Student." Following a series of trials and appeals, the teenagers involved in In-Ho Oh's death were either charged with first- or second-degree murder and received a variety of sentences ranging from ten years' probation to life imprisonment. See Schneider, *Ecology of Homicide*, 48.
38 Schneider, *Ecology of Homicide*, 37–38.
39 Schneider, 40–41.
40 "Death on the Doorstep."
41 "Attack Penn Foreign Student."
42 R. P. Brown, letter to Mayor Richardson Dilworth.
43 Dilworth, letter to Mrs. D. German.
44 Copman, letter to Mayor Richardson Dilworth.
45 Shockley, letter to Mayor Richardson Dilworth.
46 Dilworth, letter to Joseph T. Clancy.
47 Dilworth, letter to Benjamin Cohen.
48 Dilworth, "New Industry."
49 Schneider, *Ecology of Homicide*, 37 (for Steinberg quote), 41–50.
50 Schneider, 39.
51 Anderson, *Gang Unit*, 20–25. During this time period, the Philadelphia Police Department considered a gang to be a group of at least three individuals. The author of this monograph, M. Phineas Anderson, was head of Saint Augustine Academy, an all-girls school in Norristown, PA. He received his A.B. from Trinity College and his MEd from Harvard Graduate School of Education.

52 Kane, "Tops and Bottoms," 74.

53 Kane, 74–76.

54 Kane, 74, 76–77.

55 Kane, 78–79.

56 Graham et al., "Parents of Youths Shocked, Saddened by Brutal Killing."

57 Graham et al.

58 Graham et al.

59 Graham et al.

60 United Presbyterian Church in the USA, *Epistle from the Koreans*.

61 United Presbyterian Church in the USA, 16:57–17:32.

62 Perkiss, *Making Good Neighbors*, 54.

63 "Youth, 15, Stabbed to Death."

64 "Boy Stabbed to Death in Teen Gang Attack." In 1963, Thomas Edison High School was located at 8th Street and Lehigh Avenue in Fairhill, while John Wanamaker Junior High School was located at 12th Street and Montgomery Avenue in Yorktown. The two original school buildings (now demolished) were approximately 1.3 miles away from each other. The other teens involved in the gang attack were sixteen-year-olds Allen Chapman and Richard Savoy, fifteen-year-old Leroy Odom, fourteen-year-old Alexander Branch, and thirteen-year-old Larry Braxton.

65 "Boy Stabbed to Death in Teen Gang Attack."

66 Schneider, *Ecology of Homicide*, 78.

67 "Gang Slaying."

68 "Angry Judge Sentences 5 in Gang Slaying."

69 "North: Doing No Good."

70 "No Other Life."

71 "North: Doing No Good." Based on the oral histories and interviews I analyzed surrounding the 1964 Columbia Avenue event, I classify the incident as both an uprising and riot. See Countryman, *Up South*, for a thorough exploration of the 1964 Columbia Avenue Riots and Philadelphia's civil rights movement from the 1940s to 1970s.

72 Ferrick, Carvajal, and Gibbons, "25-Year-Old Scars of a Riot Violence of 1964."

73 "No Other Life."

74 Hamilton, *Rizzo*, 66–69.

75 Ferrick, Carvajal, and Gibbons, "25-Year-Old Scars of a Riot."

76 Murray and McAdams, "Subway Patrols Beefed Up."

77 "City Leaders Honor Sailor as Subway Attack Hero."

78 Murray and McAdams, "Subway Patrols Beefed Up."

79 Murray and McAdams.

80 Murray and McAdams.

81 Dixon, *Clansman*, 182.

82 Berry, *All That Makes a Man*, 1–304.

83 Cook, *Thomas Dixon*, 68.

84 Murray and McAdams, "Subway Patrols Beefed Up."

85 Murray and McAdams.

86 Murray and McAdams.

87 Murray and McAdams.

88 Murray and McAdams.

89 Murray and McAdams.

90 Murray and McAdams. Juanita Kidd Stout (1919–98) was an Oklahoma-born attorney who began her own law practice in Philadelphia in 1954. In 1988, she became the first black woman in the United States appointed as judge to a state supreme court. In 2012, Philadelphia's criminal justice center was renamed in her honor.

91 Murray and McAdams.

92 Murray and McAdams.

93 J. Clark, "Shotgun Blast Triggers Young Great Society."

94 Horton Berg, *I Cry When the Sun Goes Down*, 101.

95 McCurdy, "I Couldn't Run Away from Those Streets."

96 Horton Berg, *I Cry When the Sun Goes Down*, 151–55.

97 J. Clark, "Shotgun Blast Triggers Young Great Society."

98 J. Clark.

99 J. Clark.

100 J. Clark.

101 J. Clark.

102 *Young Great Society Members Painting a House.*

103 *Women from the New Mantua Infant Care Center Stand in Front of Wooden Shack.* Herman Wrice's wife, Jean Wrice, worked with Mrs. Ione Strauss, president of the alumnae association at University of Pennsylvania; Mrs. Hattie Thompson, president of the Day Care Center Advisory Board; and Mrs. Jane Freeman of the Family Service of Philadelphia to establish the New Mantua Infant Care Center at 651 North 35th Street in West Philadelphia on behalf of the Young Greats Society.

104 *Juvenile Gang Leaders Return from Puerto Rico.*

105 Anderson, *Gang Unit*, 7. M. Phineas Anderson's 1969 manual *The Gang Unit* was sponsored by the nonprofit corporation the Pennsylvania Advancement School. The manual consisted of sociological research on gangs, statistics on juvenile gang violence in Philadelphia, and classroom lesson plans for teachers who may encounter gang-affiliated youth in their schools.

106 Anderson, 26–27.

107 Anderson, 19.

108 Anderson, 10.

109 Anderson, 12.

110 Anderson, 20–25.

111 Anderson, 20–25.

112 Anderson, 20–25.

113 Anderson, 20–25.

114 Anderson, 20–25.

115 Anderson, 20–25.
116 Anderson, 84–85.
117 Anderson, 84–85.
118 Anderson, 2.
119 Anderson, 17–18.
120 Anderson, 20.
121 Janson, "Gangs Face Drive in Philadelphia."
122 Shuttleworth, "Sennett to Wait for Gang Study."
123 Jargowsky, Wheeler, and Gillette, "Poverty."
124 Shuttleworth, "Sennett to Wait for Gang Study."
125 Shuttleworth.
126 Larkin and Clancy, "Rizzo Pleads for Funds to Fight Gangs."
127 Larkin and Clancy.
128 Larkin and Clancy.
129 Larkin and Clancy.
130 "Billions for Safe Streets."
131 According to journalist Fred Hamilton, when Frank Rizzo was a deputy police commissioner, he worked alongside Police Commissioner Howard R. Leary to design strategies to enhance several special units of the police department. Rizzo worked with Leary to create a team of sharpshooters trained to use "high-powered rifles with telescopic sights" to function in the stakeout, antirobbery, and riot service aspects of policing. Rizzo established the policy of black and white officers patrolling together by car in black communities and equipped patrolmen with walkie-talkies that could be used to radio police district headquarters for help or reinforcements. Hamilton also claimed that Rizzo attempted to convince City Council to purchase helicopters and two bullet-proof personnel carriers to enhance criminal investigations, but the request to militarize the police department in this manner was denied.
132 Hamilton, *Rizzo*, 70–75.
133 "Hearings on Gang Warfare."
134 Thrasher, *Gang*, 286–92.
135 Thompson, "Why Mass Incarceration Matters."

4. SAFE STREETS, INC.
 1 "Philadelphia Gangs."
 2 "Arlene Urges Talks on Gangs."
 3 "City's Gang Youths."
 4 Dougherty and Griffenberg, "5 Held in 'Get Anybody' Killing of Temple Graduate Student."
 5 Murphy and Lintz, "Bullet Kills Girl, 7."
 6 Speer, "Safe Streets Project."
 7 Speer.
 8 Speer.

9 "U.S. Gives DA $80,000 for Gang Control."

10 Speer, "Safe Streets Project."

11 Speer.

12 Speer. When twenty-one-year-old Bennie Swans joined the staff of Safe Streets, Inc., around 1970, he was a Vietnam veteran looking to volunteer after hearing news about the rise in gang violence in Philadelphia. In 1975, Swans left Safe Streets, Inc., to establish the nonprofit antigang organization the Crisis Intervention Network (CIN), which remained in operation until 1991.

13 Speer.

14 The North Philadelphia location was a rowhome in a residential neighborhood, while the West Philadelphia location was a storefront connected to a row of businesses.

15 "U.S. Gives DA $80,000 for Gang Control."

16 Donner, "Rizzo's Philadelphia," 197–244.

17 T. Johnson, "Men Needed to Share Skills with Boys."

18 Lombardo, *Blue-Collar Conservatism*, 140–41.

19 "U.S. Gives DA $80,000 for Gang Control."

20 Speer, "Safe Streets Project."

21 Speer.

22 Speer.

23 Ferrick, "Safe Streets Center Seeks to Expand Effective Work."

24 Speer, "Safe Streets Project."

25 Speer.

26 Speer.

27 Ferrick, "Safe Streets Center Seeks to Expand Effective Work."

28 "U.S. Gives City $150,000 for Gang Control."

29 "U.S. Gives City $150,000 for Gang Control."

30 Speer, "Safe Streets Project."

31 "Sandy Grady . . . on the Loose."

32 "Sandy Grady . . . on the Loose."

33 "Sandy Grady . . . on the Loose."

34 "Sandy Grady . . . on the Loose."

35 "Sandy Grady . . . on the Loose."

36 "Gang Members Who Have Taken Auto Mechanic Course."

37 Daughen and Binzen, *Cop Who Would Be King*, 149–50.

38 Daughen and Binzen, 149.

39 Daughen and Binzen, 150.

40 *Black Panther Party.*

41 Blakemore, "How the Black Panthers' Breakfast Program Both Inspired and Threatened the Government."

42 The BPP's Free Breakfast for School Children Program began in January 1969 in Oakland, California. BPP members and volunteers consulted nutritionists on breakfast options and went to local grocery stores requesting donations to buy

healthy food (specifically eggs, chocolate milk, meat, cereal, and fresh oranges) to feed tens of thousands of kids nationwide. The BPP's breakfast program later influenced the federal government to authorize free breakfast in public schools by 1975.

43 Daughen and Binzen, *Cop Who Would Be King*, 147–55.
44 Daughen and Binzen, 150–55.
45 Umansky and Moore, "Economic, Racial Fears Fan Bartram Row."
46 Umansky and Moore.
47 Umansky and Moore.
48 Umansky and Moore.
49 Umansky and Moore.
50 Umansky and Moore.
51 Umansky and Moore.
52 Umansky and Moore.
53 Umansky and Moore.
54 Elkins, "'It Was like a War.'"
55 Larkin and Clancy, "Rizzo Pleads for Funds to Fight Gangs."
56 Larkin and Clancy.
57 Janson, "Gangs Face Drive in Philadelphia."
58 Janson.
59 Janson.
60 Janson.
61 Janson.
62 Janson.
63 Caparella, "Gang Leader Who Pledged Peace Held in Killing."
64 T. Johnson, "'He Said Somebody Would Be Killed.'"
65 Moore, "Slain Gang Worker to Be Honored Today."
66 Moore.
67 T. Johnson, "'He Said Somebody Would Be Killed.'"
68 T. Johnson.
69 T. Johnson.
70 T. Johnson.
71 Moore, "Slain Gang Worker to Be Honored Today."
72 Moore.
73 Moore.
74 Moore.
75 W. Brown, "'Peacemaker' Held in Murder."
76 T. Johnson, "Gang Slaying Kills Peace Dream."
77 T. Johnson.
78 T. Johnson.
79 Youth in Conflict Cooperative Service Project, *Safe Streets, Inc.*
80 Youth in Conflict Cooperative Service Project.
81 Youth in Conflict Cooperative Service Project.

82 Youth in Conflict Cooperative Service Project.

83 Youth in Conflict Cooperative Service Project.

84 Youth in Conflict Cooperative Service Project.

85 Youth in Conflict Cooperative Service Project.

86 Kotzbauer, "Safe Streets Gang Control Gets $30,000."

87 Kotzbauer.

88 "Millions for Safe Streets, and Crime Still Climbs."

89 Kotzbauer, "Safe Streets Gang Control Gets $30,000."

90 "Gang-Control Loses Bid for U.S. Aid."

91 "Gang-Control Loses Bid for U.S. Aid."

92 "Gang-Control Loses Bid for U.S. Aid."

93 "Gang-Control Loses Bid for U.S. Aid."

94 Miller, *Violence by Youth Gangs and Youth Groups*, 1–10.

95 Miller, 27.

96 Miller, 27.

97 Kotzbauer, "Cast-Off Kids Will Go to Foster Homes, Not Lockup."

98 Kotzbauer.

99 "Billions for Safe Streets Yield Failure, Fear, Fury."

100 "Billions for Safe Streets Yield Failure, Fear, Fury."

101 Paolantonio, *Rizzo*, 240.

102 Clark and Clark, "Rally and Relapse," 676.

103 Hamilton, *Rizzo*, 202–3.

104 Hamilton, 202–3.

105 "In Memoriam: Lennox L. Moak."

106 Goode and Schneider, *Reshaping Ethnic and Racial Relations in Philadelphia*, 35.

107 Mugge, *Amateur Night at City Hall*.

108 Goode and Schneider, *Reshaping Ethnic and Racial Relations in Philadelphia*, 34.

109 Mugge, *Amateur Night at City Hall*.

110 Geffen, "Industrial Development and Social Crisis."

111 Goode and Schneider, *Reshaping Ethnic and Racial Relations in Philadelphia*, 34. Today, Kensington still retains the stigma of being a blighted neighborhood, especially after the crack cocaine epidemic of the 1980s, when some blocks within the area contained open-air drug markets near intersections like Kensington and Allegheny Avenues, also known as the K&A.

5. "WELCOME TO THE JUNGLE"
Epigraph: McCaffrey, "Didn't Know It Was a Cop."

1 Morrison and Bridgeo, "Policeman in Critical Condition."

2 David, "To Live in Fear."

3 "Violence Is a Way of Life at Project."

4 "Wilson Park Homes Set for Use."

5 Walton, "Trapped."

6 Interstate 76 (I-76), which travels through South and Southwest Philadelphia, was built in 1964.

7 "Violence Is a Way of Life at Project."

8 Walton, "Trapped."

9 "Policeman's Death."

10 "Mindless Tragedy Ruins Six Lives."

11 David, "Murder Trial Told of Bullet Casings."

12 David, "Youth Falters at Murder Trial."

13 "Shot Fatal to Officer Came from Youth's Rifle."

14 It is unknown whether the youths Martin identified as boys from the "Passyunk Gang" were actually gang members. What is known is that Wilson Park housing project security guards ordered boys from the Passyunk Homes housing project to disperse and leave Wilson Park following the shooting.

15 David, "Murder Trial Pits Youth against Pal."

16 "Sniper Shoots Down Police."

17 "Shooting Jars Band."

18 David, "Murder Trial Pits Youth against Pal."

19 "Policeman's Death."

20 "$3 Million Suit over Death."

21 "Sniper Shoots Down Police." In the 1960s and 1970s, police used the military term *sniper* to refer to unidentified shooters who operated from elevated positions in undisclosed areas like windows in high-rises and on roofs. Following the Civil Rights Movement, the term became popular when racial uprisings against police brutality like the 1967 Newark Riots occurred in the era of the Vietnam War (1955–75).

22 Morrison and Bridgeo, "Policeman in Critical Condition."

23 Morrison and Bridgeo.

24 "Police Were Lawless in Terror at Wilson Park."

25 "Sniper Shoots Down Police."

26 Morrison and Bridgeo, "Policeman in Critical Condition."

27 Morrison and Bridgeo.

28 Morrison and Bridgeo.

29 "Policeman Is Shot by a Sniper."

30 McCaffrey, "Didn't Know It Was a Cop."

31 McCaffrey.

32 Morrison and Bridgeo, "Policeman in Critical Condition."

33 "Policeman Loses Fight with Sniper's Bullet."

34 Wilson, "Philadelphia Police Put Net over Crime Area." Operation FIND was a revamped version of the previous Fugitive Search Plan, where police were assigned to "strategic" locations along the perimeter of the city. See the appendix for a chart of "successful" apprehensions under Operation FIND.

35 Wilson.

36 Federal Bureau of Investigation, *FBI Law Enforcement Bulletin*.

37 Operation FIND is not commonly known by name to Philadelphians today, but
    it is still used in manhunts for suspects who murder police officers. For ex-
    ample, on October 31, 2007, twenty-five-year veteran Philadelphia police officer
    Charles "Chuck" Cassidy was shot in the head and killed by twenty-one-year-old
    Lewis M. Jordan (known as John Lewis) when he interrupted an armed robbery
    at a Dunkin Donuts at North Broad Street and Old York Road. Operation FIND
    was immediately implemented in the surrounding Northwest/North Philadel-
    phia area and remained in effect for several days. Some residents even reported
    that police broke down their homes' doors during the police's search of the
    neighborhood. Jordan was later apprehended in Florida. Once in police custody,
    Jordan confessed to the crimes of robbery and murder. He was later sentenced
    to death in 2009, and he currently sits on death row at SCI-Phoenix in Skippack,
    Pennsylvania.

38 Dougherty and Griffenberg, "Rookie Cop Is Slain."

39 Foley, *Unsolved Shooting*, 1–50.

40 Dougherty and Griffenberg, "Rookie Cop Is Slain."

41 Wilson, "Philadelphia Police Put Net over Crime Area."

42 Foley, *Unsolved Shooting*, 5–97. After more than fifty years since the murder of
    Patrolman Cione and subsequent investigation of the crime by the police depart-
    ment and the FBI, the case remains unsolved today.

43 Federal Bureau of Investigation, *FBI Law Enforcement Bulletin*, 3–6, 29.

44 "Black Clergy Give Support to Suit against Top Police."

45 "Black Clergy Give Support to Suit against Top Police."

46 Foley, *Unsolved Shooting* 5–97.

47 Heimer, "Man, 20, Arrested in Cop Shooting."

48 Lear, "Southwark Residents Protest PHA."

49 Lear, "Southwark Residents Say Police Used 'Gestapo Tactics.'"

50 "Police Were Lawless in Terror at Wilson Park."

51 Muskil, "Murder of a Millionaire."

52 "Police Were Lawless in Terror at Wilson Park."

53 Lewis, *Five Families*.

54 Lewis, "Culture of Poverty."

55 Lewis.

56 Lewis.

57 United States Department of Labor, *Negro Family*.

58 United States Department of Labor.

59 Stack, *All Our Kin*.

60 Stack, 24.

61 Davis, *Women, Race, and Class*. See Daniel Geary's 2015 book *Beyond Civil Rights:
    The Moynihan Report and Its Legacy* for more information on the life and career
    of anthropologist Oscar Lewis.

62 Frank Rizzo was police commissioner of Philadelphia from 1967 to 1972 and
    mayor from 1972 to 1980.

63 Lombardo, *Blue-Collar Conservatism*, 140.

64 Mugge, *Amateur Night at City Hall*.

65 Mugge.

66 City of Philadelphia Office of the Mayor News Release, "Remarks by Mayor Frank L. Rizzo."

67 City of Philadelphia Office of the Mayor News Release.

68 City of Philadelphia Office of the Mayor News Release.

69 Grusin, Bergman, and Bergman, *Good Times* theme song.

70 Anderson, "Project Tenants Confer with Law to Curb Crime."

71 Peters, "Triggerman Suspect Arrested in Rosen Cop Shooting."

72 Lawson, *Pruitt-Igoe Projects*, 20–21.

73 Bauman, "Black Slums / Black Projects," 336.

74 Levenstein, *Movement without Marches*, 111.

75 Coates, "Case for Reparations."

76 Bauman, "Black Slums / Black Projects," 320–23.

77 Washington, "Women Live in Fear in Southwark Unit."

78 Walton, "Trapped."

79 Hunt, *Blueprint for Disaster*, 173.

80 Washington, "Tenants Vow to Hold Rent."

81 Washington.

82 Lawson, *Pruitt-Igoe Projects*, 58–59.

83 Glover, "Factions May Fight over Drug Market."

84 Hunt, *Blueprint for Disaster*, 170–74.

85 "4th Suspect Sought in Killing of 2 Chicago Policemen."

86 Austen, *High-Risers*, 74–75.

87 Austen, 74–75.

88 Washington, "Women Live in Fear in Southwark Unit."

89 Weisenbach, "Social Worker, 2 Teens Shot." In 1965, Martin Luther King Jr. gave a speech at the Hawthorne Square housing project during the Freedom Rally in Philadelphia. In 1970, the housing project was renamed Martin Luther King Plaza.

90 Weisenbach, "Social Worker, 2 Teens Shot."

91 Terry, "5 Boys Seized in Rape Robbery."

92 Terry.

93 Washington, "Women Live in Fear in Southwark Unit."

94 Mann, "Perils of a Housing Project."

95 Mann.

96 Mann.

97 Mann.

98 Lewis, "Gang Murders Korean Student in West Phila."

99 "Stop Gang Rapings."

100 Cleveland, Benson, and Gaye, "Save the Children."

101 Trettin, "Dad's Final Tribute to a Slain Policeman."

102 "Policeman Dies of Wounds."

103 *Commonwealth of Pennsylvania v. Shirley Munson.*
104 "In Our Opinion."
105 "In Our Opinion."
106 T. Johnson, "Men Needed to Share Skills with Boys." Helen Corprew LCSW
 ACSW QCSW (1928–2018) was a Temple University–educated social worker who
 spent much of her career trying to solve the issue of juvenile delinquency with
 rehabilitation. Around 1966, Corprew became affiliated with the City of Philadelphia, and during the 1970s, she served as the assistant coordinator of the Special
 Service Office for Philadelphia's family court. According to the May 1974 *Philadelphia Daily News* article, Corprew's program, STEPS (Start Towards Eliminating
 Past Setbacks) operated on a "federally funded" budget of $65,000, granted by
 the Law Enforcement Assistance Administration (LEAA). In the 1980s, Corprew
 continued to advocate for the rehabilitation of juvenile delinquents, and her
 initiatives were advertised and promoted not only in newspapers but also on the
 radio. She later operated her own private practice until her retirement around the
 age of eighty-five.
107 David, "Jurors Can't Agree."
108 David.
109 "Martin May Claim Accidental Shooting."
110 Gibbons, "3 Youths Held Without Bail."
111 Commonwealth of Pennsylvania v. Andre Martin.
112 David, "Youth Falters at Murder Trial."
113 Schaeffer, "Defense Rests in Police Slaying at Project."
114 "Mindless Tragedy Ruins Six Lives."
115 "Murderer Draws Life."
116 Schaeffer, "Defense Rests in Police Slaying at Project."
117 David, "Jury Hears Mother Plead for Son's Life."
118 Commonwealth of Pennsylvania v. Andre Martin.
119 "2 Youths Freed in Cop Slaying."
120 Levenstein, *Movement without Marches*, 118.
121 Melamed, "For Juvenile Lifer Who Killed Policeman, 44 Years to Life."
122 Melamed.
123 Allyn, "Prosecutors Seeking 20 More Years for Philly Juvenile Life Who Killed
 Cop."
124 "Information about Inmate."
125 Scolforo, "Pennsylvania Supreme Court Rejects Juvenile Life Sentences."

6. A TRIP TO 8TH AND RACE
Epigraph: Brownworth, "Cradle Beating Witness Says Justice Was Not Served."

 1 Neumann and Marimow, "City Policeman Charged in Beating."
 2 Neumann and Marimow, "A Policeman Is Charged."
 3 Neumann and Marimow.

4 Racher, "Cop Faces Charges in 'Beating.'"

5 Neumann and Marimow, "City Policeman Charged in Beating."

6 T. Johnson, "Cradle."

7 T. Johnson.

8 T. Johnson.

9 "Cops Off the Hook."

10 "Cops Off the Hook."

11 Brownworth, "Cradle Beating Witness Says Justice Was Not Served."

12 Brownworth.

13 Brownworth.

14 Pennsylvania State Committee, *Police-Community Relations in Philadelphia*.

15 Neumann and Marimow, "Homicide Files, Parts I–IV."

16 Pennsylvania State Committee, *Police-Community Relations in Philadelphia*, iii–vi.

17 Pennsylvania State Committee, iii–vi.

18 Pennsylvania State Committee, iii–vi.

19 Pennsylvania State Committee, iii.

20 Pennsylvania State Committee, 1–88.

21 Pennsylvania State Committee, iii–14.

22 Pennsylvania State Committee, 13.

23 In 1963, the Philadelphia Police Department's headquarters moved from the basement of City Hall to the newly built Police Administration Building (colloquially known as the Roundhouse) at 8th and Race Streets in Center City. The facility remained open at that location until 2022, when police headquarters moved to the former home of the *Philadelphia Inquirer* at 440 North Broad Street. Prior to the move, the new facility was renovated and renamed the Philadelphia Public Services Building. The facility contains not only police headquarters but also the Sixth and Ninth Police Districts, the 911 call center, and the medical examiner's office.

24 Pennsylvania State Committee, *Police-Community Relations in Philadelphia*, 9.

25 Pennsylvania State Committee, 32–33.

26 Pennsylvania State Committee, 32–33.

27 Pennsylvania State Committee, 32–33.

28 Pennsylvania State Committee, 33–36.

29 Pennsylvania State Committee, 33–36.

30 Pennsylvania State Committee, 33–36.

31 Pennsylvania State Committee, 33–36.

32 Pennsylvania State Committee, 46–47.

33 Pennsylvania State Committee, 46–47.

34 Pennsylvania State Committee, 46–47.

35 "Fallen Officers-Philadelphia Police Department." The three officers murdered were black officer Charles R. Reynolds in October 1969, white officer Frederick Cione Jr. in January 1970, and black officer Harry Lee Davis in April 1970.

36 Griffin, *Philadelphia's Black Mafia*, 73.

37 Pennsylvania State Committee, *Police-Community Relations in Philadelphia*, 9.
38 Pennsylvania State Committee, 12.
39 Pennsylvania State Committee, 89–103.
40 Police Commissioner Joseph O'Neill was in office from 1971 to 1980, District Attorney Arlen Specter was in office from 1966 to 1974, Mayor James H. J. Tate was in office from 1962 to 1972, and Mayor Frank Rizzo was in office from 1972 to 1980.
41 Pennsylvania State Committee, *Police-Community Relations in Philadelphia*, 99–100.
42 Pennsylvania State Committee, 89–90.
43 Pennsylvania State Committee, 91.
44 Pennsylvania State Committee, 101–3.
45 Pennsylvania Crime Commission, *Report on Police Corruption.*
46 Public Interest Law Center of Philadelphia, miscellaneous letters.
47 Public Interest Law Center of Philadelphia.
48 Project Attorney Lucy J. Weidner of Public Interest Law Center of Philadelphia, "September 14, 1977 Letter to Commissioner Joseph O'Neill."
49 Staff Attorney Ann K. Seidman of Public Interest Law Center of Philadelphia, "January 4, 1977 Letter to Commissioner Joseph O'Neill."
50 *Slain Fairmount Park Police Officer.*
51 Griffin, *Philadelphia's Black Mafia*, 73.
52 "Two Philadelphia Policemen Killed in Shooting Attacks."
53 "Two Philadelphia Policemen Killed in Shooting Attacks."
54 "Two Philadelphia Policemen Killed in Shooting Attacks."
55 Jackson, "Statement of Anthony E. Jackson."
56 McKelvey and Shapiro, "Police Department Overtime."
57 "$3 Million Suit over Death."
58 "$3 Million Suit over Death."
59 "News Briefs."
60 *Commonwealth of Pennsylvania v. Donald Woodruff.*
61 "Policeman Acquitted."
62 "$3 Million Suit over Death."
63 Scanlon and Heimer, "Cop Kills Kensington Youth."
64 Scanlon and Heimer.
65 Scanlon and Heimer.
66 "2 Policemen Arrested, Deadly Force Not Warranted."
67 "'Brothers' Object to Order."
68 "'Brothers' Object to Order."
69 "2 Policemen Arrested, Deadly Force Not Warranted,."
70 "2 Policemen Arrested, Deadly Force Not Warranted."
71 "Philadelphia Policeman Acquitted in Shooting of Handcuffed Prisoner."
72 "2 Policemen Arrested, Deadly Force Not Warranted."
73 "Philadelphia Policeman Acquitted in Shooting of Handcuffed Prisoner."

74 "Philadelphia Policeman Acquitted in Shooting of Handcuffed Prisoner."
75 "Philadelphia Policeman Acquitted in Shooting of Handcuffed Prisoner."
76 "Police Hiring Practices Produce Time-Bombs."
77 "Police Hiring Practices Produce Time-Bombs."
78 "Police Hiring Practices Produce Time-Bombs."
79 *Demonstrations over Police Brutality.*
80 Jackson, "Statement of Anthony E. Jackson," 1–84.
81 Jackson, 1.
82 Jackson, 1.
83 Jackson, 1.
84 Jackson, 14–84.
85 Schneider, *Ecology of Homicide*, 95–96.
86 Mugge, *Amateur Night at City Hall.*
87 Mugge.
88 Mugge.
89 Skolnick and Fyfe, *Above the Law*, 140.
90 "Police Get Overtime Pay Pact, First in City's History."
91 McKelvey and Shapiro, "Police Department Overtime."
92 McKelvey and Shapiro.
93 King, "2 Years after Holmesburg Riot."
94 "Violence Hits Tasker Homes."
95 Griffin, *Philadelphia's Black Mafia*, 73.
96 McKelvey and Shapiro, "Police Department Overtime."
97 McKelvey and Shapiro.
98 McKelvey and Shapiro.
99 McKelvey and Shapiro.

CONCLUSION

1 McKelvey and Shapiro, "Police Department Overtime Runs."
2 Krasner, *For the People*, 5.
3 Clark and Clark, "Rally and Relapse," 652–54.
4 "Curb Meter Looters."
5 "Tate Asks Widening of Realty Tax Base."
6 "Moore Sees No Need for New Taxes."
7 Police Study Task Force, *Philadelphia and Its Police*, 122–23.
8 Dilworth, "New Industry."
9 Collins, "Retirement of 309."
10 Clark and Clark, "Rally and Relapse," 664.
11 Countryman, *Up South*, 1–4.
12 "Moore Brands Tate 'a Racist.'"
13 Lordan, "City's $24 Million Surplus Fund Nearly Exhausted."
14 Lordan and Hussie, "Tate Oks $12.4 Million Spending Cut."
15 Wolf, "Bicentennial City," 708–10.

16 Wolf, 710–20, 727.

17 Branham and Smith, "Hard Times, Higher Taxes and Dirty Streets."

18 Wolf, "Bicentennial City," 722–23.

19 "Frank Rizzo's Last Hurrah?"

20 Neumann and Marimow, "Homicide Files, Part I." The article "The Homicide Files" was in its entirety a four-part series detailing police brutality and corruption within the Philadelphia Police Department. The series won *Philadelphia Inquirer* staff writers Jonathan Neumann and William K. Marimow a Pulitzer Prize for their work.

21 Neumann and Marimow.

22 Neumann and Marimow.

23 Neumann and Marimow. Michael Chitwood joined the Philadelphia Police Department in April 1964. He later became the police superintendent of Upper Darby Township for fourteen years and served as a police officer for a total of fifty-five years until his retirement on December 1, 2019.

24 McKelvey and Shapiro, "Police Department Overtime."

25 Goode and Schneider, *Reshaping Ethnic and Racial Relations in Philadelphia*, 36.

26 For more microhistories on the issue of "asset stripping," in which city governments unequally invest socioeconomic resources in the neighborhoods of the majority (which are oftentimes white and wealthy) while consciously disinvesting from the communities of the minority and further disadvantaging historically marginalized groups for financial gain, see the 2017 edition of Clyde Woods's book *Development Arrested: The Blues and Plantation Power in the Mississippi Delta* along with Joaquín Villanueva, Martín Cobián, and Félix Rodríguez's 2018 article "San Juan, the Fragile City: Finance Capital, Class, and the Making of Puerto Rico's Economic Crisis."

AFTERWORD

Epigraph: Baldwin, *Fire Next Time*, 8.

1 Shubin, "Memorial to a Murder."

2 "DA to Ask Adult Trials for 8 Teeners in Killing."

3 Thrasher, *Gang*, 286–92.

4 Vitale, *End of Policing*, 170–75.

5 "Father and 4 Uncles of Oh Raise Funds for His Killers."

6 American Civil Liberties Union, "What's at Stake."

7 Krasner, *For the People*, 6.

8 "Gov. Josh Shapiro Calls on Legislature to Abolish Death Penalty." As of 2023, Pennsylvania's current governor, Josh Shapiro, has maintained the state moratorium on the death penalty.

9 Krasner, *For the People*, 6.

10 Lowrey, "Trump Says His Tax Plan Won't Benefit the Rich."

11 Alexander, *New Jim Crow*, 5, 48–49.

12 American Civil Liberties Union, "What's at Stake."

13 Krasner, *For the People*, 4–5.

14 Widra and Geffen, "Where People in Prison Come From."

15 Thompson, "Why Mass Incarceration Matters."

16 Rhynhart, "Review and Analysis of the Philadelphia Police Department." This report came into existence following the 2020 nationwide George Floyd protests against police brutality and in response to the Philadelphia City Council's Police Reform Working Group's request that the city provide "transparency and insight about how PPD [Philadelphia Police Department] spends its budgeted funds and deploys available resources." Under the supervision of the Office of the City Controller, the research firm Stout Risius Ross, LLC (Stout), assisted with the review of the Philadelphia Police Department while Horsey, Buckner & Heffler, LLP, and the Center for Policing Equity offered support for the initiative.

17 Rhynhart, 38–44.

18 Rhynhart, 27–28; 31.

19 Rhynhart, 56–57.

20 Rhynhart, 32–36.

21 Rhynhart, 54–55.

22 Sullivan and Baranauckas, "Here's How Much Money Goes to Police Departments in Largest Cities across the U.S." The City of Philadelphia describes its fiscal year as operating from July 1 through June 30.

23 Rhynhart, "Review and Analysis of the Philadelphia Police Department," vi.

24 Parker, "Neighborhood Safety and Community Policing Plan."

25 Rhynhart, "Review and Analysis of the Philadelphia Police Department," 12–24.

26 Wooten, "Philadelphia Also Facing Crisis of Funds Shortage." In 1976, Philadelphia's city budget was approximately $788 million, with $152.5 million allotted for the police department. That year, Philadelphia had approximately 8,600 police officers.

27 Pennsylvania Crime Commission, *Report on Police Corruption*.

28 Trippett, "It Looks Just like a War Zone."

29 Puckett, "Long Shadow of the MOVE Fire."

30 Ismay, "35 Years after MOVE Bombing That Killed 11, Philadelphia Apologizes." On November 12, 2020, Philadelphia City Council adopted Resolution No. 20060900, in which the city formally apologized for the MOVE bombing and recognized May 13th as an annual day of "observation, reflection and recommitment" to reconciliation, justice, and harmony.

31 Police Study Task Force, *Philadelphia and Its Police*, 164.

32 Police Study Task Force, 177.

33 Mogano, "Philly's Police Misconduct Cases Drain Taxpayer Money."

34 Mogano.

35 Rhynhart, "Review and Analysis of the Philadelphia Police Department," 8.

36 Mogano, "Philly's Police Misconduct Cases Drain Taxpayer Money."

37 Institute for Survey Research at Temple University (ISR), "City of Philadelphia 2019–2020 Philadelphia Resident Survey Report."

38 ISR.

39 Rhynhart, "Review and Analysis of the Philadelphia Police Department," 5.

40 Rhynhart, 6–7.

41 Vargas and Palmer, "Philly Eased Police Residency Requirements." The Philadelphia Fire Department's union earned a residency right similar to the police in 2016.

42 Vargas and Palmer.

43 Vargas and Palmer.

44 Wooten, "Philadelphia Also Facing Crisis of Funds Shortage."

45 Gambacorta et al., "Philly's Police Union Spent Decades Amassing Power."

46 Chappell, "Chauvin and 3 Former Officers Face New Charges over George Floyd's Death."

47 Hill et al., "8 Minutes and 46 Seconds."

48 Shammas, Bellware, and Dennis, "Murder Charges Filed against All Four Officers in George Floyd's Death."

49 Marin, "'Unprepared' Philly Police Violated Use-of-Force and Tear Gas Policies."

50 Marin, "Military Psy-Ops or ATM Explosions?"

51 Orso et al., "Philly Police Stood by as Men with Baseball Bats 'Protected' Fishtown."

52 Orso, "Day after Fishtown Residents Walked the Streets with Baseball Bats."

53 "Philadelphia City Council Approves $4.8 Billion Budget in 14-3 Vote."

54 "Philadelphia Rocked by Fresh Unrest after Police Shooting."

55 "Philadelphia Rocked by Fresh Unrest after Police Shooting."

56 Madej, "Three Arrests Related to Unrest Made since Friday."

57 Rhynhart, "Review and Analysis of the Philadelphia Police Department," 45. According to City Controller Rebecca Rhynhart's 2022 report, the Philadelphia Police Department receives an average of 200,000 calls per month, with approximately 60 percent being nonemergency calls. The 311 city services hotline was created to handle complaints of vandalism, nuisances, and illegal dumping of waste. The city controller recommends the City of Philadelphia develop a 411 hotline for mental health issues that will go beyond the "mental health delegate in the 911 radio room every day during the day shift and from 3 PM to 11 PM who assists with calls as needed" and "transfer suicidal calls to a crisis hotline" so that the Philadelphia Police Department can focus on "high-priority incidents" and increase their response time to emergency calls.

58 Spikol, "I've Had Public Mental Health Outbursts like Walter Wallace Jr."

59 Viola, *Click!*

60 "Crime: Bizarre Battle Leaves Two Dead in Philadelphia."

61 T. Johnson, "Men Needed to Share Skills with Boys."

62 Winger, "West Philadelphia's House of Umoja Strengthens Hope and Community."

63 Althouse, "7 Philly Violence Prevention Programs."

BIBLIOGRAPHY

"2 Policemen Arrested, Deadly Force Not Warranted." *Daily News*, October 12, 1978, 19. www.newspapers.com.

"2 Youths Freed in Cop Slaying." *Philadelphia Evening Bulletin*, January 14, 1977. Temple University Special Collections Research Center, *Philadelphia Evening Bulletin* clippings, call no. SCRC 169, vol. Andre Martin, collection URB.

"$3 Million Suit over Death." *Pocono Record*, April 3, 1976, 2. www.newspapers.com.

"4 in Teen Gang Jailed in Killing." *Philadelphia Inquirer*, February 16, 1957, 11. www .newspapers.com.

"4th Suspect Sought in Killing of 2 Chicago Policemen." *Philadelphia Daily News*, July 20, 1970, 33. www.newspapers.com.

"11 Lashed as 'Vermin' And Held Without Bail in Killing of Student." *Philadelphia Inquirer*, May 1, 1958, 1. www.newspapers.com.

"125 Police Ordered into Murder Area to Curb Teen Gangs: Residents Pledged Aid by Gibbons." *Philadelphia Inquirer*, April 29, 1958, 1, 3. www.newspapers.com.

A1: NPR. "To Be In A Rage, Almost All The Time." June 1, 2020, Video, 34:38, www.npr.org.

"Act 132, the Pennsylvania Equal Rights Bill of 1935." ExplorePAHistory.com. Accessed May 28, 2023. https://explorepahistory.com.

Adero, Malaika, ed. Preface to *Up South: Stories, Studies and Letters of This Century's African-American Migrations*. New York: New Press, 1993.

"A Different Black Invasion." *Birmingham News*, September 5, 1918, 8. www.newspapers .com.

Agyepong, Tera Eva. *The Criminalization of Black Children: Race, Gender, and Delinquency in Chicago's Juvenile Justice System, 1899–1945*. Chapel Hill: University of North Carolina Press, 2018.

Alexander, Michelle. *The New Jim Crow: Mass Incarceration in the Age of Colorblindness*. New York: New Press, 2010.

Allyn, Bobby. "Prosecutors Seeking 20 More Years for Philly Juvenile Life Who Killed Cop." WHYY, September 27, 2017. https://whyy.org.

Althouse, Michaela. "7 Philly Violence Prevention Programs to Know and Support This MLK Day." *Philadelphia Magazine*, January 18, 2019. www.phillymag.com.

Altschuler, Glenn C., and Stuart M. Blumin. *The GI Bill: A New Deal for Veterans*. Oxford: Oxford University Press, 2009.

American Civil Liberties Union. "What's at Stake." ACLU.org. Accessed April 16, 2023. www.aclu.org.

Anderson, Dorothy. "Project Tenants Confer with Law to Curb Crime." *Philadelphia Tribune*, August 6, 1957, 2. ProQuest Historical Newspapers.

Anderson, M. Phineas. *The Gang Unit*. Washington, DC: ERIC Clearinghouse, 1970.

An Evader. "Race Irritation." *Chicago Tribune*, March 3, 1923, 6. www.newspapers.com.

"Angry Judge Sentences 5 in Gang Slaying." *Philadelphia Daily News*, July 17, 1963, 5, www.newspapers.com.

"Another Outrage in Quaker City." *New York Age*, November 11, 1914, 5. www.newspapers.com.

Antosh, Lou. "Gus Rangnow, Who Started It All, Is Still No. 1 PAL." *Philadelphia Daily News*, June 11, 1969, 18. www.newspapers.com.

AP. "Youth Gangs Seen Growing Threat." *Morning Call*, May 1, 1976, 4. www.newspapers.com.

AP News. "Thomas Gibbons, 83 of Philadelphia Police." *New York Times*, February 7, 1988, 44. www.nytimes.com.

"Arlene Urges Talks on Gangs." *Philadelphia Inquirer*, June 24, 1969, 23. www.newspapers.com.

Asquith, Christina. *The Emergency Teacher: The Inspirational Story of a New Teacher in an Inner-City School*. New York: Skyhorse, 2007.

"Attack Penn Foreign Student." *Chicago Defender*, October 20, 1958, A2. ProQuest.

Austen, Ben. *High-Risers: Cabrini-Green and the Fate of American Public Housing*. New York: HarperCollins, 2018.

Avery, Ron. "As Neighborhoods Change, So Do the Names." *Philadelphia Daily News*, January 2, 1991, 6. www.newspapers.com.

Baldwin, James. *The Fire Next Time*. New York: Dial, 2013.

Ball, M. V. "Correspondence: The Mortality of the Negro." *Medical News* 64, no. 5 (April 1894): 389–90.

"Baltimore Resents Negro in White Block." *Philadelphia Inquirer*, March 8, 1922, 1. www.newspapers.com.

Barbour, W. Miller. "Gangs and Their Locations." Wharton Centre, 1944–47. From Temple University Special Collections Research Center, call no. URB 30, box 34, folder 2.

Bauman, John F. "Black Slums / Black Projects: The New Deal and Negro Housing in Philadelphia." *Pennsylvania History: A Journal of Mid-Atlantic Studies* 41, no. 3 (July 1974): 310–38.

Berry, Stephen W. *All That Makes a Man: Love and Ambition in the Civil War South*. New York: Oxford University Press, 2002.

"Billions for Safe Streets Yield Failure, Fear, Fury." *Philadelphia Evening Bulletin*, September 11, 1977.

Binzen, Peter, ed. *Nearly Everybody Read It: Snapshots of the Philadelphia Bulletin*. Philadelphia: Camino Books, 1998.

"'Birth of A Nation' Wins Praise of Many Mayors." *Harrisburg Daily Independent*, February 5, 1916, 14. www.newspapers.com.

"Black Clergy Give Support to Suit against Top Police." *Philadelphia Tribune*, April 28, 1970, 16. ProQuest.

"Black Invasion of Harlem Stirs Up Bitter Feud." *Evening World*, December 15, 1911, 19. www.newspapers.com.

Black Panther Party. *The Black Panther Party*. New York: Merit, 1966.

Blackmon, Douglas. *Slavery by Another Name: The Re-enslavement of Black Americans from the Civil War to World War II*. New York: Vintage Books, 2008.

Blakemore, Erin. "How the Black Panthers' Breakfast Program Both Inspired and Threatened the Government." History.com, February 6, 2018. www.history.com.

"Boy Stabbed to Death in Teen Gang Attack, Five Youths Charged." *Philadelphia Inquirer*, June 18, 1963, 25. www.newspapers.com.

Branham, Lorraine, and Pamela Smith. "Hard Times, Higher Taxes and Dirty Streets." *Philadelphia Tribune*, May 22, 1976, 1, 23. ProQuest Historical Newspapers.

"'Brothers' Object to Order." *Times-News*, November 15, 1978, 5. https://news.google.com.

Brown, Lawrence T. *The Black Butterfly: The Harmful Politics of Race and Space in America*, Baltimore: Johns Hopkins University Press, 2021.

Brown, Richard P. Letter to Mayor Richardson Dilworth, October 21, 1958. Crime Situation, box A 4400, Mayor Files, 1958, Municipal Developments (A–P), Philadelphia Municipal Archives (PMA).

Brown, Warren. "'Peacemaker' Held in Murder: Leader Disavowed Gangs a Month Ago." *Philadelphia Inquirer*, August 13, 1973, 31. www.newspapers.com.

Brownworth, Victoria A. "Cradle Beating Witness Says Justice Was Not Served." *Philadelphia Inquirer*, November 29, 1977, 13. www.newspapers.com.

Burt, Nathaniel, and Wallace E. Davies. "The Iron Age, 1876–1905." In Wolf, Wainwright, and Weigley, *Philadelphia*, 471–523.

Caddoo, Cara. "The Birth of a Nation, Police Brutality, and Black Protest." *Journal of the Gilded Age and Progressive Era* 14, no. 4 (October 2015): 608–11.

Callard, Judith, and Germantown Historical Society. *Images of America: Germantown, Mount Airy, and Chestnut Hill*. Philadelphia: Arcadia, 2000.

Caparella, Kitty. "Gang Leader Who Pledged Peace Held in Killing." *Philadelphia Daily News*, August 13, 1973, 31. www.newspapers.com.

"Capt. Rizzo Refuses to Stop Arrests." *Philadelphia Tribune*, March 25, 1952, 1–2. ProQuest Historical Newspapers.

Carlisle, Dennis. "In Logan Square, Pick of the Lock-Ups." HiddenCityPhila.org, December 10, 2012. https://hiddencityphila.org.

Cassidy, Morley. "Most Explosive Race Problem in North: Cassidy Article Reprint Is Public Service." *Philadelphia Tribune*, February 22, 1958, 1. ProQuest Historical Newspapers.

———. "The Most Explosive Race Problem Is in the North: 'Tyrannosaurus' Stalks in the City of Brotherly Love." *Human Events* 14, no. 45 (November 9, 1957): 1–4.

Chappell, Bill. "Chauvin and 3 Former Officers Face New Charges over George Floyd's Death." NPR, June 3, 2020. www.npr.org.

Children Play Ping Pong at Wharton Centre. Photograph. Philadelphia, Wharton Centre, date unknown. From Temple University Libraries, Special Collections Research Center. Accessed January 25, 2021. https://digital.library.temple.edu.

"CITIES: Hands Dripping Blood." *Time*, May 12, 1958. http://time.com.

"City Leaders Honor Sailor as Subway Attack Hero." *Philadelphia Inquirer*, March 12, 1965, 1. www.newspapers.com.

"City of Philadelphia Five Year Financial and Strategic Plan, 2023–2027." Philadelphia City Council, March 30, 2022. http://phlcouncil.com.

City of Philadelphia Office of the Mayor News Release. "Remarks by Mayor Frank L. Rizzo of Philadelphia at Pennsylvania Sons of Italy Convention Tamiment-in-the-Poconos." June 30, 1973. From Temple University Special Collections Research Center, *Peter Binzen Papers*, call no. (SPC) MSS SP 053, collection URB.

"City's Gang Youths Caught in 'Cycle of Impoverished Existence.'" *Philadelphia Inquirer*, July 18, 1971, 17. www.newspapers.com.

"City's Gang Youths Caught in 'Cycle of Impoverished Existence.'" *Philadelphia Inquirer*, July 18, 1971, 17. www.newspapers.com.

Clark, Alexis. "How 'The Birth of a Nation' Revived the Ku Klux Klan." History.com, July 29, 2019. www.history.com.

Clark, Joe. "Shotgun Blast Triggers Young Great Society." *Philadelphia Daily News*, September 1, 1965, 4–14. www.newspapers.com.

Clark, Joseph S., Jr., and Dennis J. Clark. "Rally and Relapse, 1946–1968." In Wolf, Wainwright, and Weigley, *Philadelphia*, 649–703.

Cleveland, Al, Renaldo Benson, and Marvin Gaye. "Save the Children." UMG Recordings, 1971.

Coates, Ta-Nehisi. "The Case for Reparations." *Atlantic*, June 2014. www.theatlantic.com.

Cohen, Lizabeth. *Consumer's Republic: The Politics of Mass Consumption in Postwar America*. New York: Vintage Books, 2004.

Collins, William B. "Retirement of 309 Sends City Pensions to Peak $1,237,105." *Philadelphia Inquirer*, August 7, 1960, 1. ProQuest.

Commonwealth of Pennsylvania v. Andre Martin. Municipal Court of Philadelphia County, March 1, 1976. Unified Judicial System of Pennsylvania. https://ujsportal.pacourts.us.

Commonwealth of Pennsylvania v. Donald Woodruff. Municipal Court of Philadelphia County, February 18, 1976. Unified Judicial System of Pennsylvania. https://ujsportal.pacourts.us.

Commonwealth of Pennsylvania v. Shirley Munson. Municipal Court of Philadelphia County, December 12, 1970. Unified Judicial System of Pennsylvania. https://ujsportal.pacourts.us.

Cook, Raymond A. *Thomas Dixon*. New York: Twayne, 1974.

"Cops Off the Hook." *Philadelphia Daily News*, November 23, 1977, 4. www.newspapers.com.

Copman, Jacob. Letter to Mayor Richardson Dilworth, October 31, 1958. Crime Situation, box A 4400, Mayor Files, 1958, Municipal Developments (A–P), Philadelphia Municipal Archives (PMA).

Corson, Helen H. *Article Soliciting Funds for Proposed Settlement House—a Few of the Future Patrons: The Susan Parrish Wharton Memorial*. Photograph. Philadelphia, *Friends' Intelligencer*, April 12, 1930. From Temple University Libraries, Special Collections Research Center. https://digital.library.temple.edu.

Coughlin, Brenda C., and Sudhir Alladi Venkatesh. "The Urban Street Gang after 1970." *Annual Review of Sociology* 29 (August 2003): 41–64.

Countryman, Matthew J. *Up South: Civil Rights and Black Power in Philadelphia*. Philadelphia: University of Pennsylvania Press, 2006.

"Crime: Bizarre Battle Leaves Two Dead in Philadelphia." *Jet*, November 27, 1980, 16. https://books.google.com.

Cunningham, R. M. "The Morbidity and Mortality of Negro Convicts." *Medical News* 64, no. 5 (1894): 113.

"Curb Meter Looters, Gibbons Asks Courts." *Philadelphia Inquirer*, March 2, 1958, 31. www .newspapers.com.

"DA to Ask Adult Trials for 8 Teeners in Killing." *Philadelphia Inquirer*, April 29, 1958, 3. www.newspapers.com.

Daughen, Joseph R., and Peter Binzen. *The Cop Who Would Be King: The Honorable Frank Rizzo*. Boston: Little, Brown, 1977.

David, Gunter. "Jurors Can't Agree: Cop Killer Gets Life." *Philadelphia Evening Bulletin*, September 22, 1976. From Temple University Special Collections Research Center, *Philadelphia Evening Bulletin* clippings, call no. SCRC 169, vol. Andre Martin, collection URB.

———. "Jury Hears Mother Plead for Son's Life after Slay Verdict." *Philadelphia Evening Bulletin*, September 21, 1976. From Temple University Special Collections Research Center, *Philadelphia Evening Bulletin* clippings, call no. SCRC 169, vol. Andre Martin, collection URB.

———. "Murder Trial Pits Youth against Pal." *Philadelphia Evening Bulletin*, September 8, 1976. From Temple University Special Collections Research Center, *Philadelphia Evening Bulletin* clippings, call no. SCRC 169, vol. Andre Martin, collection URB.

———. "Murder Trial Told of Bullet Casings." *Philadelphia Evening Bulletin*, September 4, 1976. From Temple University Special Collections Research Center, *Philadelphia Evening Bulletin* clippings, call no. SCRC 169, vol. Andre Martin, collection URB.

———. "To Live in Fear Everyday of Your Life." *Philadelphia Evening Bulletin*, September 15, 1976. From Temple University Special Collections Research Center, *Philadelphia Evening Bulletin* clippings, call no. SCRC 169, vol. Andre Martin, collection URB.

———. "Youth Falters at Murder Trial." *Philadelphia Evening Bulletin*, September 9, 1976. From Temple University Special Collections Research Center, *Philadelphia Evening Bulletin* clippings, call no. SCRC 169, vol. Andre Martin, collection URB.

Davis, Angela. *Women, Race, and Class*. New York: Vintage, 1981.

"Death on the Doorstep." Newspaper article sent to Mayor Richardson Dilworth. Crime Situation, Box A 4400, Mayor Files, 1958, Municipal Developments (A-P), Philadelphia Municipal Archives (PMA).

Demonstrations over Police Brutality. Photograph. *Philadelphia Evening Bulletin*, February 16, 1971. From Temple University Libraries, Special Collections Research Center. https://digital.library.temple.edu.

Desmond, Matthew, and Mustafa Emirbayer. *Racial Domination, Racial Progress: The Sociology of Race in America*. New York: McGraw-Hill Education, 2009.

Dilworth, Mayor Richardson. Letter to Benjamin Cohen, October 31, 1958. Crime Situation, box A 4400, Mayor Files, 1958, Municipal Developments (A–P), Philadelphia Municipal Archives (PMA).

———. Letter to Mrs. D. German, October 31, 1958. Crime Situation, Box A 4400, Mayor Files, 1958, Municipal Developments (A–P), Philadelphia Municipal Archives (PMA).

———. Letter to Joseph T. Clancy, October 22, 1958. Crime Situation, Box A 4400, Mayor Files, 1958, Municipal Developments (A–P), Philadelphia Municipal Archives (PMA).

———. "New Industry, Jobs Will End Period Hikes." *Philadelphia Inquirer*, August 7, 1960, 1, 14. ProQuest.

Dimitriadis, Greg. "The Situation Complex: Revisiting Frederic Thrasher's *The Gang: A Study of 1,313 Gangs in Chicago*." *Cultural Studies* ↔ *Critical Methodologies* 6, no. 3 (August 1, 2006): 335–53.

Dirkson, Menika. "Hyper-segregation, Inequality, and Murder Rates—a Review of 'The Ecology of Homicide.'" *Metropole*, Urban History Association, June 14, 2021. https://themetropole.blog.

Dixon, Thomas, Jr. *The Clansman: A Historical Romance of the Ku Klux Klan*. New York: Doubleday, Page, 1905.

Donner, Frank. "Rizzo's Philadelphia: Police City." In *Protectors of Privilege: Red Squads and Police Repression in Urban America*. Oakland: University of California Press, 1992.

D'Ooge, Craig. "'The Birth of a Nation': Symposium on Classic Film Discusses Inaccuracies and Virtues." Library of Congress, June 24, 1994. www.loc.gov.

Dougherty, Frank, and Ed Griffenberg. "5 Held in 'Get Anybody' Killing of Temple Graduate Student." *Philadelphia Daily News*, April 28, 1970, 3, 53. www.newspapers.com.

———. "Rookie Cop Is Slain in N. Phila. Street." *Philadelphia Daily News*, January 30, 1970, 3. www.newspapers.com.

Du Bois, William Edward Burghardt, and Isabel Eaton. *The Philadelphia Negro: A Social Study*. Philadelphia: University of Pennsylvania Press, 1899.

Elkins, Alex. "'It Was like a War': Encountering the State in the 1918 and 1964 Philadelphia Riots." Atlanta: OAH, 2014.

Equal Justice Initiative. "Reconstruction in America: Racial Violence after the Civil War, 1865–1876." EJI. Accessed May 28, 2023. https://eji.org.

"Fallen Officers-Philadelphia Police Department, 1960–1999." Officer Down Memorial Page. Accessed May 8, 2015. www.odmp.org.

"Fatal Beating Hearing for 11 on Wednesday." *Standard-Sentinel*, April 29, 1958, 15. www .newspapers.com.

"Father and 4 Uncles of Oh Raise Funds for His Killers." *Philadelphia Evening Bulletin*, May 12, 1958.

Farr, Gail E. "Spanish Merchants Association of Philadelphia, 1970–1988." Historical Society of Pennsylvania Balch Institute, April 1994. www.portal.hsp.org.

Federal Bureau of Investigation. *FBI Law Enforcement Bulletin*. Vol. 40, no. 11. Washington, DC: United States Department of Justice, November 1971.

Ferrick, Thomas, Jr., Doreen Carvajal, and Thomas J. Gibbons Jr. "The 25-Year-Old Scars of a Riot Violence of 1964 Devastated a Vital Neighborhood." *Philadelphia Inquirer*, August 27, 1989. http://articles.philly.com.

Ferrick, Tom. "Safe Streets Center Seeks to Expand Effective Work." *Philadelphia Inquirer*, July 13, 1970.

Finkel, Ken. "Roots of Hypersegregation in Philadelphia, 1920–1930." *Philly History Blog*, February 22, 2016. https://blog.phillyhistory.org.

"Five Typical Cases Handled by the Juvenile Aid Bureau." *Philadelphia Inquirer*, December 13, 1956, 3. www.newspapers.com.

Foley, Sharon. *The Unsolved Shooting of Patrolman Frederick Cione*. Self-published, 2017.

Forman, James, Jr. *Locking Up Our Own: Crime and Punishment in Black America*. New York: Farrar, Straus and Giroux, 2017.

Fox, Ben. "Trump Leaves Mark on Immigration Policy, Some of It Lasting." *AP News*, December 30, 2020. https://apnews.com.

Franklin, V. P. "Operation Street Corner." In *W. E. B. Du Bois, Race, and the City: "The Philadelphia Negro" and Its Legacy*, edited by Michael B. Katz and Thomas J. Sugrue, 195–218. Philadelphia: University of Pennsylvania Press, 1998.

"Frank Rizzo's Last Hurrah? Philadelphia on Verge of Fiscal Collapse." *Morning Herald*, June 17, 1976, 34. www.newspapers.com.

Gambacorta, David, Juliana Feliciano Reyes, William Bender, and Sean Collins Walsh. "Philly's Police Union Spent Decades Amassing Power. Reforms Could Cut Its Clout." *Philadelphia Inquirer*, October 6, 2017. www.inquirer.com.

Gambardello, Joseph A. "How Philly Came to Call Its Downtown 'Center City.'" *Philadelphia Inquirer*, May 14, 2019. www.inquirer.com.

"Gang-Control Loses Bid for U.S. Aid." *Philadelphia Evening Bulletin*, June 20, 1975.

Gang Killing—Raid on Gang Headquarters. Photograph. *Philadelphia Evening Bulletin*, April 20, 1971. From Temple University Libraries, Special Collections Research Center. https://digital.library.temple.edu.

"Gang Members Who Have Taken Auto Mechanic Course." *Philadelphia Evening Bulletin*, August 1, 1975. From Temple University Special Collections Research Center, *George D. McDowell Philadelphia Evening Bulletin Collection*, call no. SCRC 170, vol. Gangs—Miscellaneous, *George D. McDowell Philadelphia Evening Bulletin Photographs*, P254061B.

"Gang Slaying." *Courier-Post*, July 10, 1963, 3. www.newspapers.com.

Gearty, Robert, and Joe Kemp. "Cops Clobber Vicious Gang." *New York Daily News*, December 8, 2011, 28. www.newspapers.com.

Geffen, Elizabeth M. "Industrial Development and Social Crisis, 1841–1854." In Wolf, Wainwright, and Weigley, *Philadelphia*, 307–62.

Gibbons, Thomas J., Jr. "3 Youths Held without Bail in Sniper Killing of Officer." *Philadelphia Evening Bulletin*, March 2, 1976. From Temple University Special Collections Research Center, *Philadelphia Evening Bulletin* clippings, call no. SCRC 169, vol. Andre Martin, collection URB.

Glover, Anthony E. "Factions May Fight over Drug Market." *St. Louis Post-Dispatch*, April 8, 1973, 21. www.newspapers.com.

Glover, Katherine. "Leisure for Living." In *William Torrey Harris: The Commemoration of the One Hundredth Anniversary of His Birth, 1835–1935*. Washington, DC: Department of the Interior, 1936.

Goode, Judith, and Jo Anne Schneider. *Reshaping Ethnic and Racial Relations in Philadelphia: Immigrants in a Divided City*. Philadelphia: Temple University Press, 1994.

"Gov. Josh Shapiro Calls on Legislature to Abolish Death Penalty." *Philadelphia Inquirer*, February 16, 2023. www.inquirer.com.

Graham, Theodore W., Art Peters, J. Donald Porter, and Charles Thomas. "Parents of Youths Shocked, Saddened by Brutal Killing." *Philadelphia Tribune*, May 3, 1958, 1, 3. ProQuest Historical Newspapers.

Griffin, Sean Patrick. *Philadelphia's Black Mafia: A Social and Political History*. New York: Springer Science & Business Media, 2003.

Gross, Kali N. *Colored Amazons: Crime, Violence, and Black Women in the City of Brotherly Love, 1880–1910*. Durham, NC: Duke University Press, 2006.

Grusin, Dave, Alan Bergman, and Marilyn Bergman. *Good Times* theme song. CBS Television, 1974.

Hamilton, Fred. *Rizzo: From Cop to Mayor of Philadelphia*. New York: Viking, 1973.

Hardy, Charles, III. "Historical Overview." The Great Migration: A City Transformed. Accessed March 11, 2021. https://greatmigrationphl.org.

Harriot, Michael. "Maybe America Is Racist." The Root. Accessed April 14, 2021. www.theroot.com.

"Hearings on Gang Warfare Blasted by Mantua Group." *Philadelphia Tribune*, July 29, 1969, 1–2. ProQuest Historical Newspapers.

Heimer, Scott. "Man, 20, Arrested in Cop Shooting." *Philadelphia Daily News*, December 24, 1974, 3. www.newspapers.com.

Henri, Florette. *Black Migration: Movement North, 1900–1920*. New York: Anchor, 1975.

Hill, Evan, Ainara Tiefenthäler, Christiaan Triebert, Drew Jordan, Haley Willis, and Robin Stein. "8 Minutes and 46 Seconds: How George Floyd Was Killed in Police Custody." *New York Times*, May 31, 2020. www.nytimes.com.

Hingston, Sandy. "What Two Centuries of Census Records Taught Us about Philadelphia." *Philadelphia Magazine*, January 18, 2020. www.phillymag.com.

Hinton, Elizabeth K. *From the War on Poverty to the War on Crime: The Making of Mass Incarceration in America*. Cambridge, MA: Harvard University Press, 2016.

Hirsch, Arnold. *Making the Second Ghetto: Race and Housing in Chicago, 1940–1960*. Chicago: University of Chicago Press, 1983.

Hoffman, Frederick L. *Race Traits and Tendencies of the American Negro*. New York: American Economic Association, 1896.

———. "Vital Statistics of the Negro." *Arena*, April 1892, 539–42.

Hoffnung-Garskof, Jesse. "Answers about Dominicans in New York." *New York Times*, March 18, 2009. www.nytimes.com.

Hornblum, Allen M. *Sentenced to Science: One Black Man's Story of Imprisonment in America*. University Park: Pennsylvania State University Press, 2007.

Horton Berg, Jean. *I Cry When the Sun Goes Down: The Story of Herman Wrice*. Philadelphia: Westminster, 1975.

Hunt, D. Bradford. *Blueprint for Disaster: The Unraveling of Chicago Public Housing*. Chicago: University of Chicago Press, 2009.

"Information about Inmate: AF9705 (Andre Martin)." Pennsylvania Department of Corrections. Accessed May 7, 2015. http://inmatelocator.cor.pa.gov.

"In-Ho Oh's Parents to Give $500 to 'Help' His Slayers." *Philadelphia Evening Bulletin*, April 3, 1959. From Temple University Special Collections Research Center, *Philadelphia Evening Bulletin* clippings, call no. SCRC 169A, vol. 2412 / Oh, In-Ho—(Murdered).

"In Memoriam: Lennox L. Moak." *Public Budgeting & Finance* (Summer 1983): 120–22.

"Innocent Bystander Again: 9-Year-Old Killed as Teen Gangs War." *Simpson's Leader-Times*, April 21, 1971, 2. www.newspapers.com.

"In Our Opinion: Willing to Kill." *Philadelphia Daily News*. September 24, 1976, 17. www.newspapers.com.

Institute for Survey Research at Temple University (ISR). "City of Philadelphia 2019–2020 Philadelphia Resident Survey Report." Phila.gov. Accessed February 11, 2021. www.phila.gov.

"Interview: Beulah Collins, August 1, 1983." Goin' North. Accessed May 28, 2023, https://goinnorth.org.

"Interview: Crosby Brittenum, March 20, 1984." Goin' North. Accessed March 4, 2023, https://goinnorth.org.

"Interview: Edgar Campbell, September 26, 1984." Goin' North. Accessed May 28, 2023, https://goinnorth.org.

"Interview: Kathryn F. (Kitty) Woodard, March 26, 1984." Goin' North. Accessed May 28, 2023, https://goinnorth.org.

"Interview: Ralph Jones, February 14, 1984." Goin' North. Accessed March 14, 2023, https://goinnorth.org.

Ismay, John. "35 Years after MOVE Bombing That Killed 11, Philadelphia Apologizes." *New York Times*, November 13, 2020. www.nytimes.com.

Jackson, Anthony E. "Statement of Anthony E. Jackson, Esq., Director, Police Project, PILCOP, April 19, 1979." PILCOP, April 19, 1979. https://pubintlaw.org.

Janson, Donald. "Gangs Face Drive in Philadelphia." *New York Times*, February 13, 1972. www.nytimes.com.

Jargowsky, Paul A., Christopher A. Wheeler, and Howard Gillette. "Poverty." The Encyclopedia of Greater Philadelphia, 2017. https://philadelphiaencyclopedia.org.

Johnson, Jacqueline Joan. "ReMemory: What There Is for Us." In *Up South: Stories, Studies and Letters of This Century's African-American Migrations*, edited by Malaika Adero, 102–3. New York: New Press, 1993.

Johnson, Karl E. "Police-Black Community Relations in Postwar Philadelphia: Race and Criminalization in Urban Social Spaces, 1945–1960." *Journal of African American History: African Americans and the Urban Landscape* 89, no. 2 (Spring 2004): 118–34.

Johnson, Tyree. "Cradle: Philly Folks Would Believe Me." *Philadelphia Daily News*, November 23, 1977, 4. www.newspapers.com.

———. "Gang Slaying Kills Peace Dream." *Philadelphia Daily News*, August 14, 1973, 8. www.newspapers.com.

———. "'He Said Somebody Would Be Killed.'" *Philadelphia Daily News*, June 29, 1973, 4. www.newspapers.com.

———. "Men Needed to Share Skills with Boys." *Philadelphia Daily News*, May 15, 1974. from Temple University Special Collections Research Center, *Philadelphia Evening Bulletin* clippings, call no. SCRC 169B, collection URB, vol. Safe Streets, Inc., box 3575.

Jordan, Winthrop. *White over Black: American Attitudes toward the Negro, 1550–1812*. Chapel Hill: University of North Carolina Press, 2013.

Juvenile Gang Leaders Return from Puerto Rico. Photograph. *Philadelphia Evening Bulletin*, June 26, 1970. From Temple University Libraries, Special Collections Research Center. https://digital.library.temple.edu.

Kane, John J. "The Tops and Bottoms: The Study of Negro Gangs in West Philadelphia." *American Catholic Sociological Review* 9, no. 2 (June 1948): 74–83.

Karafin, Harry J. "The Problem of Teen-Age Street Gangs." *Philadelphia Inquirer*, December 13, 1956, 3. www.newspapers.com.

"Kid Gloves Won't End Gang Wars." *Philadelphia Inquirer*, December 16, 1956, 54. www.newspapers.com.

Kim, Hannah. "Death in Philadelphia, 1958: The Murder of In-Ho Oh and the Politics of Cold War America." *Pacific Historical Review* 89, no. 2 (2020): 232–63.

King, Maxwell. "2 Years after Holmesburg Riot: Prison Adds Drug Center, Expands Work-Release." *Philadelphia Inquirer*, July 23, 1972, 26. www.newspapers.com.

Kitzmiller, Erika M. *The Roots of Educational Inequality: Philadelphia's Germantown High School, 1907–2014*. Philadelphia: University of Pennsylvania Press, 2021.

KODX Seattle. "Robin D. G. Kelley—What Is Racial Capitalism and Why Does It Matter?" November 18, 2017. YouTube video, 1:26:46. https://www.youtube.com/watch?v=--gim7W_jQQ.

Kotzbauer, Robert W. "Cast-Off Kids Will Go to Foster Homes, Not Lockup." *Philadelphia Evening Bulletin*, August 31, 1976.

———. "Safe Streets Gang Control Gets $30,000." *Philadelphia Evening Bulletin*, January 7, 1975.

Krasner, Larry. *For the People: A Story of Justice and Power*. New York: One World, 2021.

Larkin, Mary, and John Clancy. "Rizzo Pleads for Funds to Fight Gangs." *Philadelphia Inquirer*, June 24, 1969, 1, 23–26. www.newspapers.com.

Lawson, Benjamin Alexander. *The Pruitt-Igoe Projects: Modernism, Social Control, and the Failure of Public Housing, 1954–1976*. Stillwater: Oklahoma State University, 2007.

Lear, Len. "Southwark Residents Protest PHA Giving Apartment Keys to Police." *Philadelphia Tribune*, February 4, 1975, 8. ProQuest Historical Newspapers.

———. "Southwark Residents Say Police Used 'Gestapo Tactics' in Hunt for Gunman in Apartment Complex." *Philadelphia Tribune*, January 4, 1975, 1. ProQuest Historical Newspapers.

Lee, Jae-Hyup. *Dynamics of Ethnic Identity: Three Asian American Communities in Philadelphia*. New York: Garland. 1998.

Leiter, Andrew. "Thomas Dixon, Jr.: Conflicts in History and Literature." Documenting the American South. Accessed March 11, 2021. http://unc.edu.

Levenstein, Lisa. *A Movement without Marches: African American Women and the Politics of Poverty in Postwar Philadelphia*. Chapel Hill; University of North Carolina Press, 2009.

Lewis, Maurice M., Jr. "Gang Murders Korean Student in West Phila.: Police Round Up 6 Youths after Savage Assault." *Philadelphia Evening Bulletin*, April 26, 1958. From Temple University Special Collections Research Center, *Philadelphia Evening Bulletin* clippings, call no. SCRC 169A, vol. 2412 / Oh, In-Ho—(Murdered).

Lewis, Oscar. "The Culture of Poverty." *Scientific American* 215, no. 4 (October 1966): 19–25.

———. *Five Families: Mexican Case Studies in the Culture of Poverty*. New York: Basic Books, 1959.

Lisowski, Joshua. "Police Officers Waking Teen Sleeping in Bus Station." The Encyclopedia of Greater Philadelphia, September 14, 2014. https://philadelphiaencyclopedia.org.

Litwack, Leon F. "Hellhounds." In *Without Sanctuary: Lynching Photography in America*, edited by James Allen, Hilton Als, Congressman John Lewis, and Leon F. Litwack, 8–37. Santa Fe: Twin Palms, 2000.

LoBianco, Tom, and Ashley Killough. "Trump Pitches Black Voters: 'What the Hell Do You Have to Lose?'" *CNN*, August 19, 2016. www.cnn.com.

Lombardo, Timothy. *Blue-Collar Conservatism: Frank Rizzo's Philadelphia and Populist Politics*. Philadelphia: University of Pennsylvania Press, 2018.

Lordan, Francis M. "City's $24 Million Surplus Fund Nearly Exhausted." *Philadelphia Inquirer*, December 24, 1968, 23. www.newspapers.com.

Lordan, Francis M., and E. J. Hussie. "Tate Oks $12.4 Million Spending Cut." *Philadelphia Inquirer*, January 14, 1969, 10. www.newspapers.com.

Lowrey, Annie. "Trump Says His Tax Plan Won't Benefit the Rich—He's Exactly Wrong." *Atlantic*, September 29, 2017. www.theatlantic.com.

Madej, Patricia. "Three Arrests Related to Unrest Made since Friday." *Philadelphia Inquirer*, October 31, 2020. www.inquirer.com.

Mann, Jim. "The Perils of a Housing Project: Crime." *Philadelphia Inquirer*, October 22, 1974, 1–2. www.newspapers.com.

Marin, Max. "Military Psy-Ops or ATM Explosions? Nightly Booms Spur Conspiracy Theories in Philly." Billy Penn, June 4, 2020. https://billypenn.com.

———. "'Unprepared' Philly Police Violated Use-of-Force and Tear Gas Policies during Summer Protests, Review Finds." Billy Penn, December 23, 2020. https://billypenn .com.

"Martin May Claim Accidental Shooting." *Philadelphia Daily News*, September 13, 1976, 4. www.newspapers.com.

"Mayor Names 2 Negroes to Tax Advisory Group." *Philadelphia Tribune*, November 9, 1968, 1, 4. ProQuest Historical Newspapers.

"Mayor Starts Drive for Fund to Honor Slain Student." *Philadelphia Inquirer*, May 6, 1958, 33. www.newspapers.com.

McCaffrey, Joseph D. "Didn't Know It Was a Cop Says Officer-Slaying Suspect." *Philadelphia Evening Bulletin*, March 11, 1976. From Temple University Special Collections Research Center, *Philadelphia Evening Bulletin* clippings, call no. SCRC 169, vol. Andre Martin, collection URB.

McCurdy, Glenn. "I Couldn't Run Away from Those Streets." *Philadelphia Inquirer*, July 30, 1972, 261–63. www.newspapers.com.

McGrail, Stephen. "Philadelphia Negro (The)." The Encyclopedia of Greater Philadelphia, 2013. https://philadelphiaencyclopedia.org.

McKelvey, Gerald, and Howard Shapiro. "Police Department Overtime Runs $6.3 Million in 7 Months." *Philadelphia Inquirer*, March 21, 1971, 21–24. www .newspapers.com.

Melamed, Samantha. "For Juvenile Lifer Who Killed Policeman, 44 Years to Life." *Philadelphia Inquirer*, September 27, 2017. www.philly.com.

Meyer, Stephen Grant. *As Long as They Don't Move Next Door: Segregation and Racial Conflict in American Neighborhoods*. New York: Rowman & Littlefield, 2000.

Miller, Walter B. *Violence by Youth Gangs and Youth Groups as a Crime Problem in Major American Cities*. Cambridge, MA: Center for Criminal Justice, Harvard Law School, 1975.

"Millions for Safe Streets, and Crime Still Climbs." *Philadelphia Evening Bulletin*, March 10, 1974.

"Mindless Tragedy Ruins Six Lives." *Philadelphia Inquirer*, March 7, 1976, 15-A. www .newspapers.com.

Mogano, Larissa. "Philly's Police Misconduct Cases Drain Taxpayer Money." *Philadelphia Inquirer*, October 1, 2019. https://fusion.inquirer.com.

Molina, Natalia. *How Race Is Made in America: Immigration, Citizenship, and the Historical Power of Racial Scripts*. Berkeley: University of California Press, 2014.

Monahan, Thomas P. "Police Dispositions of Juvenile Offenders: The Problem of Measurement and a Study of Philadelphia Data." *Phylon* 31, no. 2 (1970): 129–41.

Moore, Acel. "Slain Gang Worker to Be Honored Today." *Philadelphia Inquirer*, July 15, 1973, 31. www.newspapers.com.

"Moore Brands Tate 'a Racist,' Praises Police." *Philadelphia Evening Bulletin*, October 11, 1966. From Temple University Libraries, Special Collections Research Center. https://digital.library.temple.edu.

"Moore Sees No Need for New Taxes, Urges Austerity." *Philadelphia Inquirer Public Ledger*, March 8, 1959, 1B, 6B. ProQuest.

Morgan, Jennifer. "'Some Could Suckle over Their Shoulder': Male Travelers, Female Bodies, and the Gendering of Racial Ideology, 1500–1770." *William and Mary Quarterly* 54, no. 1 (1997): 167–92.

Morrison, John F., and Robert Bridgeo. "Policeman in Critical Condition." *Philadelphia Evening Bulletin*, February 26, 1976. From Temple University Special Collections Research Center, *Philadelphia Evening Bulletin* clippings, call no. SCRC 169, vol. Andre Martin, collection URB.

Mossell, Sadie Tanner. "The Standard of Living among One Hundred Negro Migrant Families in Philadelphia." *Annals of the American Academy of Political and Social Science: Child Welfare* 98 (November 1921).

Mugge, Robert, dir. *Amateur Night at City Hall: The Story of Frank L. Rizzo*. MVD Entertainment Group, 1978. Kanopy, web. Accessed November 24, 2017.

Muhammad, Khalil. *The Condemnation of Blackness: Race, Crime, and the Making of Modern Urban America*. Cambridge, MA: Harvard University Press, 2011.

"Murderer Draws Life." *Reading Eagle*, September 23, 1976, 9. https://news.google.com.

Murphy, Richard B., and James S. Lintz, "Bullet Kills Girl, 7, in Street Fighting." *Philadelphia Inquirer*, June 14, 1970, 21. www.newspapers.com.

Murray, George J., and Leonard J. McAdams. "Subway Patrols Beefed Up, Dogs to Join Guards." *Philadelphia Inquirer*, March 10, 1965, 1–5. www.newspapers.com.

Muskil, Paul. "Murder of a Millionaire." *Times-Tribune*, August 22, 1976, 62. www.newspapers.com.

Nabried, Thomas. "Uproot and Destroy Causes for Crime." *Philadelphia Tribune*, May 10, 1958, 4. ProQuest Historical Newspapers.

"Negroes Raise Film Fund: $500 Collected at Mass-Meeting to Fight Photoplay." *Evening Public Ledger*, September 27, 1915, 4. www.newspapers.com.

Neumann, Jonathan, and William K. Marimow. "A Policeman Is Charged." *Philadelphia Inquirer*, July 8, 1977, 4. www.newspapers.com.

———. "City Policeman Charged in Beating." *Philadelphia Inquirer*, July 8, 1977, 1. www.newspapers.com.

———. "The Homicide Files, Part I." *Philadelphia Inquirer*, April 24, 1977. www.inquirer.com.

———. "The Homicide Files, Parts I–IV." *Philadelphia Inquirer*, April 1977.

"News Briefs: Philadelphia." *Gettysburg Times*, February 18, 1976, 2. https://news.google.com.

Ngai, Mae. *Impossible Subjects Illegal Aliens and the Making of Modern America.* Princeton, NJ: Princeton University Press, 2014.

"No Other Life." *Pennsylvania Gazette*, March 6, 2001. www.upenn.edu/gazette.

Nurge, Dana. "Liberating Yet Limiting: The Paradox of Female Gang Membership." In *Gangs and Society: Alternative Perspectives*, edited by David C. Brotherton, Louis Kontos, and Luis Barrios, 161–82. New York: Columbia University Press, 2003.

Nutter, Michael A. "Philadelphia Homicides 1960–2020." Michael A. Nutter. Accessed August 12, 2022. https://mikenutterllc.com.

Orso, Anna. "A Day after Fishtown Residents Walked the Streets with Baseball Bats, Protesters Return to the Neighborhood." *Philadelphia Inquirer*, June 2, 2020. www .inquirer.com.

Orso, Anna, Allison Steele, William Bender, and Vinny Vella. "Philly Police Stood by as Men with Baseball Bats 'Protected' Fishtown. Some Residents Were Assaulted and Threatened." *Philadelphia Inquirer*, June 2, 2020. www.inquirer.com.

"Other Editors' Views: Why They Don't Cringe." *Evening Times*, May 5, 1958, 4. www .newspapers.com.

Paolantonio, S. A. *Rizzo: The Last Big Man in Big City America*. Philadelphia: Camino Books, 1993.

Park, Robert E., and Ernest W. Burgess. *The City*. Chicago: University of Chicago Press, 1925.

Parker, Cherelle. "Neighborhood Safety and Community Policing Plan." Philadelphia City Council, Spring 2022. https://phlcouncil.com.

Pasto, James. "'Street Corner Society' Revisited." *Bostoniano*, February 23, 2013.

Pennsylvania Crime Commission. *Report on Police Corruption and the Quality of Law Enforcement in Philadelphia*. St. Davids: Pennsylvania Crime Commission, March 1974.

Pennsylvania Historic and Museum Commission. *Pennsylvania, U.S., Death Certificates, 1906–1967*. Ancestry.com online database. Accessed April 19, 2021. Provo, UT. www.ancestry.com.

Pennsylvania State Committee. *Police-Community Relations in Philadelphia: A Report to the United States Commission on Civil Rights by the Pennsylvania State Committee to the Commission*. Philadelphia: United States Commission on Civil Rights, June 1972.

Perales, Dorothy. "Letters to the Editor: Risky Riding." *Philadelphia Daily News*, August 19, 1970, 29. www.newspapers.com.

Perkiss, Abigail. *Making Good Neighbors: Civil Rights, Liberalism, and Integration in Postwar Philadelphia*. Ithaca, NY: Cornell University Press, 2014.

Peters, Art. "Race Mortician Directed Rites for in-Ho Oh." *Philadelphia Tribune*, May 3, 1958, 1. ProQuest Historical Newspapers.

———. "Triggerman Suspect Arrested in Rosen Cop Shooting." *Philadelphia Tribune*, November 11, 1961, 2. ProQuest Historical Newspapers.

"Philadelphia City Council Approves $4.8 Billion Budget in 14–3 Vote." *6ABC News*, June 25, 2020. https://6abc.com.

"Philadelphia Gangs: Gang-Related Homicides in Philadelphia 1965–1976." *Philadelphia Evening Bulletin*, May 23, 1976. From Temple University Special Collections Research Center, *George D. McDowell Philadelphia Evening Bulletin Collection*, call no. SCRC 170, vol. Gangs—Miscellaneous, *George D. McDowell Philadelphia Evening Bulletin Photographs*, P254Z201411000174B.

"Philadelphia Policeman Acquitted in Shooting of Handcuffed Prisoner." *Evening Independent*, August 17, 1979, 2. https://news.google.com.

"Philadelphia Rocked by Fresh Unrest after Police Shooting." *BBC*, October 28, 2020. www.bbc.com.

"Philadelphia Strike in 1903 Gave Rise to 'Children's Army.'" *Philadelphia Inquirer*, June 24, 2003, C01, C04. www.newspapers.com.

"Police Capture 11 in Korean's Fatal Beating." *Indiana Gazette*, April 28, 1958, 16. www.newspapers.com.

"Police Get Overtime Pay Pact, First in City's History." *Philadelphia Inquirer*, November 15, 1961, 45. www.newspapers.com.

"Police Hiring Practices Produce Time-Bombs." *Philadelphia Inquirer*, November 20, 1978, 6. www.newspapers.com.

"Policeman Acquitted." *Reading Eagle*, November 4, 1976, 45. https://news.google.com.

"Policeman Dies of Wounds." *Philadelphia Inquirer*, March 1, 1976, 4. www.newspapers.com.

"Policeman Is Shot by a Sniper." *Beaver County Times*, February 27, 1976, 3. https://news.google.com.

"Policeman Loses Fight with Sniper's Bullet." *Philadelphia Daily News*, March 1, 1976, 3. www.newspapers.com.

"Policeman's Death: Was Vengeance the Motive?" *Philadelphia Inquirer*, March 7, 1976, 1-E. www.newspapers.com.

"Police Stop Raid on Colored Household." *Philadelphia Inquirer*, November 6, 1914, 6. www.newspapers.com.

Police Study Task Force. *Philadelphia and Its Police*. Philadelphia: Philadelphia Task Force, 1986.

"Police Were Lawless in Terror at Wilson Park." *Philadelphia Tribune*, March 6, 1976, 1. ProQuest Historical Newspapers.

Project Attorney Lucy J. Weidner of Public Interest Law Center of Philadelphia (PILCOP). "September 14, 1977 Letter to Commissioner Joseph O'Neill on the December 24, 1976 Arrest of Troy Brooks." PILCOP, Sharon Hill WHS Archives box 17, "Letters to the Commissioner, 1976–1977" folder, April 1978.

Public Interest Law Center of Philadelphia (PILCOP). Miscellaneous letters. PILCOP, Sharon Hill WHS Archives box 17, "Letters to the Commissioner, 1976–1977" folder, April 1978.

Puckett, John L. "The Long Shadow of the MOVE Fire." West Philadelphia Collaborative History. Accessed February 11, 2021. https://collaborativehistory.gse.upenn.edu.

Racher, Dave. "Cop Faces Charges in 'Beating.'" *Philadelphia Daily News*, July 8, 1977, 4. www.newspapers.com.

Rainwater, Lee. "Revolt of the Dirty Workers." *Society* 5, no. 2 (November 1967): 1–2.

Ransom, Jan, and Al Baker. "Inside the Trinitarios: How a Gang Feud Led to the Death of a Teenager." *New York Times*, July 18, 2018. www.nytimes.com.

Rhynhart, Rebecca. "Review and Analysis of the Philadelphia Police Department and Other Related Police Spending." City of Philadelphia Office of the Controller, October 2022. https://controller.phila.gov.

Ringler, Major Jack K., and Henry I. Shaw Jr. "US Marine Corps Operations in the Dominican Republic April–June 1965." Washington, DC: Historical Division USMC, 1970.

Roberts, Samuel K. "Kelly Miller and Thomas Dixon Jr. on Blacks in American Civilization." *Phylon* 41, no. 2 (Second quarter, 1980): 202–9.

Robinson, Cedric J. *Black Marxism: The Making of the Black Radical Tradition*. Chapel Hill: University of North Carolina Press, 1983.

———. *Forgeries of Memory and Meaning: Blacks and the Regimes of Race in American Theater and Film Before World War II*. Chapel Hill: University of North Carolina Press, 2012.

Romero, Melissa. "How Philly's Poverty Rate Has Changed since 1970, by District." Curbed Philadelphia, January 30, 2017. https://philly.curbed.com.

Rothstein, Richard. *The Color of Law: A Forgotten History of How Our Government Segregated America*. New York: Liveright, 2017.

Royal, Camika. *Not Paved for Us: Black Educators and Public School Reform in Philadelphia*. Cambridge, MA: Harvard Education Press, 2022.

"Sandy Grady . . . on the Loose: Garage Man Tries to Salvage a Program." *Philadelphia Evening Bulletin*, March 9, 1972.

Scanlon, Karen, and Scott Heimer. "Cop Kills Kensington Youth." *Philadelphia Daily News*, February 27, 1978, 16. www.newspapers.com.

Schaeffer, Marilyn. "Defense Rests in Police Slaying at Project." *Philadelphia Evening Bulletin*, September 16, 1976. From Temple University Special Collections Research Center, *Philadelphia Evening Bulletin* clippings, call no. SCRC 169, vol. Andre Martin, collection URB.

Schneider, Eric C. "Crime." The Encyclopedia of Greater Philadelphia, 2014, https://philadelphiaencyclopedia.org.

———. *The Ecology of Homicide: Race, Place, and Space in Postwar Philadelphia*. Philadelphia: University of Pennsylvania Press, 2020.

Schneider, Eric C., Christopher Agee, and Themis Chronopoulos. "Dirty Work: Police and Community Relations and the Limits of Liberalism in Postwar Philadelphia." *Journal of Urban History* 46, no. 5 (2020): 961–79.

Scolforo, Mark. "Pennsylvania Supreme Court Rejects Juvenile Life Sentences." *NBC Philadelphia*, June 27, 2017. www.nbcphiladelphia.com.

"SEPTA Riders Speak Out." *Philadelphia Daily News*, August 8, 1983, 5. www.newspapers.com.

Shaler, Nathaniel S. "The Negro Problem." *Atlantic Monthly* 54 (1884): 696–709.

Shammas, Brittany, Kim Bellware, and Brady Dennis. "Murder Charges Filed against All Four Officers in George Floyd's Death as Protests against Biased Policing Continue." *Washington Post*, July 3, 2020. www.washingtonpost.com.

Shertzer, Allison, and Randall Walsh. "Why US Cities Are Segregated by Race: New Evidence on the Role of 'White Flight.'" VoxEU, May 19, 2016. https://voxeu.org.

Shockley, Cereta M. Letter to Mayor Richardson Dilworth, October 26, 1958. Crime Situation, box A 4400, Mayor Files, 1958, Municipal Developments (A–P), Philadelphia Municipal Archives (PMA).

"Shooting Jars Band." *Philadelphia Daily News*, February 26, 1976, 3. www.newspapers .com.

"Shot Fatal to Officer Came from Youth's Rifle, Jury Is Told." *Philadelphia Evening Bulletin*, September 10, 1976. From Temple University Special Collections Research Center, *Philadelphia Evening Bulletin* clippings, call no. SCRC 169, vol. Andre Martin, collection URB.

Shubin, Seymour. "Memorial to a Murder." *Pittsburgh Post–Gazette*, June 11, 1961, 108. www.newspapers.com.

Shuttleworth, Ken. "Sennett to Wait for Gang Study before Acting." *Philadelphia Inquirer*, June 18, 1969, 43. www.newspapers.com.

Simon, Roger D. *Philadelphia: A Brief History*. Mansfield: Pennsylvania Historical Association, 2017.

Singer, Lawrence H. "Dawn Patrol." *Philadelphia Inquirer*, August 13, 1944, 93. www .newspapers.com.

Skolnick, Jerome H., and James J. Fyfe. *Above the Law: Police and the Excessive Use of Force*. New York: Free Press, 1993.

Slain Fairmount Park Police Officer, Frank Von Colln. Photograph. *Philadelphia Evening Bulletin*, August 30, 1970. From Temple University Libraries, Special Collections Research Center, George D. McDowell Philadelphia Evening Bulletin Photographs—Digital Collections. Accessed March 31, 2021. www.temple.edu.

Smart, James. "Old Northeast Was Built for Learning." *Philadelphia Inquirer*, August 11, 2011. www.inquirer.com.

"Sniper Shoots Down Police, Setting Off a Massive Manhunt." *Philadelphia Inquirer*, February 26, 1976, 2-A. www.newspapers.com.

Speer, William J. "The Safe Streets Project—Inroads on Phila. Gang Control?" *Philadelphia Inquirer*, February 22, 1970, 1, 3.

Spencer, John P. *In the Crossfire: Marcus Foster and the Troubled History of American School Reform*. Philadelphia: University of Pennsylvania Press, 2012.

Spikol, Liz. "I've Had Public Mental Health Outbursts like Walter Wallace Jr. I'm Alive Because I'm White." *Philadelphia Inquirer*, October 30, 2020. www.inquirer.com.

Stack, Carol. *All Our Kin: Strategies for Survival in a Black Community*. New York: Basic Books, 1974.

Staff Attorney Ann K. Seidman of Public Interest Law Center of Philadelphia (PILCOP). "January 4, 1977 Letter to Commissioner Joseph O'Neill on the April 10, 1976

Beating of Leroy Jenkins of 7943 Woolston Avenue." PILCOP, Sharon Hill WHS Archives box 17, "Letters to the Commissioner, 1976–1977" folder, April 1978.

"Stop Gang Rapings." *Philadelphia Tribune*, April 7, 1973, 8. ProQuest Historical Newspapers.

Storey, Charles J. *A Study of Municipal Recreation in Philadelphia*. Philadelphia: Playgrounds Association of Philadelphia, 1929.

"Stray-Bullet Death of Boy: Gang Youth Held in Killing." *Philadelphia Daily News*, April 22, 1971, 5. www.newspapers.com.

"Street-Corner Slaying of Youth Admitted by Two Hoodlums." *Philadelphia Inquirer*, February 11, 1956, 13. www.newspapers.com.

Suddler, Carl. *Presumed Criminal: Black Youth and the Justice System in Postwar New York*. New York: New York University Press, 2019.

Sugrue, Thomas J. *Sweet Land of Liberty: The Forgotten Struggle for Civil Rights in the North*. New York: Random House, 2008.

Sullivan, Carl, and Carla Baranauckas. "Here's How Much Money Goes to Police Departments in Largest Cities across the U.S." *USA Today*, June 26, 2020. www.usatoday.com.

"Tate Asks Widening of Realty Tax Base to Meet City Costs." *Philadelphia Inquirer Public Ledger*, February 25, 1959, 1. ProQuest.

Taub, Amanda. "Behind 2016's Turmoil, a Crisis of White Identity." *New York Times*, November 2, 2016. www.nytimes.com.

"Teagle's White Wife the Cause of Trouble at 60th and Spruce Streets." *Philadelphia Tribune*, November 14, 1914, 5. ProQuest Historical Newspapers.

TED. "The Danger of a Single Story-Chimamanda Ngozi Adichie." October 7, 2009. YouTube video, 19:16. www.youtube.com/watch?v=D9Ihs241zeg.

Terry, Robert L. "5 Boys Seized in Rape Robbery of Woman in Housing Project." *Philadelphia Inquirer*, April 3, 1973, 15. www.newspapers.com.

"The North: Doing No Good." *Time*, September 4, 1964. http://time.com.

Thompson, Heather Ann. "Why Mass Incarceration Matters: Rethinking Crisis, Decline, and Transformation in Postwar American History." *Journal of American History* 97, no. 3 (December 2010): 703–34.

Thrasher, Frederic. *The Gang: A Study of 1,313 Gangs in Chicago*. Chicago: University of Chicago Press, 1927.

"Thug Kills Businessman on Broad St." *Philadelphia Inquirer*, December 7, 1956, 1, 12. www.newspapers.com.

"To Reimburse Negro." *Evening Public Ledger Philadelphia*, November 6, 1914. http://chroniclingamerica.loc.gov.

Trettin, Walter H. "A Dad's Final Tribute to a Slain Policeman." *Philadelphia Daily News*, March 4, 1976, 4. www.newspapers.com.

"Tribune Sports: PAL Bouts on TV Beam as of Today." *Philadelphia Tribune*, June 3, 1952, 10. ProQuest Historical Newspapers.

Trippett, Frank. "It Looks Just like a War Zone." *Time*, June 24, 2001. http://time.com.

"Two Philadelphia Policemen Killed in Shooting Attacks." *St. Petersburg Times*, February 22, 1971. https://news.google.com.

Umansky, David J., and Acel Moore. "Economic, Racial Fears Fan Bartram Row." *Philadelphia Inquirer*, June 21, 1970, 17, 27. www.newspapers.com.

United Presbyterian Church in the USA. *An Epistle from the Koreans*. Directed by Lloyd Young. Burbank, CA: Film Productions International, 1959.

United States Bureau of the Census. "Migrations—the African-American Mosaic Exhibition." Library of Congress. Accessed May 28, 2023. www.loc.gov.

United States Congress Senate Committee on the Judiciary Subcommittee to Investigate Juvenile Delinquency (Philadelphia, PA). *Hearings before the United States Senate Committee on the Judiciary, Subcommittee to Investigate Juvenile Delinquency in the U.S., Eighty-Third Congress, Second Session, on Apr. 14, 15, 1954*. Washington, DC: US Government Printing Office, 1954.

United States Department of Labor. *The Negro Family: The Case for National Action*. Washington, DC: US Government Print, 1965.

United States of America, Bureau of the Census. *Fifteenth Census of the United States, 1930*. Ancestry.com online database, 1930 United States Federal Census. Provo, UT. Accessed April 19, 2021. www.ancestry.com.

———. *Fourteenth Census of the United States, 1920*. Ancestry.com online database, 1920 United States Federal Census. Provo, UT. Accessed April 19, 2021. www .ancestry.com.

———. *Seventeenth Census of the United States, 1950*, Ancestry.com online database, 1950 United States Federal Census. Lehi, UT. Accessed June 9, 2023. www.ancestry.com.

———. *Sixteenth Census of the United States, 1940*. Ancestry.com online database, 1940 United States Federal Census. Provo, UT. Accessed April 19, 2021. www .ancestry.com.

———. *Thirteenth Census of the United States, 1910*. Ancestry.com online database, 1910 United States Federal Census. Lehi, UT. Accessed April 19, 2021. www.ancestry.com.

———. *Twelfth Census of the United States, 1900*. Ancestry.com online database, 1900 United States Federal Census. Provo, UT. Accessed April 19, 2021. www.ancestry .com.

"U.S. Gives City $150,000 for Gang Control." *Philadelphia Evening Bulletin*, July 22, 1970.

"U.S. Gives DA $80,000 for Gang Control." *Philadelphia Evening Bulletin*, June 26, 1969.

Vargas, Claudia, and Chris Palmer. "Philly Eased Police Residency Requirements. Then the Exodus Began." *Philadelphia Inquirer*, October 6, 2017. www.inquirer.com.

Viola, Michael. *Click! Life through the Lens of a News Photographer*. Philadelphia: Five Corners, 1998.

"Violence Hits Tasker Homes as Police Watch Fairmount." *Philadelphia Inquirer*, August 28, 1970, 1. www.newspapers.com.

"Violence Is a Way of Life at Project." *Philadelphia Inquirer*, February 25, 1976, 2. www .newspapers.com.

Vitale, Alex S. *The End of Policing*. Brooklyn: Verso Books, 2017.

Walton, Mary. "Trapped: Housing Project an Island of Fear." *Philadelphia Inquirer*, July 14, 1975, 1-2-A. www.newspapers.com.

Ward, Matthew. "Police Athletic League." The Encyclopedia of Greater Philadelphia, 2017. http://philadelphiaencyclopedia.org.

Washington, Linn. "Tenants Vow to Hold Rent over Idle Elevators at S.P." *Philadelphia Tribune*, April 10, 1976, 2. ProQuest Historical Newspapers.

———. "Women Live in Fear in Southwark Unit." *Philadelphia Tribune*, December 2, 1975, 2. ProQuest Historical Newspapers.

Webber, Harry B. "In Philadelphia—Third Largest City: Housing Cancer Is Undermining City." *Philadelphia Tribune*, March 7, 1935, 12. ProQuest Historical Newspapers.

———. "Slum Profits in Philadelphia Run into Huge Profits Often Bringing 100 Percent Return." *Philadelphia Tribune*, April 18, 1935, 12. ProQuest Historical Newspapers.

———. "Slums No Accident Claims Tribune Housing Investigator." *Philadelphia Tribune*, March 14, 1935, 20. ProQuest Historical Newspapers.

Weisenbach, William. "Boy, 9, Is Slain after Mother Bears 5th Baby." *Philadelphia Inquirer*, April 21, 1971, 31. www.newspapers.com.

———. "Social Worker, 2 Teens Shot in Gang Ruckus." *Philadelphia Inquirer*, April 3, 1968, 45. www.newspapers.com.

"West Phila. House Stoned." *Evening Public Ledger Philadelphia*, November 5, 1914. http://chroniclingamerica.loc.gov.

Whalen, Carmen Teresa. *From Puerto Rico to Philadelphia: Puerto Rican Workers and Postwar Economies*. Philadelphia: Temple University Press, 2001.

Whyte, William Foote. *Street Corner Society: The Social Structure of an Italian Slum*. Chicago: University of Chicago Press, 1943.

Widra, Emily, and Benjamin Geffen. "Where People in Prison Come from: The Geography of Mass Incarceration in Pennsylvania." *Prison Policy Initiative*, September 2022. www.prisonpolicy.org.

Wilkerson, Isabel. *The Warmth of Other Suns: The Epic Story of America's Great Migration*. New York: Knopf Doubleday, 2010.

Wilson, Kathryn E. "From Bachelor Enclave to Urban Village: The Evolution of Early Chinatown." *Historical Society of Pennsylvania Legacies* 12, no. 1 (May 2012): 12–17. https://hsp.org.

Wilson, Kendall. "Philadelphia Police Put Net over Crime Area in Minutes." *Daily Item*, February 1, 1969, 16. www.newspapers.com.

"Wilson Park Homes Set for Use." *Philadelphia Inquirer*, March 14, 1954, 17. www.newspapers.com.

Wilson, Woodrow. *A History of the American People*. New York: Harper & Brothers, 1902.

Winger, Amelia. "West Philadelphia's House of Umoja Strengthens Hope and Community." *Global Philadelphia*, April 17, 2020. http://globalphiladelphia.org.

Wolf, Edwin, Nicholas B. Wainwright, and Russell Frank Weigley. *Philadelphia: A 300-Year History*. New York: W. W. Norton, 1982.

Wolf, Stephanie G. "The Bicentennial City, 1968–1982." In Wolf, Wainwright, and Weigley, *Philadelphia*, 704–34.

Wolfinger, James. *Philadelphia Divided: Race and Politics in the City of Brotherly Love.* Chapel Hill: University of North Carolina Press, 2007.

Women from the New Mantua Infant Care Center Stand in Front of Wooden Shack. Photograph. *Philadelphia Evening Bulletin*, May 16, 1970. From Temple University Libraries, Special Collections Research Center. https://digital.library.temple.edu.

Wooten, James T. "Philadelphia Also Facing Crisis of Funds Shortage." *New York Times*, May 20, 1976. www.nytimes.com.

Yanker. "Moving." *Chicago Tribune*, March 3, 1923, 6. www.newspapers.com.

Yax, Laura K. "Population of the 100 Largest Cities and Other Urban Places in the United States: 1790 to 1990." US Census Bureau. Accessed May 28, 2023. www.census.gov.

Young Great Society Members Painting a House. Photograph. *Philadelphia Evening Bulletin*, July 25, 1979. From Temple University Libraries, Special Collections Research Center. https://digital.library.temple.edu.

"Youth, 15, Stabbed to Death in 'Revenge' Attack, 5 Held." *Philadelphia Daily News*, June 18, 1963, 4. www.newspapers.com.

Youth Cleaning Streets and Lots. Photograph. Philadelphia, Wharton Centre, date unknown. From Temple University Libraries, Special Collections Research Center. Accessed January 25, 2021. https://digital.library.temple.edu.

Youth in Conflict Cooperative Service Project. *Safe Streets, Inc. (Six Month Evaluation Report, July–December 1974).* Washington, DC: US Department of Justice Law Enforcement Assistance Administration National Criminal Justice Reference Service, December 31, 1974.

INDEX

ABOUT THE AUTHOR

Menika B. Dirkson is Assistant Professor of African American History at Morgan State University. She previously taught at Loyola University Maryland and Temple University. She has received grants from the Philadelphia Foundation and Thomas Jefferson University's Arlen Specter Center for her research on race and policing following the Civil Rights Movement. Dirkson was born, raised, and lives in Philadelphia.

www.ingramcontent.com/pod-product-compliance
Lightning Source LLC
Chambersburg PA
CBHW031535260326
41914CB00032B/1821/J

.